Rising Life Expectancy

Between 1800 and 2000 life expectancy at birth rose from about thirty years to a global average of sixty-seven years, and to more than seventy-five years in favored countries. This dramatic change, called the health transition, is characterized by a transition in how long people expected to live and in how they expected to die. The most common age at death jumped from infancy to old age. Most people lived to know their children as adults, and most children became acquainted with their grandparents. Whereas earlier people died chiefly from infectious diseases with a short course, by later decades they died from chronic diseases, often with a protracted course. The ranks of people living in their most economically productive years filled out, and the old became commonplace figures everywhere. *Rising Life Expectancy: A Global History* examines the way humans reduced risks to their survival, both regionally and globally, to promote world population growth and population aging.

James C. Riley is professor of history at Indiana University and the author of books and articles on population and world health, most recently *Sick, Not Dead: The Health of British Workingmen During the Mortality Decline.* He is a recipient of research awards from the National Endowment for the Humanities and the National Institutes of Health.

Rising Life Expectancy

A Global History

JAMES C. RILEY
Indiana University

CAMBRIDGE
UNIVERSITY PRESS

PUBLISHED BY THE PRESS SYNDICATE OF THE UNIVERSITY OF CAMBRIDGE
The Pitt Building, Trumpington Street, Cambridge, United Kingdom

CAMBRIDGE UNIVERSITY PRESS
The Edinburgh Building, Cambridge CB2 2RU, UK
40 West 20th Street, New York, NY 10011-4211, USA
10 Stamford Road, Oakleigh, VIC 3166, Australia
Ruiz de Alarcón 13, 28014 Madrid, Spain
Dock House, The Waterfront, Cape Town 8001, South Africa

http://www.cambridge.org

© James C. Riley 2001

First published 2001

Printed in the United States of America

Typeface Erhardt 11/13 pt.   *System* QuarkXPress 4.04 [AG]

A catalog record for this book is available from the British Library.

Library of Congress Cataloging in Publication Data
Riley, James C.
Rising life expectancy : a global history / James C. Riley.
p.   cm.
Includes bibliographical references and index.
ISBN 0-521-80245-8 — ISBN 0-521-00281-8 (pbk.)
1. Life expectancy.   I. Title.

HB1322.3 .R55 2001
304.6′45—dc21   00-050242

ISBN 0 521 80245 8 hardback
ISBN 0 521 00281 8 paperback

for Sharyn

Contents

List of Figures, Maps, and Tables   *page* ix

Preface and Acknowledgments   xi

    Introduction: A Global Revolution in Life Expectancy   1

1   A Brief Overview of the Health Transition   32

2   Public Health   58

3   Medicine   81

4   Wealth, Income, and Economic Development   122

5   Famine, Malnutrition, and Diet   145

6   Households and Individuals   169

7   Literacy and Education   200

    Conclusion   220

    Index   233

List of Figures, Maps, and Tables

Figures

I.1	Four Life Expectancy Profiles	4
1.1	Life Expectancy, 1960 and 1995	37
1.2	Crude Death Rates in Four Countries, 1735–1825	37
1.3	The Pace of Gains in Survivorship	39
2.1	Jan Molenaer, *The Five Senses: Smell*	62
4.1	Per Capita GDP and Crude Death Rates in Ten Countries, 1820	125
4.2	Per Capita Output and Crude Death Rates in Six Countries, 1830–1910	126
4.3	Life Expectancy and Income in 1900	129
4.4	Life Expectancy and Income around 1940	129
4.5	Life Expectancy and Income in 1960	130
4.6	Life Expectancy and Income in 1997	130
5.1	Mortality among Children under Five, 1996	155
6.1	Pierre Auguste Renoir, *Claude et Renée*	170
7.1	Female Literacy and Child Survival, 1995	217

Maps

1.1	Life Expectancy in 1995	42

List of Figures, Maps, and Tables

Tables

I.1	Leading Causes of Death in London, 1701–1776, and Britain, 1992	17
1.1	Life Expectancy for Both Sexes	38
1.2	Leading Mortality Crises in the Twentieth Century	41
3.1	Major Vaccines	99
3.2	Life Expectancy, Per Capita GDP, and Health Spending in Thirty-Seven Countries	118
4.1	A Comparison of Per Capita GDP and Life Expectancy, 1960 and 1995	139
C.1	Surplus Mortality, 1990–1995	227

Preface and Acknowledgments

People have long imagined that they might individually live to old age. For most of human history, threats to survival overwhelmed this idea. A few people lived to be old, but most of the members of any society died young. Until the early twentieth century more people died in infancy than at any other age. Reaching old age became a commonplace thing only in the twentieth century. This is a history of the retreat of death and the democratization of survival to old age in the period since about 1800.

Survival and health should be distinguished. A person may be alive but not well. The difference matters because disease and injury have not retreated as far as death has. Morbidity, in the sense of sickness prevalence, remains high in all societies, in some because communicable diseases are so common and in some because protracted noncommunicable diseases have taken their place. Moreover, the factors that influence sickness and death seem to overlap only in part, and often to influence these two effects differently. In a future stage of the global health transition, sickness prevalence, too, may be forced back.

Two main arguments are developed in this book. The first main argument is that individual countries, sometimes even regions within countries, devise their own strategies for reducing mortality. People have always selected from the same six tactical areas: public health, medicine, wealth and income, nutrition, behavior, and education. But different countries have used these means in quite different ways, in different sequences, and at different moments in the development of each tactic. There are many paths to low death rates and generalized survival to old age. The global health transition emerged from a series of particular health transitions.

The central chapters of this book relate the history of these tactical areas, focusing on how each came to be recognized as a means of controlling risks to survival and on the human effort to understand how each tactic works in practice and what its possibilities are. The tactics appear roughly in the sequence in which they were recognized as effective means of controlling disease and injury. This structure owes more to the aim of organizing an otherwise ungainly body of information than it does to any argument that these categories should necessarily be differentiated from one another in this way or arrayed in this order. In truth, they overlap, often to the point that it is difficult to decide where to situate a certain issue. For example, the success of inoculation and, later, vaccination against smallpox might be deemed chiefly a medical remedy or a public health improvement. The capacity of a parent to react effectively to a child's sickness might be assigned to education, medicine, behavior, or social status and income.

The second main argument deals with the implications of having extended survival in this way, rather than in another way. During the last half of the twentieth century all countries and regions made some use of all six tactics, albeit in quite different mixtures and forms. That seems to be a good thing, in that different peoples and societies exhibit strong preferences in the things they are willing to do. The multiplicity of tactics, and the many forms of each tactic, are accommodations to the different characteristics and preferences of people. They allow Costa Rica and the

United States, for example, to achieve approximately the same levels of life expectancy at birth by quite different means.

There is also a cost to this particularistic approach. It leads toward overall strategies in which old schemes are often maintained even as new schemes are being adopted. In the end the strategies that limit risks to survival and foster the good health of a population may be remarkably inefficient. Students of health and health systems need to address the problem of identifying the elements of each country's health strategy. And they need to appraise the effectiveness of the tactical elements in use. Which are more effective, measured by lower cost or less stress on the habits and attitudes of a population? Which of them impede and which assist the next stage of the ongoing effort to elevate survivorship and to reduce morbidity?

I began working on this book in the mid-1980s, and I have accumulated many debts. Some of them are to colleagues at Indiana University, who read drafts, listened to papers, and provided critical advice: George Alter, Ann Carmichael, Elyce Rotella, and George Stolnitz. Ed McClellan in the Indiana University School of Education helped me find my way in the theoretical literature on education. Additionally, I am in debt to scholars elsewhere for assistance, sometimes given verbally but more often as written comments. Those are especially welcome because they require reflection and organization, and show the devotion the person giving criticism has to a project. For such help, I want to thank Jack Caldwell, Pat Caldwell, Steve Kunitz, Massimo Livi Bacci, David Lucas, and Walter Nugent. Anonymous readers for Cambridge University Press put forth much effort and gave good advice, as did my editor, Frank Smith. This book is dedicated to my wife, whom my colleagues describe as a person of extraordinary tolerance and consideration.

Introduction:

A Global Revolution in Life Expectancy

At the end of the twentieth century everyone could not expect to live an extended life, but humankind had moved closer to that goal than ever before. In 1800, with nearly one billion people alive, life expectancy at birth did not surpass thirty years. By 2000, with more than six billion people alive, life expectancy reached nearly sixty-seven years amidst a continuing rise. This is the crowning achievement of the modern era, surpassing wealth, military power, and political stability in import. Mindful of the effects of declining fertility and optimistic about the future course of survivorship, U.N. demographers project that the global average for males and females will rise from sixty-seven years at the end of the twentieth century to seventy-six years in the middle of the twenty-first century.[1]

This dramatic change is called the "health transition," in which humankind acquired an expectation of living to be old. These longer lives contributed to population growth, adding people who in earlier periods died at younger ages. Because death rates at ages above sixty-five did not

---

[1] United Nations Secretariat, Department of Economic and Social Affairs, Population Division, *World Population Prospects: The 1998 Revision*, 2 vols. (New York, 1998), I: 547.

decline until late in the health transition, these longer lives initially filled the ranks of every population with people living in their most economically productive years, 15-64. Prior to the health transition more than half of all people died before reaching adulthood. In some countries and regions more than half died before they reached age ten. Generalized survival to old age also modified the emotions of life, making death in infancy, childhood, and youth an uncommon thing and causing the modal age of death to jump from infancy to older adulthood. In the longer run, during the second half of the twentieth century, these longer lives added vastly to the quantity and proportion of people of advanced age, who possess the wisdom of experience. In 1800, people aged sixty-five and higher made up less than 5 percent of most populations; by 2000 their share had tripled to 15 percent in high life expectancy societies.

The scale of rising life expectancy can most readily be grasped by examining a rectangle, which depicts the space of life and sets of survival curves within it. Each curve begins with a full population of people born alive and diminishes as people die. The rectangle itself extends to the age to which we can imagine any people might survive. For most of human history our imagination has been limited by the age of the oldest person we know. The older limit could be set at seventy years, following the pronouncement in Psalms 90:10. It could be fixed at eighty-five years, which has sometimes been described as the maximum age to which populations can aspire to survive. Recently it has often been put at 100 or 110 years: increasing numbers of people now live to be 100, though very few live past 110. Now, on the strength of the promised discovery of the genes responsible for specific diseases and learning that will show how to modify these genes and how to manipulate proteins that cause cell destruction, some set the older limit at 150 years.[2]

---

[2] S. Jay Olshansky, Bruce A. Carnes, and Christine Cassel, "In Search of Methuselah: Estimating the Upper Limits to Human Longevity," *Science* 250 (1990): 634–40.

Four sets of curves appear in the panels of Figure I.1a–d. Figures I.1a and I.1b show the survival of French females in the 1740s and 1996 and life expectancy in each period. Figure I.1c shows the survival of Japanese females in 1891–98, 1947, and 1996, and Figure I.1d the survival of Indian females in 1901 and 1993.[3] These figures show some interesting and important things. First, they distinguish between the lived portion of the space of life, below each curve, and the unlived portion, above each curve. Compare the meager segment of the rectangle represented by survivorship before the health transition began in France or India with the much larger segment of recent years. Second, little progress was made at extending the lived portion before the eighteenth century, when the health transition began, but rapid progress has been made since then. Third, these figures show that survival prospects have improved at every age, from infancy to the oldest ages.[4] The gain in infancy has been the largest, but every age has benefited. Fourth, the unlived space, which has been pushed toward the upper right corner in each, remains large. If it is true that we can realistically imagine people in general living to be 100 or 110, then much of the transition remains to be completed.

---

[3] Here survival refers to a theoretical rather than an actual population. In an actual population the survival prospects of people at each age are known only when they live through that age. The life table, which reports the risk of death at each age for the current population, makes it unnecessary to wait until the people born in the same period have all died in order to estimate their life expectancy. The principal weakness of this approach is that it tends to understate the effect of changes under way. During the health transition survival rates rose and life expectancy calculated by means of the life table understated the average age to which people actually lived. Demographers also build cohort life tables, which show actual survival prospects for a group of people born at the same time. Of necessity, cohort tables cannot be constructed in full until the entire cohort has died.

[4] Jacques Vallin, "La mortalité en Europe de 1720 à 1914: Tendances à long terme et changements de structure par sexe et age," *Annales de démographie historique* (1989): 31–54; and, for the twentieth century, Graziella Caselli, "National Differences in the Health Transition in Europe," *Historical Methods* 29 (1996): 107–25.

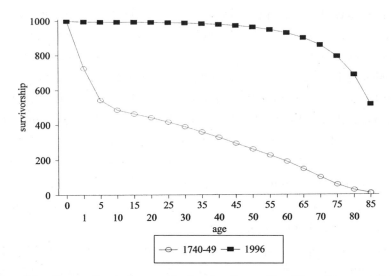

Figure I.1a. France: Survival curves for females. *Source:* Yves Blayo, "La mortalité en France de 1740 à 1829," *Population* 30, Special Number (1975): 141; *Annuaire statistique de la France,* vol. 102 (Paris, 1999), pp. 84–85.

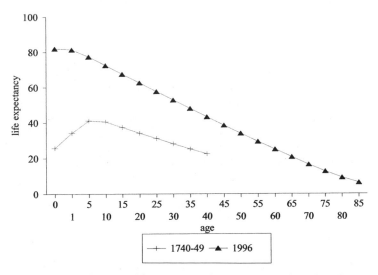

Figure I.1b. France: Life expectancy, females. *Source:* See Fig. I.1a.

4

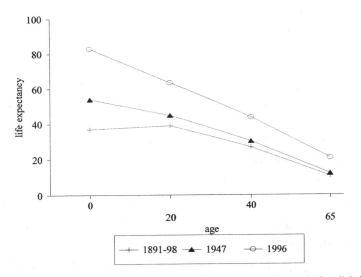

Figure I.1c. Japan: Life expectancy, females. *Source:* www.mhw.gp.jp/english/database/lifetb/part7.html, which gives official values from abridged life tables; Haruo Mizushima, "Reformation of Early Life Tables for Japan," *Minzoku Eisei* 28 (1962): 64–74 (in Japanese).

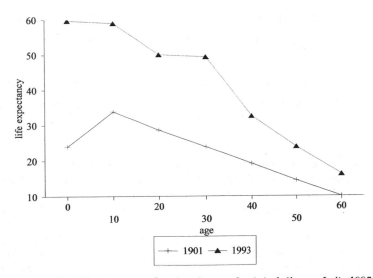

Figure I.1d India: Life expectancy, females. *Source: Statistical Abstract India 1997* (New Delhi, 1990), p. 51.

On this evidence one might argue for the image of revolution rather than transition in survival since 1800. Why, then, is it called the health transition?

The History of This History

A comparatively new term,[5] *health transition* describes the reduction of mortality in the long run. Historians often use the term *revolution* to describe changes as momentous and, on the scale of human history, as concentrated in time as the health transition. But the modern rise of life expectancy lacks the dramatic origin that usually accompanies such a usage. Whereas the industrial revolution can be said to have begun with sharp productivity gains in the manufacture of cotton textiles in Britain and Belgium before 1800, the health transition has no well-defined beginning point. It, too, was under way by 1800, but the discovery of a period or a country where it began is a quite difficult matter. The health transition also lacks singularity, or at least simplicity, in the means by which it was achieved. From the beginning, different regions and different countries advanced life expectancy by using their own tactics or combinations of tactics.

Many phrases, including "vital revolution," "mortality transition," and "mortality decline," have been used to describe the modern rise of

---

[5] Monroe Lerner, "Modernization and Health: A Model of the Health Transition," paper presented at the American Public Health Association Conference, San Francisco, 1973, seems to have used the term first, but did not win acceptance of it. On the broader meaning of the term, see Julio Frenk et al., "Elements for a Theory of the Health Transition," in Lincoln Chen, Arthur Kleinman, and Norma C. Ware, eds., *Health and Social Change in International Perspective* (Boston, 1994), pp. 25–49; W. Henry Mosley et al., "The Health Transition: Implications for Health Policy in Developing Countries," in Dean T. Jamison et al., eds., *Disease Control Priorities in Developing Countries* (Oxford, 1993), pp. 673–99; and the journal *Health Transition Review*, which began publication in 1991.

life expectancy. The term *health transition* links changes in mortality to those in morbidity, or sickness, and to the modern decline of fertility. Thus this phrase associates survival and health with the demographic transition, the movement from high mortality and fertility to low. By focusing on causes of death and sickness, it suggests a strong link between demography and epidemiology. It also reveals the incomplete nature of this change. Even though already two centuries old, the health transition has not yet stopped and probably will not stop for many decades to come. It is an ongoing thing that we manipulate and manage with great variations in skill. Much of the most helpful recent scholarly writing has focused explicitly on the problem of setting an agenda and on the task of discovering how to use past human experience in the health transition to serve better health in the future.[6]

The health transition was under way by 1800, but for a long time it was noticed more readily in individual countries than as an international, and eventually a global, development. By the early twentieth century observers understood that death rates had fallen in much of Europe and North America, but, until the 1950s, interest in the history of the mortality decline developed slowly. Since then scholars from many disciplines – especially history, demography and historical demography, medicine and medical history, public health, epidemiology, biology, anthropology, economics, and sociology – have sought to understand the history and the present development of mortality change. A huge literature has

[6] In addition to the sources cited below in this chapter, see Samuel H. Preston, "Causes and Consequences of Mortality Decline in Less Developed Countries during the Twentieth Century," in R. A. Easterlin, ed., *Population and Economic Change in Developing Countries* (Chicago, 1980), pp. 289–360; Jacques Vallin, "Theories of Mortality Decline and the African Situation," in Etienne van de Walle, Gilles Pison, and Mpembele Sala-Diakanda, eds., *Mortality and Society in Sub-Saharan Africa* (Oxford, 1992); Michael Alderson, *International Mortality Statistics* (New York, 1981); Evelyn Thiltgès, Josianne Duchêne, and Guillaume Wunsch, "Causal Theories and Models in the Study of Mortality," in Alan D. Lopez, Graziella Caselli, and Tapani Valkonen, eds., *Adult Mortality in Developed Countries: From Description to Explanation* (Oxford, 1995), pp. 21–36.

appeared. Perhaps no other topic has drawn so much multidisciplinary interest or so much discussion and learning across the ordinary boundaries of disciplines.

As is usually the case with historical dramas, the scholars of the 1950s already had some ideas about why death rates had declined. At that point most of the available information was national, and most explanations referred to leading developments in specific countries. The attempt to test explanations that seemed to account for change in one country by making explicit comparisons across countries began with a United Nations publication in 1953. There the health transition is described as a process occurring in stages with the important causative factors shifting from stage to stage. Before 1850 a higher standard of living, manifested in nutrition and better housing and clothing, enhanced survival; between 1850 and 1900 sanitary projects played the leading part; after 1900 a combination of factors came into play: economic development, public health, and biomedicine. George Stolnitz added an influential article in two parts in 1955-56 in which he stressed disease control more than economic development and called attention to the global nature of the health transition. Both approaches sought to generalize the problem by pointing out the degree to which different circumstances in another country require a reassessment of explanations offered for one country. But neither essay managed to divert scholars from attending first to national cases and leading factors.[7]

[7] United Nations, *The Determinants and Consequences of Population Trends* (New York, 1953); United Nations, *Population Studies, Age and Sex Patterns of Mortality: Model Life Tables for Under-developed Countries* (New York, 1955); and George J. Stolnitz, "A Century of International Mortality Trends," *Population Studies* 9 (1955): 24–55, and 10 (1956): 17–42. See also George J. Stolnitz, "International Mortality Trends: Some Main Facts and Interpretations," *The Population Debate: Dimensions and Perspectives*, 2 vols. (New York, 1974), I: 220–36; United Nations and World Health Organization, *Levels and Trends of Mortality since 1950* (New York, 1982); United Nations, "Mortality and Health," in *World Population Trends and Policies* (New York, 1988), pp. 116–73; H. O.

One of these national investigations in particular, Thomas McKeown's study of England and Wales, stimulated scholarly interest in the health transition. After having suggested in an earlier series of articles that public health improvements played a large part in reducing death rates in nineteenth-century England, McKeown changed his mind. Breaking down diseases causing death by their modes of transmission, he found reasons to continue to reject a medical explanation and to downgrade the public health explanation. In their place McKeown argued that a rising standard of living, especially better nutrition, mattered most. Assuming that nutritional status regulates susceptibility to disease, McKeown maintained that better nutrition helped people resist disease. His 1976 book, *The Modern Rise of Population*, has remained an influential study, with two leading effects. First, it promotes the idea that modernization, especially economic modernization, played a central role in the health transition. According to this view, populations and societies needed to develop their political, legal, and economic institutions in certain ways as a foundation for other kinds of change.[8] Modernization gets credit for having improved the standard of living and nutrition. Indeed, in McKeown's approach modernization seems to be a prerequisite for mortality decline. Second, McKeown concentrated on nineteenth-century England and Wales; his work helped focus scholarly attention on Britain, especially on nineteenth-century England.[9] Although scholars writing about England's health

Lancaster, *Expectations of Life: A Study in the Demography, Statistics, and History of World Mortality* (New York, 1990); Kenneth F. Kiple et al., *The Cambridge World History of Human Disease* (Cambridge, 1993); and World Bank, *World Development Report 1993: Investing in Health* (Oxford, 1993).

[8] For example, modernization means limitation on the powers of monarchs and imperial rulers, such as exercised in England and Wales by Parliament.

[9] Thomas McKeown, *The Modern Rise of Population* (London, 1976). McKeown also related his findings to some other countries in Thomas McKeown, R. G. Brown, and R. G. Record, "An Interpretation of the Modern Rise of Population in Europe," *Population Studies* 26 (1972): 345–82.

transition have often criticized McKeown's interpretation, those writing about rising survivorship elsewhere have often accepted that interpretation as the reigning paradigm for England and other countries, too. McKeown's interpretation suggests that the most important short-term relief measure for people facing high death rates is to augment their diets. The most effective long-term measure is to promote economic development and the capacity to buy food on favorable terms. Two of the questions that can be kept in mind while reading the chapters that follow derive from McKeown's work. Did improvements in nutrition play a major role in the retreat of early death in nineteenth-century Britain and Europe? Can McKeown's interpretation of the nineteenth-century British mortality decline be generalized to other places and times?

McKeown's writings attracted more initial interest than did a 1971 article by Abdel Omran depicting the mortality decline as an epidemiologic transition.[10] Using an implicitly comparative approach, Omran described the health transition as a series of sea changes in the leading causes of death, moving from an era of pandemic infectious diseases to an era in which chronic organ diseases dominate all causes of death. By calling his

---

[10] Abdel Omran, "The Epidemiologic Transition: A Theory of the Epidemiology of Population Change," *Milbank Memorial Fund Quarterly* 49 (1971): 509–38; Omran, "The Epidemiologic Transition Theory: A Preliminary Update," *Journal of Tropical Pediatrics* 29 (1983): 305–16; S. J. Olshansky and A. B. Ault, "The Fourth Stage of the Epidemiologic Transition: The Age of Delayed Degenerative Diseases," *Milbank Memorial Fund Quarterly* 64 (1986): 355–91; and J. C. Riley and George Alter, "The Epidemiological Transition and Morbidity," *Annales de démographie historique* (1989): 199–213.

Ronald Bennett et al., "Emerging and Re-emerging Infectious Diseases: The Third Epidemiologic Transition," *Annual Review of Anthropology* 27 (1998): 247–71, recast Omran's ideas. For an earlier version of epidemiologic transition theory, see Odin W. Anderson and George Rosen, *An Examination of the Concept of Preventive Medicine* (New York, 1960). Still useful for understanding the frequency and the array of communicable diseases is Charles Creighton, *A History of Epidemics in Britain*, 2 vols. (Cambridge, 1891–94). Judith Wolleswinkel-van den Bosch, *The Epidemiological Transition in The Netherlands* (n.p., 1998), provides a recent literature review.

interpretation a theory, Omran also tried to move study of the health transition toward abstraction and theorizing and away from description. In recent years scholars have given more attention to Omran's categories of disease and to the need to identify the disease profile of a population in order to assess how a country might initiate or accelerate rising survivorship. In Omran's approach the most important thing is to understand leading diseases.

McKeown drew attention to a single leading factor, which is nutrition, specifically, getting enough to eat. By implication the most important thing humans could learn was the lesson of balancing population with the supply of food, which Thomas Malthus addressed in his 1798 *Essay on Population*. McKeown's approach exemplifies the attempt to understand the decline of mortality by investigating leading factors that played a broad role. Omran, in contrast, focuses on the changing profile of diseases, especially those causing death. This is a single effect, but not a single cause. By implication the most important thing humans could learn is how to avoid, prevent, manage, and treat disease.

Another interpretation, which appeared in the 1950s but received little attention in the 1960s and 1970s, has reemerged in more recent scholarship.[11] This interpretation argues that the health transition had many causes rather than only a few. Even in the same country different factors led the health transition at different times. Furthermore, different regions in the same country advanced toward higher life expectancy each

[11] See the argument made by R. Schofield, D. Reher, and A. Bideau, eds., *The Decline of Mortality in Europe* (Oxford, 1991), p. 17; Jean-Claude Chesnais, *The Demographic Transition: Stages, Patterns and Economic Implications: A Longitudinal Study of 67 Countries Covering the Period 1720–1984* (Oxford, 1992); and Christopher J. L. Murray and Lincoln C. Chen, "Dynamics and Patterns of Mortality Change," in Lincoln Chen, Arthur Kleinman, and Norma C. Ware, eds., *Health and Social Change in International Perspective* (Boston, 1994), pp. 3–23. Stephen J. Kunitz, "Mortality since Malthus," in David Coleman and Roger Schofield, eds., *The State of Population Theory: Forward from Malthus* (Oxford, 1986), pp. 279–302, makes an argument in which leading factors prevailed in certain periods, but the leading factors changed over time.

at its own pace, assisted by an ever-changing set of factors. Across countries what stands out is the multiplicity rather than the singularity of strategies.

The idea that the success of the health transition is owing to many rather than to a few factors can be traced to the comparative study of survivorship. Stolnitz drew a contrast between Japan and developing countries. Sheila Johansson and Carl Mosk compared the experience of Japan with that of England and Wales and Italy, explicitly using a comparative approach to derive a theory of enhanced survivorship.[12] They examined the problem of threats to survival in two parts: some factors expose people to hazards, and some factors contribute to resistance or assist recovery. Whereas Omran, a sociologist, melded history and epidemiology, Johansson and Mosk (a historical sociologist and an economist) melded the wider range of biological and human sciences necessary to understand exposure and resistance, construing those things not at the individual but at the societal level.

That line of thought has drawn attention to what are often called proximate determinants, meaning the individual, household, and group characteristics that influence mortality: urban/rural residence, housing, nutrition, education, income, access to health services, and the like. Nineteenth-century public health thinkers, including Louis Villermé, raised these issues, but germ theory, which emphasizes the importance of microorganisms in causing disease, forced them into the background. W. H. Mosley and L. C. Chen revived this multicausal approach, arguing that a specific disease should be seen as "an indicator of the operation of the proximate determinants rather than . . . a 'cause' of illness and death." Thinking about opportunities to reduce infant and child mortality in de-

---

[12] S. Ryan Johansson and Carl Mosk, "Exposure, Resistance, and Life Expectancy: Disease and Death During the Economic Development of Japan, 1900–1960," *Population Studies* 41 (1987): 207–35.

veloping countries, Mosley and Chen directed attention away from technical innovations and toward social policy.[13]

Two research teams examined diseases causing death across the world in the 1990s in search of insights into how most effectively to reduce mortality further, and in particular to reduce it in countries where survivorship rates are not yet high. Dean Jamison, W. H. Mosley, and their associates assessed the cost-effectiveness of interventions of various types and took morbidity into account by measuring not just the deaths associated with particular diseases but also the time lost to sickness and disability.[14] They found, for example, that BCG (bacillus Calmette-Guérin) vaccine is effective against miliary tuberculosis in children but not against all forms of tuberculosis, and that oral rehydration therapy (a treatment for diarrheal dehydration) works much better in a clinic than in the community at large. Christopher Murray, Alan Lopez, and their associates examined leading causes of death and ill health in 1990 in *The Global Burden of Disease*. They formulated the problem of controlling hazards to survival as a set of global as well as national problems, deriving a detailed inventory of diseases and making a simple distinction between communicable and noncommunicable maladies. Both teams tried to produce com-

---

[13] W. H. Mosley and L. C. Chen, "An Analytical Framework for the Study of Child Survival in Developing Countries," in W. H. Mosley and L. C. Chen, eds., *Child Survival: Strategies for Research, Population and Development Review*, Supplement to vol. 10 (1984): 25–45, quote from p. 28.

A potential ally of this approach lies in study of the elements of disease and human reactions to it that are socially constructed. See esp. Charles E. Rosenberg, *The Cholera Years: The United States in 1832, 1849, and 1866* (Chicago, 1962); and J. N. Hays, *The Burdens of Disease: Epidemics and Human Response in Western History* (New Brunswick, N.J., 1998).

[14] Dean T. Jamison et al., eds., *Disease Control Priorities in Developing Countries* (Oxford, 1993). On trends in health expectation, see C. D. Mathers and J. M. Robine, "International Trends in Health Expectancies: A Review," *Australian Journal on Ageing* 17 (1998): 51–55; and Eileen Crimmins, Yasahiko Saito, and Dominique Ingegneri, "Trends in Disability-Free Life Expectancy in the United States, 1970–90," *Population and Development Review* 23 (1997): 555–72.

prehensive inventories of deaths by cause and age, to rank disease problems, and to identify solutions and policies.[15]

The comparative epidemiologic approach draws attention to factors that cross political boundaries, such as technical innovations. Stolnitz and his successors have stressed immunizations and other public health measures, chemotherapies and other medical measures, and social policy as ways to account for the retreat of mortality among infants and children, and thus as the most hopeful arenas for future action. For adults, researchers have increasingly emphasized the importance of risk factors, which consist of modes of behavior, diet, and lifestyle, some adopted in childhood, that may influence health and survival. Such an emphasis makes morbidity, conceived as both a population's sickness rate and the individual's lifelong health experience, an important issue. To this emphasis David Barker has added the idea that many adult diseases may be programmed in the prenatal period or in infancy by risk factors confronted by parents, especially mothers.[16]

[15] Christopher J. L. Murray and Alan D. Lopez, eds., *The Global Burden of Disease: A Comprehensive Assessment of Mortality and Disability from Diseases, Injuries, and Risk Factors in 1990 and Projected to 2020* (Cambridge, Mass., 1996). The project is summarized in Murray and Lopez, eds., *The Global Burden of Disease* (Cambridge, Mass., 1996); and Murray and Lopez, "Evidence-Based Health Policy – Lessons from the Global Burden of Disease Study," *Science* 274 (1996): 740–43.

See also Myriam Khlat, "La santé: Anciennes et nouvelles maladies," in Jean-Claude Chasteland and Jean-Claude Chesnais, eds., *La population du monde: Enjeux et problèmes* (Paris, 1997), pp. 435–60; and France Meslé and Jacques Vallin, "La mortalité dans le monde: Tendances et perspectives," in ibid., pp. 461–79. Robert Beaglehole and Ruth Nonita, *Public Health at the Crossroads: Achievements and Prospects* (Cambridge, 1997), incorporate this approach into a broad redefinition of public health.

[16] James C. Riley, *Sickness, Recovery, and Death: A History and Forecast of Ill Health* (Iowa City, 1989); D. J. P. Barker, "Infant Mortality, Childhood Nutrition and Ischaemic Heart Disease in England and Wales," *Lancet* (1986): 1077–81; Barker, *Fetal and Infant Origins of Adult Disease* (London, 1992); Robert W. Fogel, "Economic Growth, Population Theory, and Physiology: The Bearing of Long-Term Processes on the Making of Economic Policy," NBER working paper no. 4638, 1994; and George Alter and

Scholars studying the health transition have often focused on leading factors only to find that they could not agree on the same leading factor. One effect of this approach has been to build understanding of each tactical category piecemeal and in rich detail. Public health, medicine, wealth and income, nutrition, behavior, and education, and specific changes within each of these tactical areas, have all drawn the close scrutiny of researchers. To list these categories is therefore to introduce factors of which each is known to have had its own complex elements and complicated history. The ultimate effect of such an approach can be confusion, on the order of Henry Ford's frustration with history as just one damned thing after another. An organizing principle is needed, and the best one available is the theory of an epidemiologic transition, recast from Omran's interpretation of it. This approach makes disease the central issue.

The Epidemiologic Transition

Humans learned to shape their survival prospects very late in the course of things, long after they had learned how to limit fertility by deferring marriage, promoting celibacy, spacing children, and stopping reproduction before women reached the end of their reproductive years. In the beginning, in Omran's description of the epidemiologic transition, death was ruled by pandemic infections, which were often seasonal in their effects.[17] Omran used this characterization to describe the eighteenth cen-

James C. Riley, "How Long Does Wellness or Sickness Predict Future Health," paper presented at the Social Science History Association, Chicago, November, 1998.

On the concept of health expectation, see J. M. Robine, N. Brouard, and A. Colvez, "Les indicateurs d'espérance de vie sans incapacité (EVSI): Des indicateurs globaux de l'état de santé des populations," *Revue d'epidémiologie et santé publique* 35 (1987): 206–24.

[17] Few historians accept this description. More typically the baseline mortality regime is described as one in which endemic disease, usually communicable, caused most deaths, while mortality crises associated with epidemics, war, and famine added additional deaths but only a fraction of the long-run average.

tury and the more distant past in Northwestern Europe, which has occupied center stage because the evidence now available indicates that the health transition began there and because, by comparison with other parts of the world, the early evidence is so rich. The next stage Omran described as one of receding pandemics, and the third as one of degenerative diseases, many the unwitting products of human behavior and action.

Few commentators have agreed with Omran's terms or his periodization, but many have found these concepts useful for summing up the evolution of causes of death across time. Omran regarded it as important to point out how the decline of mortality in stages two and three contributed to population growth across the globe. In most countries death rates fell ahead of and faster than fertility, leading to explosive population growth between 1800 and 2000. Because the population in developing countries remained young at the end of the twentieth century, rapid growth in numbers can be expected to continue well into the twenty-first century even though fertility has declined. For study of the health transition, however, changes in the cause-of-death profile matter more than the timing of changes in mortality and fertility.[18]

Dramatic changes have occurred in this profile. Using the London bills of mortality, William Black compiled the causes of 1.7 million deaths in London in the period 1701–76, and in Table I.1 his compilation is compared with a recent British profile. Ten causes account for 90 percent of

Walter G. Rödel, *Mainz und seine Bevölkerung in 17. und 18. Jahrhundert* (Stuttgart, 1985), gives a good example of seasonal patterns of mortality in a city; and Masako Sakamoto-Momiyama, *Seasonality in Human Mortality: A Medico-Geographical Study* (Tokyo, 1977), provides a broad comparative study.

[18] Omran, "The Epidemiologic Transition." See also S. Jay Olshansky et al., *Infectious Diseases – New and Ancient Threats to World Health, Population Bulletin,* 52 (1997), pp. 10–12, for expansions of Omran's theory. These ideas can be interpreted within the context of the increasing frequency and pace of human contact across oceans and other geographic barriers, which had promoted the global integration of diseases. See, esp., William H. McNeill, *Plagues and Peoples* (Garden City, N.Y., 1976).

Table I.1. *Leading Causes of Death in London, 1701–1776, and Britain, 1992*

London, 1701–76	Percent	Britain, 1992	Percent
Convulsions	28.3	Diseases of the circulatory system, especially ischaemic heart disease and cerebro-vascular disease	46
Consumption	16.6	Neoplasms, led by cancer of the lung	26
Fevers (malignant, spotted, scarlet, and purple)	14.7	Diseases of the respiratory system	11
Smallpox	8.7	Diseases of the digestive system	3.4
Aged	8.0	Mental disorders	2.4
Teeth	5.2	Diseases of the nervous system	2.1
Dropsy and tympany	4.1	Diseases of the endocrine system	1.8
Asthma and tissick	2.0	Symptoms, signs, and ill-defined conditions	0.9
Cholic, gripes, and twisting of the guts	1.7	Other causes	6.4
Childbed	1.0		

Source: William Black, *A Comparative View of the Mortality of the Human Species . . .* (London, 1788), pp. 64–65, and 414ff; and John Charlton and Mike Murphy, eds., *The Health of Adult Britain 1841–1994*, 2 vols. (London, 1997), I: 45–53.

all the deaths reported by London's eighteenth-century searchers of the dead, who were lay people, mostly women who needed the extra income they earned by reporting deaths and their causes to city authorities. Only a few of the causes refer to specific diseases; most relate symptoms and effects of disease. Most of the causes can be associated with infancy and childhood and with the signs and symptoms of communicable diseases. These data do not indicate that diseases of the internal organs played a major role. The searchers glanced at a body and collected information from associates, but they did not conduct a postmortem. Even if they had, many of the internal signs that point to organ disease were discovered in the nineteenth century, after postmortem examinations began to be made in large numbers of people. No system of classification is evident in the London deaths, and the causes appear, to twentieth-century readers, to be vague.[19] As data, the London bills of mortality fairly warned residents about the waxing and waning of epidemic diseases, but provided few clues about disease management or treatment. Nevertheless, there is much evidence to indicate that acute infectious diseases dominated the eighteenth-century profile, in London and elsewhere in Europe.

The late twentieth-century profile, which is organized into the categories of the tenth edition of the *International Classification of Diseases*, shows that chronic organ diseases have become dominant. More than 70 percent of deaths in Britain in 1992 are attributed to cancers and diseases of the circulatory system. There is also the appearance of specificity in the 1992 list, compared with Black's compilation, in that deaths are attributed to named diseases. Indeed there is much more specificity in the modern approach, even though the point has not yet been reached where it can be said that the same death would be described the same way in different national medical cultures.[20] Omran meant to describe the transition from

[19] William Black, *A Comparative View of the Mortality of the Human Species . . .* (London, 1788), pp. 64–65. Although these causes appear to be vague, to eighteenth-century observers they allowed meaningful comparisons. See the comparative discussion in Johann Peter Süssmilch, *Die göttliche Ordnung in den Veränderungen des menschlichen Geschlechts. . .* , 2 vols., 2nd ed. (Berlin, 1761), II: 406–50. To understand more about seeing these diseases and the transition in context, see Arthur E. Imhof, *Die gewonnenen Jahre: Von der zunahme unserer Lebensspanne seit dreihundert Jahren oder von der Notwendigkeit einer neuen Einstellung zu Leben und Sterben: Ein historischer Essay* (Munich, 1981).

[20] Lynn Payer, *Medicine and Culture: Varieties of Treatment in the United States, England, West Germany, and France* (New York, 1988), discusses some of these differences in diagnosis and treatment in a few countries with comparatively similar medical traditions. It is particularly important to notice that, as age advances, people tend to suffer more

the stage represented by Black's list to the modern era, which is confident about the specificity of disease and the human capacity to identify and differentiate diseases.

Many authorities have noticed that Omran's epidemiologic transition theory contains little theory. It describes the health transition from the point of view of some epidemiologic traits of the leading causes of death. The implication is that humankind has learned successively to control these leading causes, the control beginning with smallpox, a viral disease transmitted through the air, and with some waterborne diseases. Both bulked large in the mortality picture of Northwestern Europe around 1800. But there is nothing in this theory to suggest *how* humans learned to control these contagions, the respiratory diseases that next emerged as leading causes, or how to begin to control the degenerative organ diseases that next took the lead. If this theory seems to predict that humans have developed to the point that they will always learn to control the leading causes of death, there is nothing in the theory that suggests why or how.

Omran's description of epidemiologic change can usefully be modified, employing the facts and insights that scholars have gained since 1971. Although pandemics sometimes occurred in the eighteenth century and earlier, the pretransition era was not one dominated by pandemics of infectious disease. It was instead an age in which diseases went unchecked, or were ineffectively checked. Thus bubonic plague could sweep into fourteenth-century Europe and reappear intermittently from then until the eighteenth century in the form of epidemics. People often died in extraordinary numbers during plague outbreaks. Life expectancy at birth could temporarily shrink to less than five years.[21] These epidemics always receded and they also spared many areas. Only rarely did they take a pan-

than one malady. The listed cause of death is meant to be the most important underlying cause, but that is not always easy to determine.

[21] George Alter, "Plague and the Amsterdam Annuitant: A New Look at Life Annuities as a Source for Historical Demography," *Population Studies* 37 (1983): 23–41. In the

demic form, extending across a wide area and affecting a large share of the
population, as bubonic plague had in the fifteenth century and as cholera
did in the nineteenth century.

Diseases usually present, and therefore endemic, caused most deaths.
Typically these diseases were capable of being transmitted from person to
person, either directly, by air or contact, or indirectly, by fomites, insects,
food, and water. Some communicable diseases remained in a locale, ever
ready to cause sickness and death. Others subsisted in the region rather
than in every locale, and were periodically reintroduced to the individual
hamlets, villages, and towns in which most Europeans lived. The diseases
of leading importance were those that caused death in a significant proportion of the people who developed an apparent, as opposed to an inapparent, case.[22] Case fatality rates among the communicable diseases of
leading importance ranged from 1 or 2 percent to about 20 percent. These
were mobile diseases. An outbreak at one locale could exhaust the supply
of potential victims within a matter of weeks or months, so that these diseases could maintain themselves only by finding ways to reach new hosts
at new sites. Human movement assured the mobility of diseases. Between
exposure to a disease, an unidentified event, and coming down sick, people moved about, and they did that more often after harvest failures and
in wartime than in ordinary times.

Disease epidemics, wars, and harvest failures sometimes produced
mortality crises, in which extraordinary numbers of people in a restricted
area died within a brief span of time.[23] These outbursts of death drew ex-

United States during the 1918 influenza epidemic, life expectancy declined from
fifty-five to less than forty years.

[22] Many people are believed to have certain diseases, such as influenza, without developing symptoms serious enough to make them aware of their illness.

[23] Hubert Charbonneau and André Larose, eds., *The Great Mortalities: Methodological
Studies of Demographic Crises in the Past* (Liège, n.d.); Jacques Dupâquier, "Les vicis-
situdes du peuplement (xve–xviiie siècles)," in Jean-Pierre Bardet and Jacques
Dupâquier, eds., *Histoire des populations de l'Europe*, 3 vols. planned (Paris, 1997), I:

Introduction

tra attention, just as they do in the modern era. But most deaths occurred in day-to-day life. The typical death took an infant or a young child. Insofar as the diseases of this era can be identified at this distance in time, they seem mostly to have been diseases familiar in the modern era: smallpox, several types of enteric diseases, acute respiratory infections, influenza, malaria, measles, diphtheria, typhus, plague, tuberculosis, bronchitis, and many others.[24] Among those, plague and typhus occurred chiefly in epidemics; the others were endemic diseases that sometimes became epidemic. Black's list of causes of death exhibits leading signs and symptoms associated with many of these diseases: skin lesions, fever, diarrhea, and convulsions.

In Northwestern Europe mortality crises began to wane in scale and frequency in some regions in the late sixteenth century. Such crises continued to occur, but by 1750 the chance that a person would die in a mortality crisis was already significantly less everywhere in Northwestern Europe, except Finland, than it had been around 1600. Thus the first stage of this recast version of the epidemiologic transition, which in Northwestern Europe lasted from about 1575 to 1900 but was concentrated in the period 1670-1750, took the form of less frequent and less devastating mortality crises. Some particular diseases, among them bubonic plague and typhus, lost force;[25] the capacity of war and harvest failure to provoke major epidemics also weakened. Because mortality

239–55; and L. Del Panta and M. Livi Bacci, "Chronologie, intensité et diffusion des crises de mortalité en Italie: 1600–1850," *Population* 32 (1977, special number): 401–46.

[24] The share of communicable diseases may be overstated, however, because so much evidence from this period reports the external signs of disease, especially skin lesions and convulsions, which are more often associated with certain communicable diseases.

[25] The isolation of plague victims within their households may have helped limit the spread of the disease within certain countries, once it had arrived. But for a long time plague kept reappearing, moving across the Mediterranean or Russia from its endemic foci in Asia. Many public health remedies were tried against plague, but none seems capable of explaining why the plague stopped reappearing.

21

crises accounted for only a small share of deaths, their retreat produced neither a large change in the death rate nor a strong trend toward longer survival.[26] Malthus, having studied the information available around 1800, concluded that most children who did not die from one disease could still be expected to die only slightly later from another. That is too pessimistic an interpretation; mortality had already begun to decline, but infant and child death rates remained high.

The second stage of this recast epidemiologic transition encompasses the waning of certain communicable diseases, of which the most important are diseases of childhood and youth. Smallpox, scarlet fever, typhoid fever, diphtheria, and whooping cough all lost weight as causes of death in Northwestern Europe during the nineteenth century, and their place was not taken, as it had been earlier, by other diseases. Children who did not die from these diseases more often survived into adulthood. Adult death rates also declined, presumably because adults, too, died less often from communicable diseases. Only infants, aged under one, and older adults, aged sixty-five and above, did not benefit in most places and parts of this second stage, which lasted from about 1750 to about 1890. At the beginning of this stage a broad variety of communicable diseases caused most deaths, and the typical victims were infants and children. By 1890 about 10 to 15 percent of a cohort still perished in infancy, but the typical newborn could be expected to live past age fifty.

The third stage, in which most respiratory diseases waned in importance and infant mortality decreased sharply, overlaps both the preceding and succeeding stages. It may have begun by 1850, when there is some evidence to suggest that tuberculosis was losing force as a cause of death in England and Wales, but it was more certainly under way by 1870. In most

---

[26] Furthermore, most crises seem to have killed the vulnerable rather than a cross-section of the population. In their aftermath death rates were often atypically low.

places in Northwestern Europe infant mortality remained high until the early twentieth century, decelerating rapidly in the early years of the new century and continuing to decline thereafter. By 1939 tuberculosis, bronchitis and chronic bronchitis, influenza, and a group of poorly differentiated respiratory diseases common among children had lost most of their force, and infant mortality had declined to less than 5 percent of a cohort.[27] World War II revived tuberculosis, especially among people facing serious nutritional deprivation, but drugs capable of curing this disease were also introduced at the war's end.

A fourth stage of epidemiologic transition began in Northwestern Europe around 1900, when cardiovascular diseases took the lead among causes of death. The most common age at which people died jumped suddenly from infancy to late adulthood. Even though deaths from an important degenerative disease, congestive heart failure, had already begun to diminish, a general decline in degenerative diseases as causes of death has been slow to develop. Heart disease in other forms, cancer, and other degenerative diseases dominated the period from 1900 into the 1960s. These diseases first acquired prominence as causes of death because of the retreat of communicable diseases and of infant and child mortality, and perhaps also because the risk factors associated with cardiovascular disease affected more and more people. Mortality from cardiovascular diseases began to decline in some countries in the 1960s, but diseases in this broad category remained the leading cause of death to the end of the twentieth century. The fourth stage of epidemiologic transition is still under way.

[27] Compilations of causes of death for the twentieth century include Samuel H. Preston, Nathan Keyfitz, and Robert Schoen, *Causes of Death: Life Tables for National Populations* (New York, 1972); Michael Alderson, *International Mortality Statistics* (New York, 1981); Jacques Vallin and France Meslé, *Les causes de décès en France de 1925 à 1978* (Paris, 1988); as well as Murray and Lopez, eds., *The Global Burden of Disease.*

This recast description of the epidemiologic transition more effectively represents the history of disease and death in Europe and North
America between 1800 and 2000. That is its most satisfactory feature. But
the sequential character of epidemiologic change in Europe and much of
the West often has not prevailed in Latin America, Asia, and Africa. In
those regions at the end of the twentieth century it is often difficult to des-
ignate one category of diseases as the most important. Water-, insect-, and
fomite-borne diseases cause many deaths among infants and children; respiratory diseases kill children, youths, and adults; and degenerative diseases victimize older adults, all at the same time.[28] This coexistence of diseases communicable and noncommunicable, acute and chronic (i.e., short
or protracted in the course), shows that the concept of epidemiologic
transition as a historical process has limited power. This concept retains
importance, however, because it shows so effectively how to categorize
diseases by their modes of transmission, and therefore how to intervene.

The key question is to explain how diseases, even whole categories of
disease, have been brought under control. The epidemiologic transition
implies that human agency accounts for most changes. That notwithstanding, researchers have investigated nonhuman agency and the unintended effects of developments in which humans were engaged. Diseases
rise and fall for reasons outside human efforts to control them. For example, new strains of influenza, some particularly lethal but most comparatively benign, often appear. The most lethal influenza epidemic in the
long period under discussion here occurred in 1918-19; that epidemic is
a statement about the continuing power of respiratory diseases to cause
death, even though the era of its unchecked effect had passed. Smallpox

---

[28] Julio Frenk, José Louis Bobadilla, and Rafael Lozaon, "The Epidemiological Transition in Latin America," in Ian M. Timæus, Juan Chackiel, and Lado Ruzicka, eds.,
Adult Mortality in Latin America (Oxford, 1996), pp. 123–39.

may have become a more virulent disease in the seventeenth century, and scarlet fever may have become a less virulent disease in the late nineteenth century.[29] In sum, diseases appear and disappear, and gain and lose virulence, for reasons outside the direct human effort to control them. Similarly, many of the things that humans do have unintended effects. Stephen Kunitz argues that smallpox and measles became comparatively benign childhood diseases because of population growth and the integration of national economies.[30] Even so, most of the explanations for declining mortality point to human agency. This book explores the principal modes of human agency.

At each passage in the epidemiologic transition larger shares of every cohort lived longer, surviving to ages at which they were at risk to diseases uncommon in childhood. One reason for the importance of tuberculosis as a cause of death in nineteenth-century Northwestern Europe, and of cardiovascular disease in the twentieth century, is the survival of people to the ages at which these diseases typically occur.[31] Thus age at death and cause of death command attention as factors that must be understood if the health transition is to be explained.[32]

[29] On smallpox, see Ann G. Carmichael and Arthur M. Silverstein, "Smallpox in Europe before the Seventeenth Century: Virulent Killer or Benign Disease?," *Journal of the History of Medicine and Allied Sciences* 42 (1987): 147–68; and on scarlet fever, McKeown, *Modern Rise of Population.*

[30] Stephen J. Kunitz, "Making a Long Story Short: A Note on Men's Height and Mortality in England from the First through the Nineteenth Centuries," *Medical History* 31 (1987): 269–80.

[31] For tuberculosis, early adulthood, ages 20–35, and for cardiovascular disease, mature adulthood, ages 50–70.

[32] Thus demographers may go to extraordinary lengths to discover causes of death. See A. Desgrées et al., "L'évolution des causes de décès d'enfants en Afrique: Une étude de cas au Sénégal avec la méthode d'autopsie verbale," *Population* 51 (1996): 845–82.

Theories and Themes

Diminishing Disease

The idea of epidemiologic transition directs attention to disease. Yet the key factor in the health transition is not disease but the actions that diminish it, reducing mortality or morbidity. Those can be divided into four categories: avoidance, prevention, treatment, and management. These four categories overlap, but important distinctions among them are clear. Avoidance refers to repetitive individual and collective efforts to escape the risk of disease. It describes the actions promoted in the eighteenth and nineteenth centuries by filth theorists, who believed that epidemic disease risks could be dampened by cleansing the human habitat. Avoidance also describes the adoption of lifestyles and the selection of foods calculated to enhance survival prospects or reduce the risk of initiating a degenerative organ disease. This form therefore describes the things that lay people do, whether on their own initiative or upon professional guidance, to try to temper disease and injury risks.

Prevention is the classic mode of public health intervention. Health authorities design a method and a program calculated to reduce the risk of disease or death. For example, they devise a vaccine and a strategy for its use. Edward Jenner pioneered prevention in this form, introducing vaccination against smallpox and anticipating a strategy – universal vaccination – by which it could be deployed to eradicate the disease. Prevention and avoidance often overlap; the principal distinction to be made between them lies in the mode of action. Lay people try to avoid diseases, whereas professionals try to prevent them. Both measures are anticipatory.

Treatment attempts to moderate the severity of disease, abbreviate its course, and reduce the risk of death. Individuals treat themselves, but the concept of treatment is usually associated with things that medical practitioners do following diagnosis. They select medications and employ other therapies calculated to diminish the power of sicknesses already in progress. In the modern understanding, successful treatments lead to cure.

Management describes another medical approach, taken when the means available do not allow a doctor or a person engaged in self-treatment to hope to cure disease but allow the effects of the disease to be modified in some useful ways. Before insulin, doctors treated diabetes by ordering a special diet, which they hoped would slow the development of this disease. Rest is often a strategy of disease management. So, too, are many of the modern medications that diminish the effects of heart disease and cancer but do not cure them. Treatment and management also overlap one another; the important difference between them lies in the anticipated effect. Treatment aims to cure while management seeks to control.

People and their health advisors deployed strategies in all of these forms before the health transition, although seldom with marked success. The remarkable thing is the success people have enjoyed during the health transition in discovering efficacious ways to do each of these things.

Countries and Their Strategies

There is more variety than similarity in the ways that countries, or even regions within countries, moved through the health transition. Northwestern Europe began around 1800 with filth theory and thereafter introduced a growing array of tactics, the mixture of which differed from place to place. Sub-Saharan Africa began toward the middle of the twentieth century and relied heavily on biomedicine with its means of prevention and treatment. Contiguous populations that have quite similar levels of life expectancy may, even if they resemble one another, have quite different levels of the immediate and the proximate factors that influence survival.[33] Single factors have sometimes led the decline of mortality in

---

[33] For concrete examples, see Frenk, Bobadillo, and Lozaon, "The Epidemiologic Transition in Latin America."

particular places and times, but, to restate an important point, the idea of a health transition draws attention to the multiplicity of factors that have been deployed to prolong life and to reduce the risk of disease.

In place of the theory of leading factors, the health transition suggests a theory of redundancy. There are several, often many, ways to reach the same level of survivorship. In the last two centuries alternative means have proliferated and gained strength. Thus the substitutability of means has gained importance to the point that, at the end of the twentieth century, diseases were avoided, prevented, treated, and managed in many different ways. Although the popular hope for prevention often rests on the idea of immunization, most diseases cannot yet be prevented in this way. And although the popular hope for treatment often rests on the idea of antibiotics, most diseases still cannot be meliorated or abbreviated in their course in the way that antibiotics do for many bacterial diseases. Because humankind relies on a multiplicity of tactics, it is an important historical problem to identify these various tactics, isolate their contributions, measure their efficacy, and discover the conditions under which each has been effective. This is also an important problem for the present and the future.

This redundancy theory leads to the idea that a population may be overprotected, in the sense of having too many backup or overlapping systems safeguarding it against specific risks. Whereas the populations of the traditional mortality regime, before 1800, lacked enough protection against risks to survivorship in nearly every area, some late twentieth-century populations may have unnecessarily elaborate systems of protection. Redundancy is a good thing when it offers a backup for every protection that may falter, but it is not a good thing when it provides an unnecessarily large number of backup systems or when it costs more than people can afford. Social scientists need to do more than they have yet done to gauge the efficacy of each element of survivorship and health, present and past.

When Will the Health Transition End?

This book examines how the current level of life expectation has been achieved. At the end of the twentieth century that level ranged from a high of eighty years in Japan for males and females taken together to a low of thirty-seven years in Sierra Leone, with a global average of 66.7 years.[34] The health transition remains incomplete. It is, in the first place, a means to an end rather than an end in itself. The goal of a long and healthy life for everyone will not fulfill our desire to improve the human condition.

Historical experience provides many useful insights into how to deepen the reach of the health transition. One of the lessons of the past, however, is that the circumstances surrounding the control of risks to survival constantly shift. Thus the historical record is not always pertinent. The things done by people living in Northwestern Europe in the first half of the nineteenth century may not always prove helpful for understanding how mortality risks can be controlled today. This characteristic may be even truer of the future than it has been of the past because so much of the territory in which life expectancy can still be extended deals with ages to which comparatively few people have survived in the past. Clearly the potential life span of the human species has not been reached. More and more people are living to be 100, indicating that it is realistic to hope that life expectation will continue to rise, even in countries such as Japan, where it is already high.[35] (The number of centenarians in Japan jumped from 113 in 1920 to 989 in 1980, and to 3,223 in 1990.) Many more people could live to advanced ages if more were known about how people can protect themselves against mortality risks at all lower ages. The scale of

---

[34] United Nations Development Programme, *Human Development Report 1999* (New York, 1999), pp. 134–37, giving estimates for 1997.

[35] Väinö Kannisto et al., "Reduction in Mortality at Advanced Ages: Several Decades of Evidence from 27 Countries," *Population and Development Review* 20 (1994): 793–810.

change in life expectancy that occurred between 1800 and 2000 is unlikely to be repeated because in much of the world there is so little room for further gains before old age. But it may be that the hazards to survival at older ages, which are now understood mostly in terms of lifestyle choices, genetic characteristics, and the accumulation of insults to health, are more complex. To extend survival time at ages above 100, it may be necessary to learn many new things about human health at high ages. In any event, one path into the future consists of extended old-age survival.

Another path leads toward better survival rates up to and into old age for people living in the less favored regions of the world which, roughly speaking, are those where life expectancy at birth falls short of seventy years. At the end of the twentieth century about half the global population lived in less favored countries. In some of those countries infant death rates were high, and many children died of diseases that could be prevented by well-known public health and medical measures. In other regions high rates of communicable disease, which cause sickness and death in infancy and childhood, coexisted with high rates of degenerative diseases. The human effort to elevate life expectancy in less favored countries enjoyed notable success in the years 1960-2000, and it can be continued. Vast differences separate the world's people in income, and those did not narrow. The narrowing of differences in life expectancy is one of the most noteworthy achievements of the second half of the twentieth century. Indeed, it is the best news of the twentieth century.

Yet another option lies in mobilizing resources to fight the things that most imperil holding on to current levels of life expectancy. AIDS is already reducing life expectancy in those regions where infection and disease are widespread: southern Africa and parts of southeast Asia. Despair and hardship have cut sharply into survival, especially among adult males, in many countries formerly in the Soviet bloc.

There is a fourth path, too. It leads toward a narrowing of the differentials in life expectancy within populations. In 1800, sex, income, education, housing, and ethnicity rarely conveyed much advantage in life expectancy within the same national population. By 1900 differentials caused or influenced by such factors were commonplace and large, and they remained large throughout the twentieth century. Those gaps can be closed by applying knowledge already available to the task of improving survival prospects among the less favored groups.

Because humankind has learned so much about how to manage risks to survival and because there is so much interest in learning more, we may be able to take all of these paths at the same time.

Suggestions for Further Reading

José Luis Bobadilla et al. "The Epidemiologic Transition and Health Priorities." In Dean T. Jamison et al., eds., *Disease Control Priorities in Developing Countries* (Oxford, 1993), pp. 51–63.

Kei Kawabata et al., eds. "Special Theme – Health Systems." *Bulletin of the World Health Organization* 78 (2000): 715–865. Available at www.who.int/bulletin/pdf/2000/issue6.

Stephen J. Kunitz. "Mortality since Malthus." In David Coleman and Roger Schofield, eds., *The State of Population Theory: Forward from Malthus* (Oxford, 1986), pp. 279–302.

Mark Lalonde. *A New Perspective on the Health of Canadians.* Ottawa, 1974.

Christopher J. L. Murray and Alan D. Lopez. *Summary: The Global Burden of Disease.* Cambridge, Mass., 1996.

Marek Okolski. "Health and Mortality." In United Nations Economic Commission for Europe and United Nations Population Fund, *European Population Conference: Proceedings,* 2 vols. (Strasbourg, 1994), I: 119–205.

R. Schofield, D. Reher, and A. Bideau, eds. *The Decline of Mortality in Europe.* Oxford, 1991.

1

A Brief Overview of the Health Transition

In some places and times before 1800 life expectancy at birth may have reached or even slightly surpassed forty years. E. A. Wrigley and R. S. Schofield estimate that in England between 1541 and 1871, survival time ranged from a high of 41.7 years (in 1581–85) to a low of 27.8 years (in 1561–65), and averaged 35.5 years.[1] In itself that represented an achievement. England's seventeenth-century population was favored in its survival levels, compared with most others. One of its advantages was to escape mortality crises – famines, epidemics, and wars – earlier than its neighbors. The Japanese, too, seem to have enjoyed atypically high life ex-

---

[1] E. A. Wrigley and R. S. Schofield. *The Population History of England, 1541–1871: A Reconstruction* (Cambridge, 1989), p. 230. Compare E. A. Wrigley et al., *English Population History from Family Reconstitution, 1580–1837* (Cambridge, 1997), p. 295. Russell estimated British life expectancy in the period 1250 to 1450 to have ranged between 17.3 years, in 1348–75, amidst the first bubonic plague epidemics, to 35.3 years. Josiah Cox Russell, *British Medieval Population* (Albuquerque, 1948), p. 186.

   The Wrigley-Schofield estimates rely on assumptions about the age distribution of survivorship that are open to debate.

pectancy in the centuries before the health transition.[2] So did the Nordic people and perhaps also people in some other world regions.

But an expectation of 35 years was unusually high. In France between 1740 and 1790 the life expectancy of males fluctuated between 24 and 28 and of females between 26 and 30 years.[3] In some regions of the world life expectancy at birth did not surpass 20 years. Low values are often an effect of high infant and child mortality. Where life expectancy at birth ranged between 20 and 35 years, the life expectancy of young adults was often much higher, even 35 or 40 years. A heavy toll of infant and child mortality brought survival time from birth down. Thus it is important to remember that life expectancy may be misleading unless the pattern of death rates has been examined at each age.[4] Across the globe in 1800 it seems unlikely that the average life lasted 30 years; indeed it may not have lasted 25 years.[5] A few people lived to be old, but many died in infancy or early childhood.

Chronology and Geography of the Health Transition

The evidence now available indicates that the health transition began in Northwestern Europe during the eighteenth century, taking the form of

---

[2] See Alan McFarlane, *The Savage Wars of Peace: England, Japan, and the Malthusian Trap* (Oxford, 1997).

[3] Yves Blayo, "La mortalité en France de 1740 à 1829," *Population* 30, Special Number (1975): 123–42.

[4] Similar life expectancies can be produced by dissimilar patterns of survivorship at particular ages.

[5] Alfred Perrenoud, "La mortalité," in Jean-Pierre Bardet and Jacques Dupâquier, eds., *Histoire des populations de l'Europe*, 3 vols. planned (Paris, 1997), I: 288–90, discusses European possibilities, given estimated levels of fertility and population trends. Higher fertility outside Europe allowed wider boundaries. On Chinese demography before and during the health transition, see James Lee and Wang Feng, "Malthusian Models and Chinese Realities: The Chinese Demographic System 1700–2000," *Population and Development Review* 25 (1999): 33–65.

a continuing although not always continuous rise in life expectancy.[6] France, Sweden, and England and Wales, three of the pioneer countries, have been studied closely, but there is limited similarity in the problems that people in those countries faced.[7] Sweden was a poor country with a largely rural population. England and France were rich countries, by the standards of the day. England's towns were abuilding and with them came the urban penalty of higher mortality, but France's level of urbanization remained lower and its death rates higher than England's. Across Northwestern Europe death rates in cities did not decline to the level of those in rural districts until about 1900, but in the twentieth century in Europe and other continents cities have often been favored and a rural penalty has emerged.[8]

Across the nineteenth century in the pioneer countries and in newcomers alike death rates declined among all ages between one and 65, but rarely in infancy (Sweden is an exception) and rarely at higher ages. Infant mortality, which had dropped in some countries in the eighteenth century, began to decline in the early twentieth century, and that decline

---

[6] Jean-Claude Chesnais, *The Demographic Transition: Stages, Patterns, and Economic Implications* (Oxford, 1992); and Massimo Livi-Bacci, *A Concise History of World Population*, 2nd ed. (Oxford, 1997), provide helpful context, placing mortality within the larger scheme of things. On European demography before the transition, see Michael W. Flinn, *The European Demographic System, 1500–1820* (Baltimore, 1981), and, among a rich variety of local and regional studies, Claude Bruneel, *La mortalité dans les campagnes: Le duché de Brabant aux XVIIe et XVIIIe siècles*, 2 vols. (Leuven, 1977).

[7] See, esp., Wrigley and Schofield, *Population History of England;* Wrigley et al., *English Population History from Family Reconstitution;* Jacques Dupâquier et al., eds., *Histoire de la population française*, 4 vols. (Paris, 1988), vol. 3; Erland Hofsten and Hans Lundström, *Swedish Population History: Main Trends from 1750 to 1970* (Stockholm, 1976); and Anders Brändström and Lars-Göran Tedebrand, eds., *Society, Health and Population during the Demographic Transition* (Stockholm, 1988).

[8] Kingsley Davis, "Cities and Mortality," *International Population Conference, Liège 1973,* 3 vols. (Liège, 1973), III: 259–81. Cities are favored, but neighborhoods within cities may still be under a penalty. See Colin McCord and Harold P. Freeman, "Excess Mortality in Harlem," *New England Journal of Medicine* 322 (1990): 173–77.

has continued. Survivorship of people aged 65–79 decreased first in the 1960s, and of people aged 80+ first in the 1980s. Among sizable countries Sweden appears to have led the world in life expectancy from the eighteenth century until about 1978, when Japan took the lead. Japan is expected to hold its lead through the next half century.[9]

Very little hard information is available about life expectancies in many world regions before 1800, or indeed before 1900. In places where the history of survivorship has been pushed back decades or even centuries before the health transition began, such as England and the Nordic lands, life expectancy fluctuated. This supports the assumption that life expectation fluctuated everywhere before the health transition. In that era life expectancies, where they are known, usually ranged between 20 and 35 years. Some evidence suggests that people enjoyed longer lives in a much earlier era, before humans domesticated plants and animals. Human settlement and more intensive communication brought more exposure to disease, which reduced life expectancy. The range of 20 to 35 years describes most populations and most periods across the world between the Neolithic Revolution and the beginning of the health transition.[10]

The sustained shift to longer survivorship that began in Northwestern Europe before 1800 expanded in the early nineteenth century into other regions of the world. By 1850 the health transition was under way

[9] Machiko Yanagishita and Jack M. Guralnik, "Changing Mortality Patterns That Led Life Expectancy in Japan to Surpass Sweden's: 1972–1988," *Demography* 25 (1988): 611–24; and United Nations Secretariat, Department of Economic and Social Affairs, Population Division, *World Population Prospects: The 1998 Revision* (New York, 1998), I: 555.

[10] Lee and Feng, "Chinese Realities," assemble estimates of male life expectancy in China since c. 1650. Scholars continue to discover the absence of either low death rates or a secular trend toward lower mortality in historical populations. For example, Zhongwei Zhao, "Long-Term Mortality Patterns in Chinese History: Evidence from a Recorded Clan Population," *Population Studies* 51 (1997): 117–27. For the case of India, see *Statistical Abstract India 1997* (New Delhi, 1997), p. 41; and Veena Bhasin, *People, Health and Disease: The Indian Scenario* (Delhi, 1994), who puts these data in context.

in the western half of Europe except Finland and probably also in Canada, Australia, and New Zealand. It had not yet begun in Japan, the United States, or in most of the remainder of the world.

By 1900 the health transition was in progress in the same area as in 1850 plus Japan, the United States, Eastern Europe, Finland, and some countries in Latin America (at least Costa Rica, Paraguay, and Mexico).[11] Between 1900 and 1960 the remaining countries joined in, most of them initiating a health transition in the 1920s and 1930s.

From about 1950 the continuing retreat of mortality can be depicted quantitatively using estimates calculated by international agencies, chiefly the United Nations Population Division and the World Bank. Figure 1.1 shows life expectancy in 150 countries in 1960 and 1995. The countries are arrayed according to their level of development around 1995, judged by the human development index, which assesses life expectancy, education, and per capita gross domestic product. The largest gains occurred in countries where development levels, assessed by these three gauges, were already lower.

Gains in survivorship have often been unequal from one country to another in the short run, but in the long run they have tended to converge toward high survivorship. Thus death rates in France and the Low Countries, which had stood well behind England and the Nordic lands, moved toward them by 1800 (Fig. 1.2). A strong global pattern of convergence developed in the second half of the twentieth century. In life expectancy and literacy, although not in per capita income, less favored nations converged toward favored nations. Table 1.1 shows regional life expectancies, actual and projected, across the century from 1950 to 2050, and the spread between the highest and lowest regions. During the second half of the

[11] Eduardo E. Arriaga, *New Life Tables for Latin American Populations in the Nineteenth and Twentieth Centuries* (Berkeley, 1968).

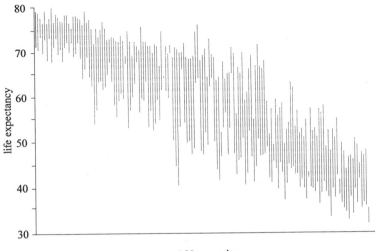

150 countries

Figure 1.1. Life expectancy, 1960 and 1995. *Source:* United Nations Development Programme, *Human Development Report 1998* (New York, 1998), pp. 128–33 and 148–49; and United Nations, *Demographic Yearbook 1961–1967* (New York, 1962–68).

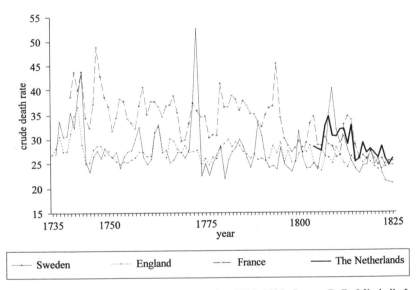

Figure 1.2. Crude death rates in four countries, 1735–1825. *Source:* B. R. Mitchell, *International Historical Statistics: Europe, 1750–1988* (New York, 1992), pp. 90–93; Sweden, Statistiska Centralbyrån, *Historisk statistik för Sverige*, 3 vols. (Stockholm, 1969), I: 86–93; and E. A. Wrigley and R. S. Schofield, *The Population History of England, 1541–1871* (Cambridge, 1989), pp. 499–501.

37

Table 1.1. *Life Expectancy for Both Sexes (in years)*

	1950–55	1995–2000	2045–50
World	46.5	65.4	76.3
Africa	37.8	51.4	70.4
Asia	41.3	66.3	77.2
Europe	66.2	73.3	80.3
Latin America and the Caribbean	51.4	69.2	77.6
North America	69	76.9	81.9
Oceania	60.9	73.8	80.7
Spread from highest to lowest	31.2	25.5	11.5

Source: United Nations Secretariat, Department of Economic and Social Affairs, Population Division, *World Population Prospects: The 1998 Revision*, 2 vols. (New York, 1998), I: 546–73.

twentieth century that spread closed; its rate of closure is expected to quicken in the next half century.

The later the health transition began in a country, the more compressed it has usually been. Figure 1.3 illustrates this by comparing the length of time during which England, Japan, and the Indian state of Kerala added years of life expectancy.[12] Although scholars have often failed to agree among themselves about which factors mattered most in any given case, this quickening pace suggests that policy makers and individuals have been able to select progressively more efficacious courses of action, compared with those adopted by the pioneers.

The twentieth century witnessed a number of cases of rapid gains in life expectancy telescoped in time. As a region Latin America added 0.2 years to life expectancy at birth each year between 1900 and 1930, but 0.7

[12] The beginning dates used in Figure 1.3 are 1790 for England, 1880 for Japan, and 1915 for Kerala.

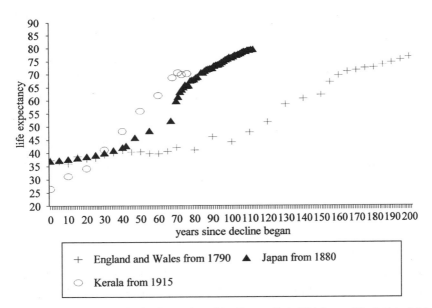

Figure 1.3. The pace of gains in survivorship. *Source:* E. A. Wrigley and R. S. Schofield, *The Population History of England, 1541–1871* (Cambridge, 1989), p. 230; E. A. Wrigley et al., *English Population History from Family Reconstitution, 1580–1837* (Cambridge, 1997), p. 295; Great Britain, *Annual Abstract of Statistics* (London, various years); Masaaki Yasukawa and Keijiro Hirooka, "Estimates of the Population Size and of the Birth- and Death-Rates in Japan, 1865–1920," *Keio Economic Studies* 11 (1974), 46; Japan, *Statistical Yearbook 1996* (Tokyo, 1996), p. 64; P. N. Mari Bhat and S. Irudaya Rajan, "Demographic Transition in Kerala Revisited," *Economic and Political Weekly* 25 (1990), 1959; Kerala, Bureau of Economics and Statistics, *Demographic Report of Kerala 1901–61* (with addendum for 1971) (Trivandrum, 1977), pp. 167–80; and *National Family Health Survey: Kerala 1992–93* (Bombay, 1995), p. 6.

years between 1930 and 1960.[13] Japan made progress at a stunning rate between 1947 and 1980, as did the Soviet Union between 1945 and 1965. Many African states attained sharply higher life expectancies in the two decades after independence, roughly 1960 to 1980. Nigeria's expectation jumped from 36 years in 1963 to about 50 years in 1980, but then stagnated.

[13] Eduardo E. Arriaga, *Mortality Decline and Its Demographic Effects in Latin America* (Berkeley, 1970), pp. 19–20 and 35.

Arabic-speaking countries in Western Asia, some countries in Central America, China, and Vietnam have matched these gains in some periods.

Led by countries that came late to the health transition, life expectancy at birth for the entire world population moved upward rapidly from about 50 years in 1960 to 64 years in 1995 and 66.7 years in 1997.[14] The gap separating poor from rich countries fell from about 30 years in 1960 to 23 years in 1995. Many more people acquired the expectation of living to old age. Map 1.1 shows life expectancy levels in 1997 in 174 countries. Regional differences persist, but they have been shrinking.

Interruptions

Although global survivorship has advanced at a pace gaining speed, the health transition includes periods of stagnation or regression. In Northwestern Europe life expectancy improved little between 1820 and 1870 because death rates were higher in cities and that was a period of rapid urbanization.[15] Breaking things down, which can be done by standardizing for age and other characteristics, survivorship improved in rural and urban areas separately in most countries. Thus a change in population composition – the urbanization of populations – masks the underlying trends, which are the important ones. Life expectancy actually improved, but urbanization conceals that development.

The most important examples of stagnation or regression in life expectation have affected the general population, and they have been the re-

---

[14] United Nations Development Programme, *Human Development Report 1998* (New York, 1998), p. 149, and *Human Development Report 1999* (New York, 1999), p. 137.

[15] On England, see Robert I. Woods, "The Effects of Population Redistribution on the Level of Mortality in Nineteenth-Century England and Wales," *Journal of Economic History* 45 (1985): 645–51; and Simon Szreter and Graham Mooney, "Urbanization, Mortality, and the Standard of Living Debate: New Estimates of the Expectation of Life at Birth in Nineteenth-Century British Cities," *Economic History Review* 51 (1998): 84–112.

sult of mortality crisis in a new form. In the classical form mortality crises usually affected restricted areas, albeit sometimes in a pattern of successive epidemics that sprawled over wide areas. The bubonic plague appeared and reappeared in Europe after 1347, each time spreading from one locale to another, often producing a catastrophic loss of life. Areas where troops moved during the Thirty Years' War suffered horrible losses, a combined effect of temporary emigration and of disease and death associated with the war. Nevertheless, in the period before 1800 in Europe, the effects of mortality crisis are much more evident at the local than the national level because the geographic reach of most crises was limited.

During the health transition local crises in Europe waned in effect, but their place was taken by international or even intercontinental mortality crises, some of immense scale. The largest twentieth-century crises are listed in Table 1.2. Human agency has played a major part in some modern crises, not just in the two world wars but also in the deliberate execu-

Table 1.2. *Leading Mortality Crises in the Twentieth Century*

Event	Estimated deaths
World War I	19 million
Influenza epidemic, 1918–19	40+ million
World War II	52 million
Famine in China 1959–61	14–26 million
AIDS epidemic, to 1999	16 million

Source: Angus Maddison, *The World Economy in the 20th Century* (Paris, 1989), p. 51; Gina Kolata, *Flu: The Story of the Great Influenza Pandemic of 1918 and the Search for the Virus that Caused It* (New York, 1999), pp. 285–86; Penny Kane, *Famine in China, 1959–61: Demographic and Social Implications* (New York, 1988), pp. 89–90; and, for the estimate of AIDS deaths, *New York Times*, Nov. 24, 1999, p. A10, citing U.N. officials.

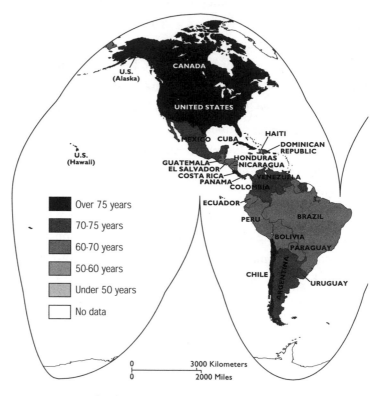

Map 1.1. Life expectancy in 1995. *Source:* United Nations

42

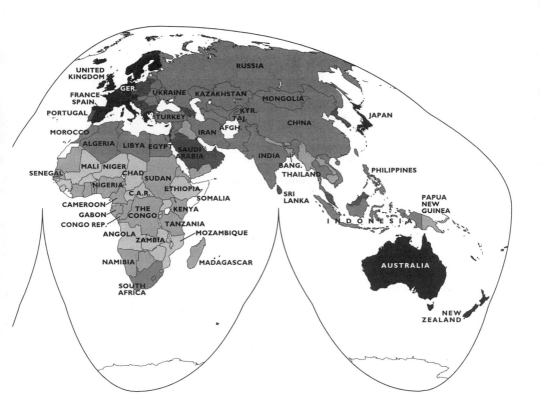

Development Programme, *Human Development Report 1998* (New York, 1998), pp. 128–30.

43

tion of six million Jews and three million gypsies during the Holocaust. The Chinese famine that began in 1959 can also be counted as a crisis that people made, in this case by forcing agricultural collectivization on reluctant peasants.

Two mortality crises have developed since 1980. Each has shown the capacity to stop life expectancy gains or to erode existing levels not just temporarily but for many years in succession. Each has slowed or halted the health transition in the countries and regions most gravely affected.[16]

Russia and Eastern Europe

In Russia and Eastern Europe gains in survivorship, which were especially rapid in the period 1945–65, have stopped in some countries and been reversed in others. The largest country in the region, the Russian Federation, entered the twentieth century with life expectancy at birth of 31 years for males and 33 years for females. The twentieth century saw recurrent progress and regression. Survivorship improved rapidly during the 1920s but deteriorated in the 1930s and early 1940s, owing to the famine associated with agricultural collectivization, Stalin's purges, and World War II. Between 1945 and 1965 life expectancy improved at a pace greater than one year of added survival per calendar year, rising to 64 years for males and 72.1 years for females. From 1965 to 1990 females gained a little, to 74.4 years, while male life expectancy fluctuated around 64 years. Then in the 1990s life expectancy deteriorated, especially for males, falling to 59.2 years in 1995, resulting in a "human security crisis."[17]

---

[16] On other cases of reversal of downward trends in mortality, see Terence H. Hull and Gavin W. Jones, "International Mortality Trends and Differentials," in United Nations, *Consequences of Mortality Trends and Differentials* (New York, 1986), pp. 1–9.

[17] Lincoln C. Chen, Friederike Wittgenstein, and Elizabeth McKeon, "The Upsurge of Mortality in Russia: Causes and Policy Implications," *Population and Development Review* 22 (1996): 517–30.

Higher death rates for males aged 15–64 due to cardiovascular diseases and external causes, especially accidents and alcohol poisoning, led the deterioration. By 1995 females could be expected to outlive males by nearly 13 years. Just as declining mortality contributed to population growth in earlier decades, rising mortality helped reverse the trend in 1992 to one of population decline.

There were also signs of a troubled health care system. Cardiovascular deaths increased among adult females; infant mortality rose; deaths from some communicable diseases, including tuberculosis, occurred more often. Although environmental toxins contributed to the crisis of the 1990s, the leading factors behind it can be associated with the collapse of the Soviet economic, political, and health care systems. Housing, food, and medical care all suddenly became expensive in a period when real incomes declined. Russia maintained living standards well above those in poor countries, but the sudden reversal of economic conditions posed a difficult adjustment. Confidence in the future waned. Older males, aged 45 and above, bore heavier emotional costs and confronted the economic deterioration more directly than did people in other age groups. But the higher mortality of infants and higher death rates from some immunizable diseases, such as diphtheria, and the numerous age groups affected show that the array of problems has widened. Survival safeguards erected since the 1940s began to unravel in the 1990s.[18]

---

[18] Vladimir M. Shkolnikov and France Meslé, "The Russian Epidemiological Crisis as Mirrored by Mortality Trends," in Julie DaVanzo and Gwendolyn Farnsworth, eds., *Russia's Demographic "Crisis"* (Santa Monica, Calif., 1996), pp. 113–62; and Vladimir Shkolnikov, France Meslé, and Jacques Vallin, "La crise sanitaire en Russie," *Population* 50 (1995): 907–42 and 945–82.

On Eastern Europe, see France Meslé, "Mortality in Eastern and Western Europe: A Widening Gap," in David Coleman, ed., *Europe's Population in the 1990s* (Oxford, 1996), pp. 127–43; and Charles M. Becker and David Bloom, eds., *The Demographic Crisis in the Former Soviet Union*, special issue of *World Development* 26 (1998): 1913–2103.

The Russian case indicates that the health infrastructure relies on the continued good performance of political, economic, and emotional support systems. Russia still has one of the highest ratios of physicians to the general population and an extensive network of clinics and hospitals, but it lacks enough equipment and medications. There has not been enough redundancy in the Russian scheme of protecting against risks to survival to compensate for failures in health care, alcohol use, and diet.

AIDS

Disease for disease, it is communicable rather than noncommunicable diseases that have most often been avoided or managed by human intervention. As later chapters make clear, however, means of avoidance and management have been tailored to specific diseases, each of which has its own signature. Systems already in place cannot be expected to protect against diseases that have novel signatures. In the long run, organisms that are dependent on one another tend to accommodate in ways that allow both to survive. Thus diseases may become benign, because either pathogens or hosts have accommodated. But accommodation is not a law. Many familiar diseases appear in new forms, which may be virulent. The history of human disease is also a history in which diseases new to humans appear.[19] Such is the case with acquired immune deficiency syndrome, or AIDS.

About half of the people infected with HIV (34.3 million as of 2000) are below age 25. In Africa, where this epidemic has caused the largest number of deaths, most infected people are women; elsewhere most are men. Between 1981, when the disease was first recognized, and 2000, more than 50 million people became infected across the world. Among

[19] S. Jay Olshansky, Bruce Carnes, Richard G. Rogers, and Len Smith, *Infectious Diseases – New and Ancient Threats to World Health*, Population Bulletin 52, no. 2 (1997); and Arlo Karlen, *Man and Microbes: Disease and Plagues in History and Modern Times* (New York, 1996).

them nearly 19 million died, with mortality rising to an estimated 2.8 million deaths in 1999. By the 1990s the largest numbers of infected people, disease cases, and deaths were found in sub-Saharan Africa, where about 8 percent of the population was infected. Across the world nearly 6 million people became infected each year.

In most regions life expectancy continued to rise because the people who died from AIDS, most of them in young adulthood, were not numerous enough to counterbalance deaths from other causes that had been deferred. But in sub-Saharan Africa life expectancy declined, and may by 2010 fall to 45 years. That would return life expectancy in the region to its level in the 1950s.

AIDS appeared in the 1980s in high-risk groups to which comparatively small numbers of people belonged: homosexuals and intravenous drug users in the West, and, in other regions, people who buy and sell sex.[20] In the 1990s the disease maintained its place in these groups and spread to the general population of much of the eastern and southern parts of sub-Saharan Africa. Typically latent for four to eleven years, the virus strains associated with AIDS are often transmitted before an infected person shows any symptoms or has any clue that he or she has been infected. The sexual routes of transmission can be broken by using condoms. Often they have not been broken, with the result that in the middle 1990s HIV infection spread in far more countries than it remained stable.[21]

[20] John C. Caldwell and Pat Caldwell, "Toward an Epidemiological Model of AIDS in Sub-Saharan Africa," *Social Science History* 20 (1996): 559–91; John C. Caldwell, "The Impact of the African AIDS Epidemic," *Health Transition Review* 7 (1997, supplement): 169–88. *Health Transition Review* contains many valuable scholarly essays on the demography of AIDS in Africa.

[21] John K. Anarfi, "Initiating Behavioural Change among Street-Involved Youth: Findings from a Youth Clinic in Accra," in John C. Caldwell et al., eds., *Resistances to Behavioural Change to Reduce HIV/AIDS Infection in Predominantly Heterosexual Epidemics in Third World Countries* (Canberra, 1999), pp. 81–90.

Morbidity

AIDS is a nearly unique disease in that it can victimize large numbers of people, its case fatality rate is virtually 100 percent, and death is usually preceded by a lengthy period of sickness and incapacity. AIDS therefore adds to both mortality and morbidity. Its additions to morbidity help illustrate the various meanings of this term, of which three are particularly important. First, morbidity refers to the rate of initiation of a new episode of sickness in people who are well. In most Western countries and in Uganda the rate of new AIDS cases has stabilized, but in other parts of sub-Saharan Africa, Haiti, and several countries in South Asia the rate of new cases has continued to rise. Second, morbidity refers to the prevalence of a disease or of sickness in general. Since people infected with HIV often survive many years before developing AIDS, and since people with AIDS often live for many months, the prevalence of this disease has increased everywhere. Part of that increase has been driven by medications that limit the replication of HIV in the people treated and keep the disease at bay; part has been driven by the rising rate of new cases. Third, morbidity refers to time lost from active life owing to sickness. Statistics on sickness prevalence can be used to modify the life table in a helpful way, making it possible to think not just about survival prospects but also about the prospects of survival in a state of wellness. Thus healthy life expectancy refers to the number of years people can be expected to survive in good health.[22]

Interest in this gauge developed first in the 1950s and 1960s, when gains in life expectancy slowed in many developed countries. Some ob-

---

[22] J. M. Robine and K. Ritchie, "Healthy Life Expectancy: Evaluation of a New Global Indicator for Change in Population Health," *British Medical Journal* 302 (1991): 457–60. For an example of the practical use of this measure, see A. C. Bebbington, "The Expectation of Life without Disability in England and Wales: 1976–88," *Population Trends* 66 (1991): 26–29.

servers concluded that the future offered less from further additions to life expectancy than from an improved quality of life, especially fewer sickness events and less sickness time. Unexpectedly, death rates began to decline among people at ages 65+ in the 1960s in many Western countries, and by the 1990s death rates were decreasing even among people in their 80s and 90s. These developments nevertheless heightened interest in the quality of life because of the heavy toll of sickness at higher ages, and because many of the diseases causing sickness and death at those ages could be traced to diet, exercise, tobacco use, and other habits adopted much earlier in life. Data on healthy life expectancy showed that it was rising more slowly than life expectancy, or not at all.[23]

The investigation of morbidity in its incidence and prevalence, and its contribution to healthy life expectancy, shows also that sickness rates have not followed the path taken by death rates. The risk of initiating a new episode of a communicable disease declined during the health transition; thus sickness incidence fell. But it fell at a slower pace than did the death rate. The incidence of noncommunicable diseases rose. Since the average duration of noncommunicable diseases is longer than that of communicable diseases, sickness prevalence increased at each age. Aggregate sickness time increased, even holding age constant. In countries where fertility declined early and the population aged, the overall burden of sickness rose the most rapidly.[24] In recent decades sickness prevalence has remained stable in some countries, increased in some, and decreased in

---

[23] Jean-Marie Robine, "Lengthening of Life and Health Status of the Population," in *Demografia: Analisi e sintesi: Cause e conseguenze dei processi demografici* (Rome, 1996), pp. 51–69.

[24] James C. Riley, "Mortality and Morbidity: Trends and Determinants," *World Health Statistics Quarterly* 51 (1998): 177–90; and Riley, "Long-Term Morbidity and Mortality Trends: Inverse Health Transitions," in John Caldwell et al., eds., *What We Know about the Health Transition: The Cultural, Social and Behavioural Determinants of Health*, 2 vols. (Canberra, 1990), I: 165–88.

some.[25] That explains why healthy life expectancy has not risen as much as life expectancy.

These differing trends show that sickness events, sickness prevalence, and mortality do not share exactly the same causes.[26] The policies that bring one under control may have little effect on the other, or may even aggravate it. The concept of healthy life expectancy suggests the possibility of living a long life free of sickness until the end. But the study of disease trends shows that this goal will be more difficult to achieve than high life expectancy alone. The relationship between mortality and morbidity, and more specifically between health and survival, requires more exploration. In the meantime every consideration of survivorship must be tempered by consideration of health and the possibility that longer survival has not led to higher levels of population health.

Health can also be appraised by looking at the accumulation of sickness events or sickness time over the life course. People who have suffered significant loads of sickness appear even after their recovery to carry effects of that experience forward, toward more future sickness and earlier death, compared with people who have been well. Some of these pathways are specific to certain diseases; childhood rheumatic fever may damage heart valves in a way that threatens health in middle age. Others appear to be effects of disease and injury in general.[27] The implication is that populations that experience less morbidity have an advantage in later health and survival.

[25] Robine, "Lengthening of Life."

[26] James C. Riley, *Sick, Not Dead: The Health of British Workingmen during the Mortality Decline* (Baltimore, 1997).

[27] George Alter and James C. Riley, "How Long Does Wellness or Sickness Predict Future Health?," paper presented at the Social Science History Association, Chicago, November, 1998.

Imports and Indigenous Remedies

Some of the innovations that contributed to the health transition can be identified with certain inventors or pioneers. Edward Jenner introduced vaccination against smallpox in 1796. Britain revived and intensified the idea of making cities safer places to live by providing pure water and disposing safely of human waste. Louis Pasteur and Robert Koch, working separately and competitively, demonstrated that many diseases are caused by specific pathogens and explained some of the ways to block those pathogens. These, among many examples of key innovations, emphasize the role of the West in interventions that prolonged life. But it is easy to exaggerate the degree to which the West discovered how to extend survivorship and to which other societies borrowed Western ideas. Jenner's vaccination spread, at a stately pace, to Asia and the Americas, and sometimes displaced the practice of inoculation against smallpox, which was already known in much of Asia at least. But Britain's public health innovations proved much more difficult for other countries to adopt. They were and remain costly; they are suited for dense and rich populations, especially for cities, but not for dispersed populations or poor people. Even in many of the countries where life expectancy at birth by 2000 surpassed seventy years, sanitary improvements remained incomplete. In Asia and Africa, systems for the delivery of purified water and the waterborne disposal of human waste usually exist in older urban neighborhoods, but less often in squatter neighborhoods or in the countryside.[28]

The leading example of a technology devised in developed countries

---

[28] For descriptions of the provision of state services to people in urban slums, see James Manor, *Power, Poverty, and Poison: Disaster and Response in an Indian City* (New Delhi, 1993); and Tade Akin Aina, "Housing and Health in Olaleye-Iponri, a Low Income Settlement in Lagos, Nigeria," in Sandy Cairncross, Jorge E. Hardoy, and David Satterthwaite, eds., *The Poor Die Young: Housing and Health in Third World Cities* (London, 1990), pp. 56–88.

and exported to the remainder of the world is biomedicine. Its main elements – germ theory, immunizations, and antibiotics – were worked out in Europe, North America, and Japan between the 1870s and the 1950s by a large number of scientists making piecemeal contributions to a complex edifice. Biomedicine was then adopted by many poor countries hoping to find a crash-course strategy for raising life expectancy. In many ways the export of biomedicine from the developed world to developing countries can be counted a success. Immunizations and antibiotics have done much to curtail the effects of communicable diseases, especially since 1950. It is difficult to imagine as rapid a pace of gains in life expectancy as seen in developing countries between 1950 and 1980 by any other means. But there are two important ways in which biomedicine has fallen short. First, it has been exported as a single tactic for extending survival, whereas in the developed countries it was always employed in alliance with other means of prevention and remedy. Biomedicine has controlled many diseases in developing countries, but that control requires the immunization of successive cohorts of infants even though the infrastructure needed to mount successful immunization campaigns may not be present. Biomedicine would be a stronger tactic if accompanied by complementary means of disease control and treatment. Second, biomedicine demands the acceptance of a theory of disease that is valuable but also incomplete and inaccurate. Germs do cause disease, but it is not necessarily a good thing to hope to control germs by means of biomedicine. Pathogens develop drug-resistant strains. What is more, constant vigilance and an ever-present supply of biomedical servants – nurses and doctors and medications – are necessary to make biomedicine continue to work. In the absence of improvements that reduce exposure to disease, biomedicine can at best take a population only part of the way toward a life expectancy at birth surpassing seventy years.

In each particular country, and often also in separate regions of the same country, indigenous resources and characteristics have often assisted the health transition. In many areas of the world people heated water before drinking it because they preferred tea to plain water. Before the health transition some societies embraced bathing while others feared it, suspecting, as many Europeans did, that bathing augmented the risk of falling sick. Some societies developed the habit of listening to and cooperating with the advice given by authorities or experts, and that habit helped in the implementation of remedies when those became available. The Indian state of Kerala urged the education of females as well as males long before parental, especially maternal, education had been shown to be a means of protecting children's survival. Many societies here and there across the globe have opted for a more egalitarian distribution of food, fuel, and housing, and in that way have reduced the proportion of people whose poverty aggravates the hazards to survival. These are just a few examples of indigenous means of mortality control. They illustrate the point that many elements of the health transition derive from traditional practices, which acquired or were given new importance. This aspect of the health transition – the mixture of imported and indigenous means of limiting hazards to survival and the identity of the indigenous means – cries for more attention from scholars.

In particular cases, such as Japan, the health transition often combined outside with indigenous ideas. There survivorship improved between the 1870s and World War II, dropped sharply during the war, and then resumed its rise. For most of that period Japan remained much poorer than European countries, whose progress in survivorship Japan matched. Gross domestic product (GDP) per capita rose by 35 percent between 1870 and 1900, but remained only a quarter of its level in the United Kingdom.[29] Judging by stature and official statistics on calorie intake, the Japanese also remained poorly nourished, their diets meager and unbalanced in vitamins, minerals, and fats. Nutritional diseases, even beriberi,

[29] Angus Maddison, *Monitoring the World Economy, 1820–1992* (Paris, 1995), pp. 23–24.

remained significant causes of death into the 1920s. Waterborne diseases, such as typhoid fever, persisted, and the Japanese continued to put off the modernization of sanitary systems. In 1937 not quite 87,000 households among some 13.8 million possessed modernized means for the disposal of human waste, and only 26 percent of houses were connected to public waterworks.

In the earlier phase of its health transition Japan mixed imported and indigenous programs. Among the imported programs, vaccination against smallpox began in the 1870s and quickly brought under control a leading cause of death in childhood. Quarantines restricted cholera. Those techniques can be counted as imports. The Japanese began a shift from Chinese to Western medicine after 1850, but even in the 1890s few doctors had yet been trained in Western medicine. Government policies promoted training many doctors rather than specialization; most people were not attended by medical practitioners when they died. From the 1920s on, the central government diverted resources to military expansion. In the meantime the Japanese people, already favored by habits and attitudes that reduced mortality risks, cooperated willingly with central-government health programs. Nowhere were tactics of enhanced survivorship spread more effectively than in Japan. The Japanese also favored a comparatively egalitarian distribution of incomes, which modern research suggests contributes to lower mortality. Imported programs were therefore used selectively, with the selection based more often on their price – vaccination was cheap compared with sanitary improvements – or their adaptability to Japanese preferences than on their efficacy.[30]

---

[30] Irene B. Taeuber, *The Population of Japan* (Princeton, 1958); S. Ryan Johansson and Carl Mosk, "Exposure, Resistance, and Life Expectancy: Disease and Death during the Economic Development of Japan, 1900–1960," *Population Studies* 41 (1987): 207–35; and Gail Honda, "Differential Structure, Differential Health: Industrialization in Japan, 1868–1940," in Richard H. Steckel and Roderick Floud, eds., *Health and Welfare during Industrialization* (Chicago, 1997), pp. 251–84. On the effects of income

After 1945, too, Japan selected imports and modified them to complement indigenous preferences. National programs to screen for tuberculosis and the risk factors associated with stroke and cancer drew a willing population into a campaign to identify health problems, leading to more effective treatment of tuberculosis and stroke. From the 1950s the Japanese ate more fruits, vegetables, and animal products without increasing intake of calories: average daily calorie intake in 1992 was slightly lower than it had been in 1955. For males the body mass index, a gauge of nutritional status, moved toward the center of the preferred range, at 25, but among females it shifted from the middle to the lower end of the preferred range, which is 20 to 30.[31] Yet females added years of life expectancy faster than males.

Even in the developed countries where the aim was to use much the same means of controlling hazards, neighboring countries often adopted distinctive approaches. This is Peter Baldwin's argument after examining the ways that Britain, France, Sweden, and Germany dealt with cholera, smallpox, and syphilis in the nineteenth century.[32] This reality will become more evident as scholars undertake more comparative histories of the health transition.

distribution, see G. B. Rogers, "Income and Inequality as Determinants of Mortality: An International Cross-Section Analysis," *Population Studies* 33 (1979): 343–51.

On the postwar period, see Takao Shigematsu et al., "Factors Contributing to the Improvement and Predominance of the Longevity of the Japanese Population," NUPRI Research Paper Series No. 65, 1994; Takeshi Hirayama, *Life-Style and Mortality: A Large-Scale Census-Based Cohort Study in Japan* (Basel, 1990); and Shigemi Kono and Shigesato Takahashi, "Mortality Trends in Japan: Why Has the Japanese Life Expectancy Kept on Increasing," Working Paper No. 1, July 1989, Institute of Population Problems, Ministry of Health and Welfare.

[31] Body mass index is calculated by dividing weight in kilograms by height in meters squared.

[32] Peter Baldwin, *Contagion and the State in Europe, 1830–1930* (Cambridge, 1999).

Conclusion

The attempt to control hazards to survival has evolved into one of the three most elaborate structures that people have overtly built, along with polities and economies. Of the three, the health transition has been the most successful, delivering a larger quantity of long life to a larger share of the world population than polities have delivered good government or economies wealth. There are only the reservations that health may not always have improved as much as survival, and that not all countries or all people enjoy the benefits of the health transition.

There is a health infrastructure. It encompasses the institutions and practices built and selected with the specific purpose of improving survival or health, and other institutions and practices that affect health and survival without have been designed to do so. Both elements are present in each of the six tactics into which this study divides the examination of the health transition's history: public health, medicine, wealth and income, nutrition, behavior, and education. They rarely have the same immediacy of effect as do the elements of political and economic infrastructures. A particular health innovation – building a sewage disposal system, a hospital, a school, an economy producing rising incomes – is expected to have a beneficial effect. But we do not often measure the payoff in lengthened survival or diminished sickness, nor do we usually try to draw direct cause-and-effect associations. Life expectancy is, for survival at least, a counterpart to gross domestic product for measuring economic performance. But the latter is much more in evidence in thought and practice than is the former.

How curious that assessment of the means meant to improve health or survival is so casual. Of course few of the elements in the health infrastructure are meant to contribute solely to health and survival. Nevertheless, assessment of the degree to which they do so would help us understand better how the health infrastructure works. As a first step toward

that end, the chapters that follow try to identify the various parts of the
health system and describe them in their historical contexts.

Suggestions for Further Reading

Lawrence A. Adeokun. "Problems of Health Intervention Programmes: The Case of
Nigeria." In Jacques Vallin and Alan D. Lopez, eds., *Health Policy, Social Policy and
Mortality Prospects* (Liège, 1985), pp. 179–93.

Alain Bideau, Bertrand Desjardins, and Héctor Pérez Brignoli, eds. *Infant and Child Mortality in the Past*. Oxford, 1997.

Alastair Gray, ed. *World Health and Disease*, rev. ed. London, 1993.

Kevin G. Kinsella. "Changes in Life Expectancy 1900–1990." *American Journal of Clinical Nutrition* 55 (1992): 1196S–1202S.

Tom Kirkwood. *Time of Our Lives: The Science of Human Aging*. Oxford, 1999.

John Landers, ed. *Historical Epidemiology and the Health Transition*, supplement to vol. 2
of the *Health Transition Review*, 1992.

Alan Macfarlane. *The Savage Wars of Peace: England, Japan and the Malthusian Trap*. Oxford, 1997.

Carl Mosk. *Making Health Work: Human Growth in Modern Japan*. Berkeley, 1996.

Neil Poulter. "The Coronary Heart Disease Epidemic: British and International Trends."
In Neil Poulter et al., eds., *Cardiovascular Disease: Risk Factors and Intervention* (Oxford, 1993), pp. 1–11.

Scott C. Ratzan et al. *Attaining Global Health: Challenges and Opportunities. Population
Bulletin* 55, no. 1 (2000).

Itsuzo Shigematsu and Hiroshi Yanagawa. "The Case of Japan." In Jacques Vallin and Alan
D. Lopez, eds., *Health Policy, Social Policy and Mortality Prospects* (Liège, 1985), pp.
399–417.

2

Public Health

Communities have long sought to cope with the toxic effects of human settlement.[1] They buried their dead and designated and trained some people to act as healers. They also built cities, which are almost unthinkable in epidemiologic terms because cities mean more hosts for communicable diseases, easier transmission of water- and airborne diseases, and a more concentrated problem of disposing of human waste. Nevertheless, people across the globe from late prehistoric times forward found ways to make cities safe enough for their inhabitants to survive, even to increase in number. Some measures were tactics of cunning: people fled the city when dread diseases appeared there. Others were tactics of protection: the collection and disposal of human waste; the quarantine, which isolated sea vessels and the sick and well people thereon for periods long enough for the disease to exhaust itself; and the *cordon sanitaire*, which was meant to

---

[1] See three classics: René Dubos, *Mirage of Health: Utopias, Progress, and Biological Change* (New York, 1959); Dubos, "The Evolution of Microbial Disease," in René Dubos and J. G. Hirsch, eds., *Bacterial and Mycotic Infections of Man*, 4th ed. (Philadelphia, 1965), pp. 20–36; and [Frank] Macfarlane Burnet and David O. White, *Natural History of Infectious Disease*, 4th ed. (Cambridge, 1972).

block the entry of disease at a land frontier.[2] Such measures, best known for their implementation in Renaissance Italy, laid the foundations of modern public health, directing concern toward the problem of crowded urban space and to strategies of disease avoidance and prevention that allow cities to exist.

Public health acquired a more precise meaning in the eighteenth and nineteenth centuries from the contributions of European, chiefly French and British, experts.[3] The new public health involved a conscious and overt attempt to impede disease processes. It was aided by collecting and analyzing data, training specialists, and educating the public in the principles of disease avoidance and prevention as cast by the experts. In Europe public health complemented and sometimes displaced an earlier community medicine remarkable for its preoccupation with the external signs of disease, especially the skin lesions associated with plague, smallpox, measles, and other diseases. In its new form public health deployed an aversion to filth, sanitary improvements, mass immunizations, the mass provision of medical services, and community education as the leading elements of a strategy of community health. Its aim was to forewarn and protect against disease and to prevent disease.

[2] E.g., Kido Sugita, "Public Health in Ancient India," in Teizo Ogawa, ed., *Public Health: Proceedings of the 5th International Symposium on the Comparative History of Medicine – East and West* (Tokyo, 1981), pp. 75–81; and George Rosen, *A History of Public Health,* expanded ed. (Baltimore, 1993).

Nevertheless, the ways that urban inhabitants protected themselves against disease remain poorly understood.

[3] On Britain, see, esp., John M. Eyler, *Victorian Social Medicine: The Ideas and Methods of William Farr* (Baltimore, 1979); and on France, Ann F. LaBerge, *Mission and Method: The Early Nineteenth-Century French Public Health Movement* (Cambridge, 1992), and William Coleman, *Death Is a Social Disease: Public Health and Political Economy in Early Industrial France* (Madison, 1982). For an appreciation of the effect of sanitary reforms on urban health in France, see S. H. Preston and E. van de Walle, "Urban French Mortality in the 19th Century," *Population Studies* 32 (1978): 275–97.

Environmentalism and the Origins
of European Public Health

Human waste carries bacteria, worms, and other pathogens, some of which cause disease. Contact with waste when it is fresh enough for the pathogens in it to survive poses a risk. The chief threats are enteric diseases, such as typhoid fever, cholera, and dysentery, and diseases associated with parasites, such as hookworm infestation. The enteric diseases that humans suffer range in effect from mild, subclinical cases to serious morbidity preventing a person from carrying on with ordinary activities. Many of them, especially cholera and typhoid fever, pose a serious risk of death. Parasites and humans often accommodate to one another, so that both survive. But human hosts are debilitated by heavy worm loads, often being made more susceptible to other diseases.

People may long have had some sense of these particular hazards. Our distant ancestors often disposed of feces in pits dug away from dwellings or in moving waters (which, at a certain speed for volume, will decontaminate waste). But children and sometimes adults, too, also defecated around human dwellings. People came into contact with human waste by walking through it, by eating food on which flies that had fed on human waste landed, and by means of other routes.

Renaissance and Enlightenment era literary sources in Europe suggest at once an affectionate tolerance for waste's odor and an aversion to the stench of decomposing matter. Noah Webster, the lexicographer, wrote a two-volume history of epidemic diseases. He portrayed neither animal nor human waste as being so dangerous as the refuse that accumulated in streets, and distinguished the stench of other refuse from the healthy odor of feces.[4]

---

[4] Noah Webster, *A Brief History of Epidemic and Pestilential Disease,* 2 vols. (Hartford, Conn., 1799; rpt., New York, 1970), II: 222–23 and 225.

In seventeenth- and eighteenth-century Europe, environmentalists, who were medical and nonmedical observers seeking to apply Hippocratic ideas about the disease hazards of the human milieu to the problem of reducing mortality, associated odor with the danger of epidemic disease. They fixed on decomposing organic waste of many types, but not particularly on human waste, as a source of danger. And they believed initially that the danger was transmitted through the air. The disease matter itself escaped specification: that was not an important question to them.

Environmentalists hypothesized that many epidemic diseases originate in nature and are passed from inanimate objects to people. Some speculated further that, once in existence, these diseases might acquire a specific character and might even be transmitted from person to person. A rotting refuse heap, made up of household garbage, could create disease. The alert and cautious person avoided malodorous sites and promoted civic programs to collect and dispose properly of refuse. These ideas revived older insights into how the public health of a city could be safeguarded, refined them, and added new elements. To environmentalists the pathogenic milieu signaled by a foul odor seemed capable of altering the epidemic constitution, a term used to describe the prevailing complex of epidemic diseases of the moment. Such a change drew special interest when it seemed to provoke an epidemic of lethal and incapacitating disease, such as plague or typhus. The particular innovation of environmentalism lay both in the idea that useful action might be taken to protect against epidemic disease and in the novel intensity of the risk faced. Rapidly growing eighteenth-century cities aggravated the scale of the urban penalty, the term coined later to describe the extra losses in mortality associated with cities. But in the eighteenth century, intervention in the public's health remained chiefly a matter of civic engagement rather than a means for adding to and exercising state power.

Figure 2.1. Jan Molenaer captured the attitude of amused tolerance to the odor of human waste in this seventeenth-century painting depicting the sense of smell (*The Five Senses: Smell*; courtesy of the Royal Cabinet of Paintings, Mauritshuis, The Hague).

In ideas current by the 1730s or 1740s and still often encountered in public health advice in the 1890s,[5] environmentalists urged the collection and disposal of refuse, especially organic matter; ventilation of dwellings; and drainage of standing water. They also advocated the use of disinfectants, by which they meant substances (such as simmering vinegar) believed to counteract odor.

Toward the end of the eighteenth century a new idea emerged: water and air alike carry danger. Water fouled by refuse and waste may cause disease. Thus environmentalism intuited the effect of rapid urban growth and of growing efforts to collect and dispose of refuse, which was to contaminate the water that people drank and used in cooking. But human waste was not singled out as a contaminant. Water was pure if it seemed fresh and tasteless, or sweet. The key innovation of this period consisted of filtration: London introduced sand filtration of Thames water in 1829.

Environmentalism turned attention away from the victim of disease and from the sick person toward epidemic disease and its putative sources. It proposed that epidemics spring from such simultaneities as a shift in the weather that coincides with decomposition and malodor. And it promoted human action toward preventing disease. Along one route, therefore, the new public health emerged as an attempt to identify hazards in the human environment so that they could be avoided or redressed. In this form environmentalism transformed itself into sanitary science, which aimed to make the habitat safe.

Environmentalism also provoked an opposing reaction, whose proponents argued that epidemic disease arises not from nature but from con-

---

[5] Jose A. Lopez del Valle, *The Development of Sanitation and Charities in Cuba during the Last Sixteen Years (1899–1914)* (Havana, 1914), pp. 3–8, describes the sway of environmentalist ideas in initial plans to combat the 1899 yellow fever epidemic. Filth theory arguments continue to play a prominent role in popular and medical explanations for epidemic disease. On those arguments regarding the 1994 plague epidemic in Surat, India, see Ghanshyam Shah, *Public Health and Urban Development: The Plague in Surat* (New Delhi, 1997), esp. pp. 173 and 234.

gregations of people, especially people living in urban poverty. Long seen chiefly as a reservoir of disease and thus of danger, the poor came to be described by early nineteenth-century anti-environmentalists as possessing certain habits and characteristics that put them at particular risk to disease. Both of these ideas deserve attention. One led toward identification of disease agents and the other toward the sociology of disease.

The Sanitary Revolution

Two discoveries identified human waste as a particular threat among the various types of refuse that are by-products of the human mode of living, and linked certain diseases to waste. The first was an empirical inference suggested by John Snow, an English epidemiologist. The second was a breakthrough in ideas about disease origins called germ theory.

Epidemiology

Snow studied the pattern of cholera, now known to be a bacterial disease transmitted through fecal contamination of drinking water, in the London epidemic of 1849. He reached the conclusion (which he stated in 1849 and restated more persuasively in 1854) that this disease was transmitted by water rather than through the air or from person to person. His 1854 essay pointed specifically to the Broad Street pump, sited next to a leaky sewer itself adjacent to the residence of a cholera victim. Snow did not identify a disease agent, which is characteristic of environmentalist theory. Although many observers were reluctant to accept Snow's argument that a particular disease was communicated by water, sanitarians began to favor separate systems for the delivery of water to households and the removal of sewage and to promote enclosed waterborne sewage removal. They accepted water along with air as a means of disease communication. Gradually, from the 1850s forward, private individuals and municipalities in Britain and elsewhere spent more money on creating such a system, while more householders added flush toilets. Paris expanded its underground sewers in the first half of the century; London began work on a general system in 1858. Other cities, in Europe and European colonies abroad, followed suit, although often sluggishly.[6] Calcutta began to build a sewerage system in 1865 and a filtered water system in 1869.[7] In nearly every case the new systems served elite and bourgeois neighborhoods first and, in the colonies, European neighborhoods. Non-Europeans sometimes resisted sanitary improvements.[8]

While cities built underground sewage drains and separate water delivery systems, private householders would, in a grand plan devised by Edwin Chadwick, float thirty-year mortgages to outfit their homes with a water closet, a sink, fresh-water piping, and the drains needed to carry off waste and waste water. That mortgage plan failed to materialize. But it illustrates the scale of the investment that householders had to make if they wanted to implement a system of waterborne sewage removal and piped water.[9]

---

[6] Lion Murard and Patrick Zylberman, *L'hygiène dans la république: La santé publique en France, ou l'utopie contrariée (1870–1918)* (Paris, 1996), castigates France for sanitary backwardness. But waterborne diseases decreased there, too.

[7] David Arnold, *Colonizing the Body: State Medicine and Epidemic Disease in Nineteenth-Century India* (Berkeley, 1993), p. 167.

[8] E.g. in Hong Kong. See Daniel R. Headrick, *The Tentacles of Progress: Technology Transfer in the Age of Imperialism, 1850–1940* (New York, 1988), p. 150.

[9] On the role of sanitary improvements in Britain's mortality decline, see Simon Szreter, "The Importance of Social Intervention in Britain's Mortality Decline c. 1850–1914: A Re-interpretation of the Role of Public Health," *Social History of Medicine* 1 (1988): 1–37; Anne Hardy, *The Epidemic Streets: Infectious Disease and the Rise of Preventive Medicine, 1856–1900* (Oxford, 1993); Gerry Kearns, "The Urban Penalty and the Population of England," in Anders Brändström and Lars-Göran Tedebrand, eds., *Society, Health and Population during the Demographic Transition* (Stockholm, 1988), pp. 213–36; and Alex Mercer, *Disease, Mortality and Population in Transition: Epidemiological-Demographic Change in England since the Eighteenth Century as Part of a Global Phenomenon* (Leicester, 1990).

By the mid-nineteenth century the traditional sanitary facilities of European cities had been overrun by rapid urban growth and thus rapid growth in the volume of human feces.[10] Urban authorities collected waste, transporting it outside the city or depositing it in streams and rivers. People also used pit latrines, built without any method of reducing odor or controlling seepage into groundwater. But by the 1850s city authorities could not keep pace with the volume.[11] Thus the sanitary revolution focused on a massive building project designed to counteract one effect of crowding: building street and household drains, filtering and piping water to households, removing human waste in fully enclosed waterborne systems, and treating sewage to render it harmless. In particular cities, these reforms were often driven by cholera epidemics, which persuaded parsimonious taxpayers and city fathers to spend the immense sums required to build systems to deliver pure water and dispose of human waste.[12] These installations constitute the largest public health building project ever mounted, one remarkable for the sums dispersed and for the collaboration of public authorities and private householders. Public officials and many physicians expected these projects to reduce diseases of all types, not just cholera and typhoid fever.[13] In that sense the results were disappointing.

[10] See, esp., Anthony S. Wohl, *Endangered Lives: Public Health in Victorian Britain* (London, 1983), for working-class conditions.

[11] In recent times Europeans and North Americans have produced an average of 100 to 200 grams of solid waste per day, and people in developing countries 130 to 520 grams (plus from each group about 1.2 kilograms of urine, which is generally sterile and harmless). Because of diet, quantities of solid waste are somewhat larger among rural poor, and stools are also more frequent. See Richard G. Feachem et al., *Sanitation and Disease: Health Aspects of Excreta and Wastewater Management* (Chichester, 1983), p. 4. But the threat of contact with waste is greater in cities because people live so close together.

[12] Richard J. Evans, *Death in Hamburg: Society and Politics in the Cholera Years, 1830–1910* (Oxford, 1987).

[13] E.g., the physician J.H.C. Dalton, *Cambridge To-day: Its Health, Life and Social Conditions* (n.p., 1908), believed that Cambridge's just-completed sewer system had reduced mortality from tuberculosis and cancer.

Three things are especially important to notice. First, the scheme to separate water from sewage worked, protecting people from disease. Mortality and morbidity from waterborne diseases decreased swiftly. Second, the new system demanded a huge investment, nothing less than the construction of a subterranean city, plus the ongoing maintenance of the system. Third, flush toilets, sewerage systems, and piped water systems were designed and construction was begun before anyone had found how water transmitted disease or the nature of the contaminant contained in water. This protective system was conceived and built on the basis of the ideas of the environmentalists, who wished to avoid stench, and sanitarians, who associated disease with filth.[14]

Germ Theory

Did filth cause disease? The filth theory of disease created a category called zymotic diseases. Smallpox, typhoid fever, typhus, and other fevers and diarrheal diseases seemed to arise from decaying organic matter. As that theory was being discussed, however, more and more observers began to refer to particles of disease matter. In an 1876 summary of his views, a leading filth theorist, John Simon, footnoted the "microphyte" as the specific agent of disease. But he focused on filth.[15]

The suspicion that small organisms might have pathogenic qualities deepened in the 1870s and 1880s. Louis Pasteur and Robert Koch first provided compelling evidence for the germ theory, which holds that particular organisms cause particular diseases, and that these organisms are necessary (but not sufficient) causes of disease. They must be present. Thus germ theorists sought to direct the attention of public health au-

---

[14] "Public health began with little scientific basis for action." C. Fraser Brockington, "The History of Public Health," in William Hobson, ed., *The Theory and Practice of Public Health*, 4th ed. (London, 1975), p. 5.

[15] John Simon, *Filth-Diseases and Their Prevention* (Boston, 1876).

thorities away from filth, in which such pathogens were often to be found, toward germs themselves and things that carry germs: insects, small animals, and fomites (inanimate objects). The key work of science shifted from the public health doctor's visits to homes and disease sites to the bacteriological laboratory, where germs were identified. This line of thinking also led to successful attempts in the early twentieth century to identify chemicals that would kill certain germs found in water systems. Adding chemicals such as chloride to drinking water was never taken as adequate in itself: it was meant to supplement the separation of water and sewage and water filtration/sewage disposal systems. Germ theory confirmed the usefulness of sanitary improvements even as it also demanded new forms of scientific expertise and new investments in health and survival.[16]

Surveillance and Control

The management of communicable diseases through surveillance and control is an old human ambition. Renaissance Italian cities kept books of the dead as barometers of danger, watching for the spikes in mortality that signaled a new epidemic, and tried to quarantine vessels carrying diseased people. Seventeenth-century British authorities confined to their homes those families in which a dread disease, such as plague, had been reported. In the nineteenth and early twentieth centuries the hospital, long a refuge for the poor and the sick, added infectious disease wards, isolating people with dread infections. Isolation implies a theory of disease communicability from person to person, which the environmentalists often rejected. Thus public health authorities in the late eighteenth and early nineteenth centuries rarely used isolation. They also rarely applied quarantines, believing that disruptions to trade and the resulting unemployment and

---

[16] See Chapter 6 for a continuation of the history of germ theory.

poverty outweighed the risk of disease transmission. The hospital redefined served working people and the middle class, not just indigents.[17]

New techniques of surveillance and control emerged in the nineteenth century. Armed with inoculation and, later, vaccination, public health authorities promoted compulsory mass immunization. They tracked the prior contacts of infected people, alerting people exposed to disease to their danger. They persuaded the public to recognize a category of people called carriers (Typhoid Mary is the classic example of a person who carried and transmitted the disease but was not sick) and to restrict such people's freedom of movement.[18] Each of these measures could be justified by medical logic, and each seemed, on the evidence, to be effective. But it is important to notice that there was no construction of public consensus for public health restraints on individual freedom of action. Across an era of transition from monarchical to representative government, a public consensus emerged favoring the new form of government, which in many ways was more powerful and demanding than its predecessor in the things required of citizens. Public health surveillance and control gained no similar consensus. Governments often used public health innovations to expand and specify their powers, but it would be misleading to suggest that public health reforms led in the policies promoted by political leaders. On the side of the populace, each public health reform could become a matter of contention even when the measures proved effective. Nineteenth-century public health authorities showed that they could sometimes command the power to enforce intrusive measures, but not that they had wide public support for the measures they advocated.[19]

[17] On the French case, see Timothy B. Smith, "The Social Transformation of Hospitals and the Rise of Medical Insurance in France, 1914–1943," *Historical Journal* 41 (1998): 1055–87. Guenter B. Risse, *Mending Bodies, Saving Souls: A History of Hospitals* (Oxford, 1999), describes the broader context.

[18] Judith Walzer Leavitt, *Typhoid Mary: Captive to the Public's Health* (Boston, 1996).

[19] Peter Baldwin, *Contagion and the State in Europe, 1830–1930* (Cambridge, 1999), ar-

Sweden deployed Edward Jenner's vaccination against smallpox aggressively, and deaths from smallpox decreased from 12,000 in 1800 to a mere eleven in 1822 even though less than 40 percent of the susceptible population had been vaccinated.[20] Thomas Malthus had argued against the hope that eradication of one disease would benefit humankind on grounds that other diseases would rush in to take its place in a world he believed to be governed by the relationship between population density and economic resources. Jenner maintained that smallpox could be eradicated and that the children saved from smallpox would not be lost to other causes of death. Experience favored Jenner; the retreat of smallpox drove much of the early nineteenth-century mortality decline across Western Europe.

From the point of view of the community, the problem of smallpox control lay in inducing, persuading, or compelling parents to have their children vaccinated. In vaccination it was not the sick who came under surveillance, but the unvaccinated. The procedure of vaccination, virtually identical to the earlier procedure of inoculation,[21] carried fewer risks because the disease matter rubbed into the incision was not smallpox itself but a relative, probably cowpox, that caused only mild symptoms. Many parents nevertheless resisted, and many others failed to hear about vaccination. Some vaccinated people later developed smallpox, stirring

gues that European states engaged in the national discussion of health policy needed to create effective and acceptable strategies for control of cholera, smallpox, and syphilis, but he does not generalize this argument to other diseases.

[20] Alfred Pettersson, "Mortalité par la variole en Suède de 1776 à 1875," *Annales de l'institut Pasteur*, 26 (1912), 637–52.

[21] In inoculation some disease matter, taken from a smallpox pustule, was rubbed into small and shallow incisions made at some point on the body. It induced a case of smallpox, by plan a mild case, and left the inoculee infectious. In smallpox vaccination the same process was used, but the disease matter was taken from an animal, usually a cow, suffering an animal form of the disease. As later research showed, vaccination stimulated the immune system without causing disease, although people vaccinated suffered some minor signs of disease.

reservations about the effectiveness of the technique and leading to the realization that people had to be revaccinated after ten to twenty years. In Leicester, England, intense popular resistance to vaccination encouraged local authorities to adopt a system of notification, isolation, and surveillance. Remarkably, Leicester's smallpox control methods proved as effective as the mass vaccination campaigns used elsewhere.[22]

In the longer run the two approaches, vaccination and surveillance, complemented one another. Health authorities usually tried mass vaccination first. That approach eradicated smallpox in Europe and the Americas. The World Health Organization collaborated with local authorities in mounting a global vaccination campaign in the 1960s. But mass vaccination failed to eradicate smallpox in Asia and Africa, where authorities turned instead to a combination of surveillance and isolation and selective vaccination. They monitored villages for smallpox cases, isolated the sick, and vaccinated people who had been in contact with the sick person. The campaign, begun with mass vaccination and ended successfully with surveillance, isolation, and selective vaccination, eradicated smallpox by 1978.[23]

We celebrate the eradication of the disease that had been the leading cause of death in eighteenth-century Europe and probably also in the Americas and an important killer across the globe.[24] But 180 years passed between Jenner's suggestion that smallpox could be eradicated and its actual eradication. What are we to make of such a long period of waiting? Perhaps the best insight we have into the difficulties of eradication comes

[22] Stuart M. F. Fraser, "Leicester and Smallpox: The Leicester Method," *Medical History* 24 (1980): 315–32.

[23] See F[rank] Fenner et al., *Smallpox and Its Eradication* (Geneva, 1988); and Donald R. Hopkins, *Princes and Peasants: Smallpox in History* (Chicago, 1983). Cases of monkeypox in humans continue to lead to occasional alarms about whether the eradication has been complete.

[24] Jayant Banthia and Tim Dyson, "Smallpox in Nineteenth-Century India," *Population and Development Review* 25 (1999): 649–80.

from David Arnold's study of India.[25] Hindus, who had long practiced inoculation, were suspicious of vaccination. Arnold concludes that small-pox was not an eradicable disease in nineteenth-century India because of the political and cultural antagonism of Hindus to the way British colonial authorities tried to introduce vaccination. But in the nineteenth century it was also not an eradicable disease in Britain or anywhere else.

Public Health and the Sociology of Disease in Europe

In his 1842 *Report on the Sanitary Condition of the Labouring Population of Great Britain,* Chadwick incriminated squalor and poor housing as sources of disease, but he focused on filth, stagnant water, and foul air.[26] Louis Villermé, who set out in the 1820s to test environmentalist ideas, focused instead on crowded living conditions and poverty: the poor of France, he argued, did not earn enough for an adequate standard of living; hence they died earlier and were more often sick. Charles Booth, Seebohm Rowntree, Henri Monod, and others who studied the conditions of life in nineteenth-century slums came to similar conclusions.

Enteric diseases, certainly cholera, occurred more often among the poor. But the preeminent disease of poverty in the nineteenth century was pulmonary tuberculosis. People transmit tuberculosis to one another by coughing or sneezing droplet nuclei, which harbor bacilli, into the air. Uninfected people breathe in the droplets, which lodge in the respiratory tract, where lesions develop. In the early twentieth century, when populations were first tested, infection rates as high as 90 percent were often

---

[25] David Arnold, *Colonizing the Body: State Medicine and Epidemic Disease in Nineteenth-Century India* (Berkeley, 1993), pp. 115–58.

[26] Ed. by M.W. Flinn (Edinburgh, 1965). John V. Pickstone, "Dearth, Dirt and Fever Epidemics: Rewriting the History of British 'Public Health,' 1780–1850," in Terence Ranger and Paul Slack, eds., *Epidemics and Ideas: Essays on the Historical Perception of Pestilence* (Cambridge, 1992), pp. 125–48, develops this distinction between Chadwickian sanitary reforms and poverty as factors in high urban mortality.

reported. Nearly everyone had been exposed to tuberculosis, usually before age fourteen. Only a fraction of those infected became sick. Infections may be activated into sickness by influenza and other febrile diseases or pregnancy, as well as by other, unidentified means, but they must be activated before it can be said that a person is diseased. Tuberculosis was the leading cause of death in nineteenth-century Western Europe. High rates of infection were still characteristic in the 1940s, but fewer active cases developed as time passed, and fewer people died. Some evidence suggests that tuberculosis mortality began to wane in Britain in the 1840s, but the evidence of declining mortality is not compelling until the 1870s.[27]

Crowded housing, often in old warehouses converted to tenements, seems to have been tuberculosis's strongest ally. Sunlight, deadly to the tuberculosis bacillus, did not reach dark, dank, and ill-ventilated urban housing. Thus the early mortality decline, which promoted population growth, unwittingly assisted tuberculosis, as did migration to cities. European societies did not build housing fast enough to keep up with demand, and cities felt this failure most. The risks were especially burdensome for industrial workers, who were exposed to the disease at home and at work.[28] Housing construction began to catch up with demand at the end of the nineteenth century. There was no dramatic point of improvement in housing space, although municipal regulations favoring ventilation and light may have had good effect. The decline of tuberculosis mortality remains incompletely explained. New therapies, which promoted convalescence away from work and home, probably helped. Effective

---

[27] W. Robert Lee, "The Mechanism of Mortality Change in Germany, 1750–1850," *Medizinhistorisches Journal* 15 (1980): 244–68, finds that tuberculosis mortality in Germany rose from the eighteenth to the nineteenth century.

[28] William Johnston, *The Modern Epidemic: A History of Tuberculosis in Japan* (Cambridge, Mass., 1995), finds young women working in urban textile factories most at risk in early twentieth-century Japan.

medications appeared only later. Tuberculosis mortality began to decrease well before the introduction of BCG vaccine (1921) or effective drugs (streptomycin in 1943, and isoniazid in 1951).[29]

Continuing evidence of wholesale exposure to tuberculosis across decades of declining mortality suggests that the most important novelty lay in how so many people managed to fight off the conversion from infection to disease. If that idea is correct then public health was the leading arena of tuberculosis control. Reexposure of people who were infected but not diseased seems to have become less of a risk because, by the late nineteenth century, the sick were more often segregated in sanitariums and hospitals.[30] Better nutrition may also have protected people from tuberculosis. In the meantime, bovine tuberculosis, transmitted in milk, was controlled through the pasteurization of milk.

Vector Control

By the early twentieth century much of the energy of public health was directed toward finding ways to control mosquitoes (malaria and yellow fever), rats (plague), houseflies (filth diseases in general), and other insects and rodents known to be disease vectors. Rodenticides, new chemical compounds, reduced rat populations. Ronald Ross's 1897 demonstra-

---

[29] Public health authorities tried to control spitting, which they believed to be the principal route by which the sick transmitted the bacillus to the well. See, e.g., S. Adolphus Knopf, *Tuberculosis as a Disease of the Masses and How to Combat It*, 7th ed. (New York, 1911), who argues the case against spitting and shows spittoon models, including pocket models.

[30] Leonard G. Wilson, "The Historical Decline of Tuberculosis in Europe and America: Its Causes and Significance," *Journal of the History of Medicine and Allied Sciences* 45 (1990): 366–96; and Amy L. Fairchild and Gerald M. Oppenheimer, "Public Health Nihilism vs. Pragmatism: History, Politics, and the Control of Tuberculosis," *American Journal of Public Health* 88 (1998): 1105–117. Arthur Newsholme, *The Elements of Vital Statistics in Their Bearing on Social and Public Health Problems,* new ed. (New York, 1924), pp. 452–62, makes the case for the effectiveness of isolating tubercular patients.

tion that female anopheline mosquitoes play a necessary role in transmission of malaria, and Walter Reed's discovery that *Aedes aegypti* mosquitoes transmit yellow fever, led to a flourishing period in medical entomology.

Malaria, a parasitic disease that makes its victims more susceptible to other ailments while it also debilitates them and, in certain forms, causes many deaths, and schistosomiasis, caused by infestation of the body by flukes, expanded their reach in the late nineteenth century. Forest clearance and the construction of irrigation networks in areas of Asia and Africa colonized by Europeans provided disease vectors – especially mosquitoes, biting flies, and snails – with additional opportunities for breeding and parasites with readier access to humans and livestock.[31] By the 1920s public authorities across the world used larvicides, such as Paris green; bred fish for their appetite for mosquitoes and mosquito larvae; cleared ditches; and applied chemicals that inhibited nesting and reproduction. Even before the introduction of DDT, mosquito control campaigns reduced malaria mortality and morbidity in much of Asia. Similar efforts in Europe's malarial regions stressed quinine treatment plus better housing and improved socioeconomic conditions. During the period of its widespread use, 1957–69, DDT led a rapid contraction of malarial regions. The southeastern United States, most of China and all of the Korean peninsula, most of the European and Asiatic regions touching the Mediterranean, the Black, and the Caspian Seas were rid of the disease. But the very property that makes DDT effective, its residual capacity when used as a house spray to continue to kill insects long after the initial application, proved harmful to other life forms. Withdrawal of DDT led to the revival of malaria in southern and southeastern Asia and in Latin America. India reported fewer than 100,000 cases in 1961, but 30 million

---

[31] Charles C. Hughes and J. M. Hunter, "Disease and 'Development' in Africa," *Social Science and Medicine* 3 (1970): 443–93.

or more in 1977. In the 1980s about half the global population lived in malaria areas, and about 100 million cases, including new and ongoing, were reported each year.

Control of Waterborne Disease without Sewerage Systems

Several societies have achieved high life expectancy and low levels of enteric disease without investing in sanitary reforms on the British model, or by delivering piped water but not building sewerage systems. Japan was the first country to adopt such a strategy; it has been followed also by Costa Rica, China, Sri Lanka, and many others, often from necessity rather than strategy. In these countries by the 1990s, life expectancy surpassed seventy years at birth even though waterborne diseases were somewhat more common than in societies with fully enclosed systems of sewage disposal.[32]

These successes have two major implications. First and foremost, they show that the huge investment in toilet and sewage treatment and disposal systems that would be required to duplicate the British system throughout the world may not be necessary. An estimate from around 1980 suggests that the cost of building waterborne sewerage systems across the world where they are lacking would have totaled $800 billion,[33] an impossibly large sum. Second, they suggest that the British system was overdesigned in its costliness, its aim to protect people from the odor of feces as well as contact with waste, and the elaborate structure of local government required to erect and maintain it. A more economical version may be all that is required to protect populations from waterborne dis-

---

[32] Further research will be required to show how waterborne diseases were controlled in these countries, and to find practical alternatives to the overdesigned British system.

[33] John M. Kalbermatten et al., *Appropriate Sanitation Alternatives: A Planning and Design Manual* (Baltimore, 1982), p. ix.

eases. Ironically, the pit latrines that people used before introduction of sanitary systems, somewhat modified, seem to provide the least expensive safe means of waste disposal.[34] Most of the modern effort to improve sanitary facilities in developing countries has focused on water purification and the delivery of piped water to households. Those campaigns have helped reduce the burden of diarrheal disease, especially among children. But the disposal of human waste remains a serious problem in many countries where neither modern nor traditional systems are adequate.[35]

Conclusion

The approach to public health devised in nineteenth-century Europe contributed significantly to the reduction of mortality. It suppressed waterborne diseases in much of Western Europe, it inaugurated study of the disease problems of poverty, it added new and effective means of disease surveillance and control, it introduced mass vaccination, and it launched insect control. Moreover, it pioneered the purposeful application of medical, social, and scientific knowledge and insight to the control of hazards to health and survival. In country after country, strategies of population health were derived from public health reforms, and governments used public health measures to refine their powers and augment them.

Each achievement also had some negative features. Sanitary improve-

---

[34] E.g., Quartal Ain Bakhteari and Laique Azam, "Pakistani Women Lead a Low-Cost Sanitation Project," in Bertha Turner, ed., *Building Community: A Third World Case Book* (London, 1989), pp. 53–58, describe the installation of soakpits in Karachi in the 1980s as an alternative to flush toilets. Soakpits protect people from wasteborne disease and use much less water.

[35] For examples, see Richard E. Stren, "The Administration of Urban Services," in Richard E. Stren and Rodney R. White, eds., *African Cities in Crisis: Managing Rapid Urban Growth* (Boulder, 1989), pp. 37–67, esp. pp. 43–47; K. C. Sivaramakrishnan and Leslie Green, *Metropolitan Management: The Asian Experience* (Oxford, 1986); and Vacliv Smil, *The Bad Earth: Environmental Degradation in China* (Armonk, N.Y., 1984), pp. 100–104.

ments were so costly that they could be implemented only gradually, even in rich countries, and have usually remained piecemeal in poor countries. Thus sanitary improvements played a bigger role in reducing mortality in Europe and North America than elsewhere on the globe. Waterborne diseases pose much less of a threat at the end of the twentieth century than they did in the 1850s, but in the 1990s they still accounted for just under 6 percent of all deaths worldwide. Cholera and typhoid fever now occur much less often than they did before the construction of sanitary systems, but enteric diseases still play a leading role as causes of death among infants and children in developing countries.[36] Virtually all of these deaths are avoidable, in epidemiologic terms.

The public health measures discussed here show the purposeful application of ideas that had an empirical basis. As the sanitary reforms illustrate, however, the desire to control death is so strong that people regularly implemented new ideas before the ideas had been fully elaborated or tested. Europeans began building sanitary systems before the germ theory had been proved and on the expectation that these systems would control communicable diseases in general. A fully waterborne system for the disposal of human waste protected people from disease. In retrospect, however, it appears that well-designed pit latrines would have done as much at less cost. Germ theory, devised after the sanitary system had been designed, showed that attention could be focused more narrowly and more cheaply. It is apparently this insight that has permitted a few poor countries in the modern world to control waterborne disease even though

---

[36] A good description of the environment in which such diseases thrive appears in Alfred A. Buck, Tom T. Sasaki, and Robert I. Anderson, *Health and Disease in Four Peruvian Villages: Contrasts in Epidemiology* (Baltimore, 1968), esp. pp. 23–27. The statistical case for adding sanitary facilities to households lacking them is made by Erica Hertz, James R. Herbert, and Joan Landon, "Social and Environmental Factors and Life Expectancy, Infant Mortality, and Maternal Mortality Rates: Results of a Cross-National Comparison," *Social Science and Medicine* 39 (1994): 105–14.

their systems of water supply and, in particular, of sewage disposal are incomplete.

The thorniest problems about the part of public health in disease control came to the fore in the nineteenth century and remain unresolved. These deal with personal liberty. Sanitary authorities argued that the means they promoted – compelling the householder to clean the interior and exterior of the dwelling and to install sanitary devices – served a useful end: disease control. But they did not take the trouble to devise a theory or a philosophy adequate to persuade individuals to sacrifice for the common good. No one like Montesquieu stepped forward to reflect on how the tension between individual liberties and their suppression for the public good might be negotiated in the realm of public health. Political philosophy continued to develop, but a field of epidemiologic philosophy did not emerge. Nor did health authorities succeed in making the case that sacrifice must be shared. Leicester's successful experiment in smallpox control through surveillance showed that health authorities, who insisted on mass vaccinations, could err, which weakened their moral authority.

AIDS brought these issues to the forefront again in the 1980s. Public health authorities initially proposed to monitor the disease, which meant testing everyone's blood; to trace the contacts that infected persons had had, in order to warn them of the possibility of disease; and to educate the public about the modes of HIV transmission. The public rejected the first two approaches. At the end of the twentieth century the capacity to control disease still outruns actual disease control.[37]

In sum, public health reforms played a significant role in the reduction of mortality in Europe by controlling waterborne disease. They served also, and on a global scale, as a demonstration of the efficacy of ap-

[37] Many of these issues are considered in "Forum: What Are the Limits?," *Health Transition Review* 7 (1997): 73–107. Jonathan Mann, "Human Rights and the New Public Health," *Health and Human Rights* 1 (1994): 229–33, indicates that sensitivity to the issue of popular acceptance of public health measures is growing.

plying scientific evidence to human problems. Their legacy is twofold: hydraulic systems protect people from waterborne diseases, but they may be archaic and are certainly costly to build and maintain; in service of society, public health abridges individual freedom, but the rationale remains philosophically underdeveloped and often provokes antagonism. We have not yet learned how to negotiate conflict between individual freedoms and the need all of us have to be protected from disease and injury.

Suggestions for Further Reading

John Cassel. "The Contribution of the Social Environment to Host Resistance." *American Journal of Epidemiology* 104 (1976): 107–23.

Stuart Galishoff. *Newark: The Nation's Unhealthiest City: 1832–1895.* New Brunswick, N.J., 1988.

J. E. Hardoy and D. Satterthwaite. "Environmental Problems of Third World Cities: A Global Issue Ignored?" *Public Administration and Development* 11 (1991): 341–61.

Jacques Leonard. *Archives du corps: La santé au XIXe siècle.* N.p., 1986.

Constance A. Nathanson. "Disease Prevention as Social Change: Toward a Theory of Public Health." *Population and Development Review* 22 (1996): 609–37.

Maureen Ogle. *All the Modern Conveniences: American Household Plumbing, 1840–1890.* Baltimore, 1996.

Katherine Ott. *Fevered Lives: Tuberculosis in American Culture since 1870.* Cambridge, Mass., 1996.

Dorothy Porter. *Health, Civilisation and the State: A History of Public Health from Ancient to Modern Times.* London, 1999.

Dorothy Porter, ed. *The History of Public Health and the Modern State.* Amsterdam, 1994.

Donald Reid. *Paris Sewers and Sewermen: Realities and Representations.* Cambridge, Mass., 1991.

James C. Riley. *The Eighteenth-Century Campaign to Avoid Disease.* New York, 1987.

Charles E. Rosenberg. *The Cholera Years: The United States in 1832, 1849, and 1866.* Chicago, 1962.

Wally Seccombe. *Weathering the Storm: Working-Class Families from the Industrial Revolution to the Fertility Decline.* London, 1993.

Jörg Vögele. *Urban Mortality Change in England and Germany, 1870–1913.* Liverpool, 1998.

3

Medicine

Two forms of medicine complement one another in trying to alleviate the suffering associated with diseases and injuries, and sometimes also to reduce the risk of dying while sick. One form, traditional medicine, is old and richly varied. The other, biomedicine, is comparatively new, having appeared in the late nineteenth century, and specific. People have long turned to traditional medicine in the effort to relieve suffering, and they continued to do so after the appearance of biomedicine. The new medicine has much greater efficacy in certain areas. But the behavior of people across the world suggests that they continue to find comfort and relief in traditional medicine. They may consult folk or alternative practitioners, and they may go to their doctors in search of traditional treatments. A thriving arena of traditional medicine consists of self-treatment: people diagnose their own ailments, especially ones they deem minor, select treatments, and try to make themselves well. In this chapter the issue is not the history of medicine but the history of medicine's contribution to the health transition in a world of dramatically different medical and health cultures. In some cultures good health is a physical issue, in others an issue of the spirit, and in still others a mixture of body, emotions, and soul. Across cultures both traditional medicine and biomedicine have helped reduce mortality and the incidence of many diseases. Both, using disease treatment and management, have also helped sick people live longer. Among all the categories of action in the health transition, medicine's approach is the most varied; it uses prevention and advice about disease avoidance as well as treatment and management.

Traditional medicine itself has taken two forms. It consisted, first, of bodies of belief about what individuals and their loved ones can do for themselves. People prescribe changes in behavior for themselves; they select therapies and medications. Second, it has been made up of a body of experts to whom people turn when they decide that self-help will not suffice. These experts may specialize in devising therapies; finding troubled aspects of the sick person's relationship with the community, with an eye toward treating those; discovering emotional problems; appraising the well-being of a person's spirit; reviewing the tenets of health and giving advice about behavior when sick; or a number of other approaches. Traditional medicine distinguishes itself, across human history and human cultures, by having searched for ways to reassure the sick person that something useful can be done to relieve suffering.

That task has become more difficult over time, in the sense at least of two underlying forces, population growth and the microbial unification of the globe. When human settlements were sparse, few communicable diseases could sustain themselves in human populations alone. The history of the last two millennia, and especially of the last two centuries, has been one of rising densities. These provide frequent enough contacts and enough susceptible hosts to sustain many communicable diseases.

Microbial unification – the emigration of pathogens and vectors into the climates and ecologies they can tolerate – is partly a result of population growth and partly of interregional and intercontinental migrations, trade, and travel. Diseases formerly restricted to certain areas have spread; many of them have become cosmopolitan. Asiatic cholera moved toward Europe between 1817 and 1831, illustrating one form of microbial unification. In those fourteen years cholera caused some 18 million deaths in India, where for some time it had been a familiar malady. But it began to spread, reaching Astrakhan in 1823 before retreating temporarily. In 1826 it surged forth once more, traveling caravan routes across the Kyrgyz steppe and Russia. Cholera arrived at Moscow in August 1829, at Hamburg in October 1831, and the eastern coast of Britain the same month. Asiatic cholera spread outward again and again. The European and North American epidemic of 1829–32 was the first of seven global pandemics. The new territories were inhospitable to cholera, so that for a long time it retreated after each outbreak.[1] For many other diseases, however, the new territories proved as welcoming as the old, so that microbial unification meant permanent exposure to additional diseases in ever larger territories.

The Healer's Effect

The sick do not appear, in any historical or contemporary system, to turn first to therapists. Respondents in one modern survey reported that for 37 percent of the health problems identified, they took no action. For another 35 percent they treated themselves with patent medications. They consulted doctors or dentists in 9 percent of cases.[2] The proportions must

---

[1] Cholera no longer works just this way. Harbored apparently in fresh and salt water in an unknown number of areas of the world, cholera can break out when water purification collapses. On the history of this disease and its modes of transmission, see Patrice Bourdelais and Jean-Yves Raulot, *Une peur bleue: Histoire du choléra en France, 1832–1854* (Paris, 1987).

[2] The Proprietary Association, *Health Care Practices and Perceptions* ([Washington, D.C.], 1984), p. 15, regarding a U.S. survey of 1982–83. The similarity in response between Americans in this survey and people in quite different settings is often striking. See, for example, Stephen Frankel, *The Huli Response to Illness* (Cambridge, 1986), pp. 75–80 and 176, where the categories range from no action and self-help to hospital attendance.

vary by time and place, but it remains true that, in the early stages of many of their ailments, people deem those ailments unworthy of treatment or needing only household remedies. Today, when chemotherapies play such a large role in medical treatment and in countries where physicians control access to drugs, people turn to doctors when they want a diagnosis and access to such medication. In Europe on the eve of the health transition in the eighteenth century, people turned to doctors and pharmacists for help in selecting medications that would restore a balance among bodily humors by inducing a patient to sweat, vomit, evacuate, or bleed. Patients believed that these humoral treatments restored internal balance, and in that way contributed to recovery. To treat smallpox, for example, practitioners used many therapies: tar water; mercury and antimony; repeated bleedings, emetics, and purges; and quinine. Few of these medicaments had much beneficent effect, judged by later standards, which stress the alleviation and abbreviation of symptoms. Nor did they enhance the likelihood of survival. But people wanted those therapies nevertheless.

Traditional doctors in Europe often wondered about the efficacy of the drugs they administered. That is apparent from the variety of the regimens they recommended. But they did not usually doubt the efficacy of their advice about behavior.[3] Popular manuals of health advice began to appear in the late seventeenth century, some written by laypeople and some by healers. Luigi Cornaro urged his readers to deny themselves fruits and vegetables in order to live as long as he had lived, to exercise, and to eat less than their appetites called for. George Cheney recommended a daily regime of denial. John Wesley believed that horseback rid-

---

The Huli live in the southern highlands of Papua New Guinea. Also see John D. Williamson and Kate Danaher, *Self-Care in Health* (London, 1978), esp. p. 39.

[3] On the need for doctors to feel confident in the therapies they deployed, see Stephen J. Kunitz, "The Personal Physician and the Decline of Mortality," in R. Schofield, D. Reher, and A. Bideau, eds., *The Decline of Mortality in Europe* (Oxford, 1991), pp. 248–62.

ing made him healthy. Stressing temperance and moderation, the manuals advised readers to make health practices part of a daily regimen.

Increasingly the manuals added inventories of diseases, suggestions about how to distinguish one malady from another, and advice about medicaments.[4] William Buchan, whose *Domestic Medicine* appeared in at least 142 editions between 1769 and 1871, called this "laying medicine open." Whereas physicians argued the need for treatments specific to the individual case, the domestic manuals made diagnosis – something the relatives or friends of the sick person could do with the aid of a printed text – the key to treatment. Successful diagnosis led to the selection of an appropriate therapy, usually one that produced a humoral response regarded as helpful, such as sweating or vomiting. Otherwise the same medication might be recommended for an entire class of diseases, as quinine was for fevers. The manuals were inherently optimistic about curing maladies. They share an eighteenth-century change of mood, in which Western people thought less often of their ailments as spiritually edifying or tests of character and began to cultivate an expectation of good health in this life. For the sick the manuals advised bed rest, more moderate eating with a careful eye on the foods consumed, cleanliness (from filth) in the sick room, and open windows.

Late twentieth-century Western medical advice replicates much of the character of this earlier advice and many of the specifics, too. The Alameda County (California) study, an important prospective study begun in 1965,

---

[4] See John Wesley, *Primitive Physick; or, An Easy and Natural Method of Curing Most Diseases* (London, 1747); William Buchan, *Domestic Medicine; or, The Family Physician . . .* (Edinburgh, 1769); Bernhard Christoph Faust, *Gesundheits-Katechismus zum Gebrauche in den Schulen und beym häuslichen Unterrichte (Bücheburg, 1794);* Samuel Auguste David Tissot, *Avis au peuple sur sa santé* (Lausanne, 1761); Thomas Willis, *The London Practice of Physick* (London, 1692).* On this genre of medical literature, see Charles E. Rosenberg, "Medical Text and Social Context: Explaining William Buchan's *Domestic Medicine,*" in Rosenberg, *Explaining Epidemics* (Cambridge, 1992), pp. 32–56.

recommends seven daily practices: don't smoke, get at least seven hours of sleep, eat breakfast, keep your weight down, drink only in moderation, exercise each day, and don't eat between meals.[5]

Perhaps people derived benefits from traditional physicians and healers in other ways, too. Modern studies indicate that people who are attended recover from their operations and ailments more quickly than do people who are not attended, other things being equal. Patients benefit when doctors and nurses show concern, especially by listening carefully to their complaints. Western doctors are known also to have used certain devices and tricks on their patients, which may have been calculated to augment the healer's effect. Moreover, in dispensing medications doctors take advantage of a mysterious placebo effect. People often report that drugs help or hurt them even when they have been administered placebos.[6]

On the eve of the health transition in Europe few people consulted physicians. Most called on healers, including surgeons, who in many places still barbered and treated wounds, broken bones, and skin diseases but who were becoming general practitioners who treated internal as well as external maladies. People also consulted leeches, medical people who specialized in bloodletting; bonesetters; and wise women, who knew the herbal and folk remedies of the locale; and they turned to apothecaries for advice in selecting medications.

---

[5] Lisa F. Berkman and Lester Breslow, *Health and Ways of Living: The Alameda County Study* (New York, 1983).

[6] In clinical trials of drugs, compounds believed to have efficacy are tested along with placebos, for purposes of control. The people given placebos often report and experience improvements. Moreover, nearly the same proportion of people taking placebos report adverse experiences as in the test group. That is so even to the point of showing up in laboratory measures of body function. For example, when Merck & Co. tested Singulair®, 18.4 percent of the test group and 18.1 percent of the placebo group reported headaches as a side effect. Some of this can be explained by the mere passage of time and recoveries and ills that would have occurred in any case. See the February 1998 enclosure included in this medication. On the history of the clinical trial, see Ted J. Kaptchuk, "Intentional Ignorance: A History of Blind Assessment and Placebo Controls in Medicine," *Bulletin of the History of Medicine* 72 (1998): 389–433.

Unconventional healers were pushed to the fringes of medicine in nineteenth-century Europe. University-trained physicians swallowed enough of their pride to cooperate with two groups they had previously scorned: surgeons and apothecaries. That cooperation rested on adding formal training and licensing to the requirements for practice as a surgeon or an apothecary. Other informal healers lost out in the professionalization of medicine. They lost out, too, in the medicalization of society; physicians, surgeon-general practitioners, and apothecaries set out to monopolize patients, treatment, and the dispensing of medications.[7] With the aid of licensing laws, a serious oversupply of health workers that developed during the nineteenth century, and the emergence of new types of informal healers, formal practitioners drove many of their old rivals into medical unemployment. When people sought medical assistance, increasingly they turned either to formal practitioners or to nurses and trained midwives.[8]

During the nineteenth century people in the central ranks of the population in Western Europe who worked with their hands joined the ranks of these formal practitioners' patients.[9] In the process people sought health services from professionals much better placed than healers had been to obtain compliance with their advice and their therapies. Medicalization refers not merely to the increasing frequency of contact with doctors, but also to the growing authority of doctors over the behavior of the sick. Doctors advised rest and recuperation, and their professional au-

---

[7] Medicalization refers also to the assertion of medical authority over problems that had not previously been seen as medical. Doctors, the medical model of diagnosis and treatment, and, later, laboratory medical science claimed greater authority over social ills.

[8] Olivier Faure, *Les français et leur médecine au XIXe siècle* (Paris, 1993).

[9] For example, by 1900, 42 percent of Amsterdammers relied on sick funds for medical and pharmaceutical services, 36 percent depended on private resources, and 22 percent drew on relief agencies. J. A. Verdoorn, *Volksgezondheid en sociale ontwikkeling: Beschouwingen over het gezondheidswezen te Amsterdam in de 19e eeuw* (Utrecht, 1965), p. 169.

thority seems to have legitimized taking time off work to recuperate from sickness. (Modern evidence suggests that rest helps the immune system combat many pathogens.[10]) Jean-Jacques Rousseau condemned doctors for making sicknesses last longer. But more deliberate convalescence may have aided recovery from disease.[11]

During the nineteenth century the rationale that formal practitioners advanced for their work changed.[12] In 1800 patients expected doctors to induce bleeding, vomiting, or sweating as an aid to restoring balance among the four humors, and doctors thought they knew how to do those things. By 1900 patients and doctors alike expected to be able to identify a particular disease and to shape therapy around that identification. Doctors sought no longer to alter the patient's symptoms by rebalancing humors; they continued to believe in such therapies as bloodletting, but used them much less often. Instead they associated particular symptoms with particular diseases and tried to relieve symptoms. Ironically, physicians seem more often to have lacked confidence in their own procedures around 1900 than around 1800. Doctors in 1800 understood far better how to produce a humoral response than their counterparts in 1900 understood how to relieve disease symptoms. Nevertheless, Charles Minor, who practiced in Asheville, North Carolina, in the 1920s, counted on medications as a part of any resourceful therapy: his confidence in himself rested on his confidence in the drugs he used.[13]

---

[10] Paul W. Ewald, *Evolution of Infectious Diseases* (New York, 1994), p. 20.

[11] On the effect in the later nineteenth century in Britain and the United States, which was rising sickness prevalence, see James C. Riley, *Sick, Not Dead: The Health of British Workingmen during the Mortality Decline* (Baltimore, 1997); and Cheryl Elman and George C. Myers, "Geographic Morbidity Differentials in the Late Nineteenth-Century United States," *Demography* 36 (1999): 429–43.

[12] J. H. Warner, *The Therapeutic Perspective: Medical Practice, Knowledge, and Identity in America, 1820–1885* (Cambridge, Mass., 1986), discusses these changes of perspective among American physicians.

[13] Kunitz, "Personal Physician," p. 249. In an instructive article, Paul Beeson assesses changes in the efficacy of available drugs between 1927 and 1975, showing rapid and

Traditional and Modern Healers

In the West biomedicine accommodated traditional medicine, albeit after initial resistance. In each of its aspects biomedicine was suited to adaptation. Germ theory identified the disease agent, which filth theory had not done. It offered an explanation about why smallpox inoculation and, later, vaccination worked. And its drugs fit well within medical and patient cultures that had, for at least a century and a half, tried to use chemical compounds to treat sickness. Even the most traditional of Western doctors hoped that Robert Koch's tuberculin would inoculate against tuberculosis and that Paul Ehrlich's Salvarsan would cure not merely syphilis but other diseases, too.

In many respects, however, traditional Western medicine survived.[14] Its ideas about injuries and diseases not associated with germs, its doctor-centeredness, its advice about how individuals might preserve health, its capacity to treat certain kinds of sickness, and its identification of poverty as an underlying cause of disease all remained unchallenged by biomedicine. Looking back at the melding period, which lasted from the 1880s to about the 1940s, few observers noticed how easily new ideas had been incorporated into old or how much the flexible way that biomedical ideas had been adopted by educators in medical schools assisted this integration. Moreover, an important struggle had begun and been partly resolved before the advent of germ theory. Formal practitioners had gained exclusive rights to practice medicine, displacing bonesetters, bleeders, wise

concentrated gains: "Changes in Medical Therapy during the Past Half Century," *Medicine* 59 (1980): 79–99.

[14] This is a collateral point in Cecil G. Helman, "'Feed a Cold, Starve a Fever' – Folk Models of Infection in an English Suburban Community, and Their Relation to Medical Treatment," *Culture, Medicine and Psychiatry* 2 (1978): 107–37. Helman's main argument is that the germ theory failed to change many of the ways in which patients and practitioners explain disease.

women, clergymen who treated their parishioners, and other healers less likely to have absorbed the tenets of biomedicine.

Elsewhere in the world, that displacement and the professionalization of traditional medicine accompanying it did not usually occur before biomedicine was introduced. Thus elsewhere the contrast between traditional and modern medicine has been more sharply drawn, pitting familiar indigenous schemes for healing against novel ideas from the outside.[15] Western medicine has sometimes been rejected, as it was in India in the mid-nineteenth century. There Western practitioners and their ayurvedic and unani counterparts alike (i.e., Hindu and Islamic, respectively) concluded that Western medical knowledge was not applicable in India. After the advent of biomedicine, rejection became more difficult because efficacy could be demonstrated in the treatment of many sicknesses.

Peter Schröder studied the effects of this struggle between traditional and modern medicine in Botswana in the 1980s among people with tuberculosis, interviewing patients, biomedical healers, and traditional healers.[16] Healers in each camp saw the treatments they administered as effective. Traditional healers took pride in the putative efficacy of their regimens in preventing sickness; they also treated sickness, often trying to identify how evil spirits had poisoned the sick person, selecting herbal regimens, or reassuring the sick person that recovery was possible. Biomedical healers took pride in the therapies they administered; they believed they could cure many diseases, including tuberculosis, if patients complied faithfully with the treatment regimens they recommended. One healer often disparaged another. Biomedical healers described their traditional counterparts as witch doctors, a term more biting even than the terms physicians used to disparage their unlicensed counterparts in the

---

[15] Of the large literature dealing with this struggle, see Nancy Elizabeth Galagher, *Medicine and Power in Tunisia, 1780–1900* (Cambridge, 1983); and Arthur Kleinman, *Patients and Healers in the Context of Culture* (Berkeley, 1980), dealing with Taiwan.

[16] Peter Schröder, *Tuberculosis and Traditional Medicine in Botswana* (Berlin, 1986).

West in the early nineteenth century: charlatans and quacks. Traditional healers urged their patients not to consult biomedical practitioners, pointing out the many patients for whom modern practitioners were able to do little or nothing. Meanwhile, patients believed both types of healers to be helpful. In the words of one tuberculosis patient: "When I am ill, I want to try every possible help from any possible person, because I want to be healthy again and one never knows who can help you."[17]

Schröder found that people with tuberculosis accepted some arguments from biomedicine and others from traditional medicine. Many believed that tuberculosis is a dangerous bacterial disease that can be treated by modern medicines. Many also believed that *thibamo,* the traditional term that many people used for tuberculosis, is caused by some or all of the following: violation of sexual taboos, divine punishment for misbehavior, ancestral influence, or witchcraft, as well as by germs, stress, and dust.[18] Hence traditional healers can play a role in its relief.

Tuberculosis patients responded to their sickness in a familiarly human way. Typically, at the onset of mild symptoms, they tried to treat themselves, seeking advice from family members. (For healers this stage is often considered a period in which the sick try to deny their symptoms. It is especially protracted in tuberculosis, cancer, and other diseases marked both by a long course of symptom development and social stigma, which suggests that many people diagnose themselves, at least in rough terms. This in turn suggests a rational-expectations model of health, in which people who fall sick have informed expectations about the social hazards of sickness, debility, and death.) When the mild symptoms of tuberculosis gave way to spitting or coughing blood, its victims turned to traditional healers or to a clinic or hospital with its modern healers. As Schröder noticed in Botswana, tuberculosis patients invested more con-

[17] Ibid., p. 20. On the failure of Western medicine in colonial Africa, see Megan Vaughan, *Curing Their Ills: Colonial Power and African Illness* (Cambridge, 1991).
[18] Schröder, *Tuberculosis and Traditional Medicine,* pp. 38 and 91–98.

fidence in modern medicine for the treatment of symptoms, even though many traditional drugs and herbs successfully treat coughs and pain, and more confidence in traditional medicine for disease prevention. Completing his investigations, Schröder decided that patients would have been better advised to use both treatment regimens at the same time.[19]

Tuberculosis brings out these contrasts in belief with particular effectiveness because, as a disease, its development and cure are so protracted. Modern treatment regimens require up to eighteen months; Botswana's public health plan at the time of Schröder's visit called for hospital treatments lasting two months, followed by a prolonged course of treatment at clinics. During the period of clinical treatment, patients often noticed that symptoms were disappearing. That, and perhaps also exhaustion, cost, or inconvenience, explain why so many people – Schröder estimates the proportion at 30 to 50 percent in developing countries in general – stop taking drugs after a few months. That is unfortunate. Exposure of the patient's particular strain of the bacterium to drugs for an incomplete course, during which some but not all of the bacteria are eliminated, seems to help the pathogens acquire resistance to these drugs. Thus biomedical healers usually blame the failure of treatment with modern drugs, a problem of growing scale across the world in the 1980s and 1990s, on patients who did not follow their advice.

Many observers suggest that the mutual disdain modern and traditional practitioners in many cultures feel for each other, but especially the disdain of modern practitioners for traditional, has made it more difficult to incorporate modern into traditional medicine in the twentieth-century developing world than it was in nineteenth-century Europe. Traditional practitioners, who may be spiritual healers, herbalists, specialists in arts such as bone-setting, or birth attendants, are numerous, accessible, and

[19] Ibid., p. 123.

often inexpensive. Modern practitioners are few and costly. Whereas modern healers stress their ability to treat disease and its symptoms, traditional healers stress their ability to treat the psychological, social, and cultural dimensions of ill health.[20] The two systems seem to be complementary: one deals better with communicable diseases, the other with social and emotional disorders. Although the time may come when biomedical healers are numerous and accessible, traditional healers seem likely to retain their role as alternative sources of therapy for physical ailments and as the main sources of help for social and emotional maladies.[21]

Traditional and modern medicine also collaborated in China, where the Maoist revolutionaries who seized power in 1949 showed a touching faith in the capacity of even a little medicine to improve health. At the 1950 National Health Conference, revolutionary leaders adopted a health program. They promoted public health initiatives: re-dig irrigation canals to reduce schistosomiasis, cultivate an aversion for insect and rodent vectors of disease, and persuade people to trap and kill flies, rats, mosquitoes, and other disease-vector pests. And they sought to augment the supply of medical personnel while reorienting medicine from traditional toward biomedical. Together the two programs helped in a rapid and substantial reduction of mortality risks. Life expectancy at birth rose by nearly 1.5 years per year between 1949 and the mid-1970s.

[20] Frants Staugård, *Traditional Medicine in a Transitional Society: Botswana Moving towards the Year 2000* (Stockholm, 1989), p. 129. This point has often been made by anthropologists, and I suggest only one further source: Paul Brodwin, *Medicine and Morality in Haiti: The Contest for Healing Power* (Cambridge, 1996).

[21] In addition to Schröder, *Tuberculosis and Traditional Medicine,* and Staugård, *Traditional Medicine,* see Gilles Bibeau et al., *Traditional Medicine in Zaire: Present and Potential Contribution to Health Services* (Ottawa, 1980); Charles M. Good, *Ethnomedical Systems in Africa: Patterns of Traditional Medicine in Rural and Urban Kenya* (New York, 1987); and Indrani Pieris, "Health Treatment Behaviour in Sri Lanka," in G. W. Jones et al., eds., *The Continuing Demographic Transition* (Oxford, 1997), pp. 332–62.

In 1949 China counted some 520,000 health workers for a population of 570 million, a ratio of 1,100 persons per doctor. Nearly all of those health workers practiced traditional medicine. Maoist policy introduced a category of "barefoot" doctors, who trained for periods as short as three months in a mixture of Western and Chinese medicine. Barefoot doctors could make a diagnosis, advise about treatment, and, where no other recourse offered itself, provide treatment.[22] Over time the ratio of health workers, excluding barefoot doctors, improved to about 900 persons per doctor and included a larger share of people trained in Western medicine. But the principal change in the supply of health services came in the form of 1.6 million barefoot doctors (by 1979).[23] Most people who consulted doctors, especially in rural areas where most of the Chinese population lived, saw barefoot doctors first. Those doctors dispensed a mixture of traditional Chinese medicine, Western ideas about the transmission and prevention of infectious and parasitic diseases, and chiefly traditional remedies. China remained poor and its people remained poorly nourished, but life expectancy improved rapidly.

Both of these histories – tuberculosis in Botswana and China's mortality decline – suggest that traditional medicine has had and continues to have much value to alleviate suffering and reduce the risk of death. Its value lies in advice about how to stay well and how to act when sick, in the doctor's concern for a patient, in a selective adoption of biomedical ideas about disease causation, in the acceptance of Western ideas about specific diseases, and in the adoption of public health improvements.

---

[22] See *A Barefoot Doctor's Manual* (Philadelphia, 1977), which translates the official manual; and Willy De Geyndt, Xiyan Zhao, and Shunli Liu, *From Barefoot Doctor to Village Doctor in Rural China*, World Bank Technical Paper No. 187 (Washington, 1992).

[23] Penny Kane, "The Case of China," in Jacques Vallin and Alan D. Lopez, eds., *Health Policy, Social Policy and Mortality Prospects* (Liège, 1985), pp. 383–98. For the later period, see Shaikh I. Hossain, "Tackling Health Transition in China," World Bank Policy Research Working Paper 1813 (Washington, 1997).

Germ Theory and Biomedicine

In the mid-nineteenth century, Western medicine typically described epidemic diseases as zymotic, signaling that they arose from something akin to fermentation and could cause infection or contagion. This was a compromise between older theory, which held few diseases to be communicable from person to person, and compelling evidence of the swift communication of diseases such as cholera. Increasingly, attention fell upon possible means of communication.

Germ theory rejected the association with fermentation and replaced it with a biological agent of disease, the germ. Identifying these agents, germ theory revised two existing ideas. One of those, suggested now and again for many centuries but advanced with increasing urgency in the nineteenth century, held that diseases may be transmitted from person to person by particles too small to be detected by the unaided eye. The other old idea concerned agents, which had been identified by the aided eye in the late seventeenth century. In the 1670s Antony van Leeuwenhoek assembled microscopes that let him see single-celled "animalcules": protozoa, spermatozoa, and bacteria. He and his followers recognized these things as being alive but construed them as harmless vegetables. Agostino Bassi proved otherwise in 1835 by showing that a microscopic fungus causes silkworm disease.

The chemist Louis Pasteur took the key step in reformulating familiar ideas in an 1857 paper in which he argued that microorganisms generate one another, rather than arising spontaneously, and that they *cause* fermentation and decomposition. The claim that pathogens cause disease, rather than being produced by it, and the allied claim that specific pathogens cause specific diseases, remained contested until 1879, when the physician Robert Koch, using sheep anthrax as his model, showed that living organisms of a particular type cause a particular disease. Koch went on to identify the tuberculosis bacillus as the sole cause of this human disease, thereby making one of the most important and widely heralded scientific discoveries of the age. He also formulated postulates that settled the question of how to decide when a pathogen found in the blood of a diseased person was responsible for the disease: do pathogens produce the same disease when introduced into a healthy animal in sufficient numbers? During the last two decades of the nineteenth century scientists identified some twenty disease-causing bacteria;[24] ultimately that number grew to slightly more than 100 bacteria that may cause disease in humans or animals.

In 1865 Joseph Lister adapted to surgical practice the idea of using bacteria-destroying substances, such as diluted phenol, as external disinfectants, a technique called asepsis when applied prospectively and antisepsis when applied after the fact. But, Lister's innovations notwithstanding, germ theory did not have an immediately large impact on medical care. It drew attention away from the disease itself and toward the microorganisms that cause disease. Just as filth theory had been taken to explain many diseases rather than just a few, germ theory, too, led people to think that pathogens of the kind Pasteur and Koch had discovered cause most diseases. Moreover, doctors and the public at large expected that germ theory would lead quickly to the control of germs by either antisepsis or immunization. Koch tried to find an antimicrobial agent but failed. Until the 1930s and 1940s the main effect of germ theory on mortality lay in teaching people how to avoid specific germs and how to avoid infecting others.

Immunization

Pasteur, a chemist, suspected that he could use living microorganisms to develop substances that would prevent disease. He worked on four dis-

---

[24] Thomas D. Brock, *Robert Koch: A Life in Medicine and Bacteriology* (Madison, Wisc., 1988), p. 290, lists the twenty bacterial pathogens, the date of their discovery, the disease they cause, and the discoverer.

eases, three of them – anthrax, fowl cholera, and swine erysipelas – important in agriculture and the fourth, rabies, a disease sometimes transmitted from dogs to people. In each case Pasteur employed living but attenuated disease cultures to induce immunity. In place of Jenner's substitution of cowpox for smallpox as a way to reduce risk, Pasteur modified pathogens in his laboratory.

Koch directed his laboratory assistants to follow up on another idea: injecting test animals with nonlethal doses of toxins produced by diphtheria and tetanus. The animals' serum neutralized these toxins, allowing extraction of a diphtheria antitoxin in 1890 that could be used to immunize humans against the disease without employing either live or killed pathogens. Diphtheria patients treated with antitoxin early in the course of the disease recovered more often than did patients treated with conventional remedies. In separate work, Almroth Wright developed a typhoid fever vaccine in 1897. But these advances had little effect on mortality. Wright's typhoid vaccine provided only temporary protection; other vaccines were often administered during the incubation period of a disease, on the model of Pasteur's rabies vaccine, rather than to the unexposed population, with the result that they had little value. And the antitoxins developed for diphtheria, tetanus, and scarlet fever spread slowly and had little effect on morbidity or mortality. Jenner's technique of preserving a supply of active cowpox across great distances by successively vaccinating a series of subjects came to be replaced by refrigeration and, for some diseases, by the development of vaccine matter that required no special preservation, such as the freeze-dried BCG vaccine introduced around 1950.

Between 1881 – when Pasteur found an attenuated culture of the anthrax bacillus, the first post-Jenner vaccine – and 2000, vaccines were developed for some twenty diseases. Important gains occurred also in understanding the immune system and thus in the capacity to plot plausible strategies for making vaccines for diseases such as malaria and AIDS. But many of the hopes of immunology, among them a vaccine against cancer, remained disappointed. Table 3.1 sums up the history of vaccines.

Mass Immunization

Each new vaccine carried with it the possibility of eradicating a disease. But each vaccine also bore a high cost in that, unlike most public health remedies, it required individual and direct administration. Completely universal vaccination programs may never have been a practical option, but every program presented the need to vaccinate large numbers of people. The Expanded Program on Immunization (EPI), launched by the World Health Organization (WHO) in 1974, aimed to vaccinate the world's children, especially children living in developing countries, against six diseases: diphtheria, pertussis, tetanus, measles, polio, and tuberculosis.[25] A seventh vaccine, protecting against hepatitis B, was added to parts of this program in the 1980s.[26] The EPI was organized on the be-

[25] Some of these same diseases were targeted in the Selective Primary Health Care program, which deemed immunizations as the most cost-effective health service that could be provided. See below, this chapter.

[26] The viral disease hepatitis B, identified in the 1950s, occurs almost universally, often in inapparent or asymptomatic cases, in many developing countries. Its victims suffered usually mild symptoms and then recovered. Some remained carriers, transmitting the virus to uninfected people, mostly infants, along a huge variety of routes. In addition, hepatitis B carriers showed themselves at high risk to developing cirrhosis and liver cancer some thirty to forty years after their initial infection. Because carriers were numerous – comprising up to 20 percent of the population – these carcinomas led among causes of death from cancer in developing countries. A vaccine would therefore protect against a viral disease and against liver cancer. A proto-vaccine, made by heating blood samples from infected people, was introduced in the 1960s and an effective vaccine in 1982. But that vaccine was costly, nearly $100 for the required series of three shots. While such an expensive product might be used to control hepatitis B in developed countries, where fewer cases occurred, it was out of reach for developing countries. A Korean pharmaceutical firm developed a cheaper version of the vaccine, costing under $1 for the series of shots, making it possible in the mid-1980s to initiate a series of country-by-country trials of adding hepatitis B vaccination to the existing

Table 3.1. *Major Vaccines*

Disease	Year initially introduced	Effectiveness
Viruses:		
Smallpox	1796	Effective for 10–20 years
Rabies	1885	Effective
Yellow fever	1936	Effective
Influenza	1943	Temporary and partial
Polio	1954, 1957	Effective
Measles	1963	Effective
Mumps	1968	Effective
Rubella	1969	Effective
Adenovirus	1970	
Hepatitis B	1980	Effective
Bacteria:		
Cholera	1884	Possible short-term immunity
Tuberculosis	1890	Tuberculin: ineffective except as a diagnostic tool
	1906–21	BCG vaccine: often effective for children[a]
Diphtheria	1890	Unresolved, but may have reduced the lethality of the disease
Tetanus	1890	Effective
Plague	1895	Temporary and partial immunity
Scarlet fever	1907	Ineffective
Whooping cough	1933	Reduced the severity of the disease
Pneumonia	1945	Effective
Bacterial meningitis	1998	Expected to be effective

[a]BCG vaccines have a highly variable effectiveness. See Paul E. M. Fine, "The BCG Story: Lessons from the Past and Implications for the Future," *Reviews of Infectious Disease* 11, Supplement 2 (1989): S353–S359.

Source: Paul Weindling, "The Immunological Tradition," in W. F. Bynum and Roy Porter, eds., *Companion Encyclopedia of the History of Medicine*, 2 vols. (London, 1993), I: 196–201; Kenneth F. Kiple, ed., *The Cambridge World History of Human Disease* (Cambridge, 1993).

lief that neither individuals nor governments in many developing countries could afford even inexpensive immunizations on their own.

The six diseases initially targeted by the EPI caused several million deaths a year. Although it proved difficult to provide all six immunizations, even partial coverage promised to reduce mortality. Given scarce resources in the combined total of what developing countries could spend and donor countries would spend on such programs, the EPI seemed to its advocates to have had the grandest effect of all health programs in the latter part of the twentieth century. Coverage rose from about 5 percent of the target population of infants and children in 1977 to nearly 80 percent in 1990. At that level of coverage this program may have saved about three million lives a year. About half that effect comes from vaccinations against measles, a disease with a low case fatality rate, below 2 percent, but one that is particularly widespread.[27] Critics have described the EPI as a Western technocratic program that failed to build the capacity of communities in developing countries to provide health services for themselves.[28] Some object to the extent to which the program relied on social

WHO program. See Louis Galambos and Jane Eliot Sewell, *Networks of Innovation: Vaccine Development at Merck, Sharp & Dohme, and Mulford, 1895–1995* (Cambridge, 1995), pp. 194–95 and 206–8, discuss cost issues from Merck's perspective. William Muraskin, *The War Against Hepatitis B: A History of the International Task Force on Hepatitis B Immunization* (Philadelphia, 1995), provides the international context.

[27] Stanley O. Foster, "Potential Health Impact of Immunization," in Hoda Rashad, Ronald Gray, and Ties Boerma, eds., *Evaluation of the Impact of Health Interventions* (Liège, 1995), pp. 47–74; Peter Aaby, "Measles Immunization and Child Survival: Uncontrolled Experiments," in ibid., pp. 11–45; and, for a general assessment, Douglas C. Ewbank and James N. Gribble, eds., *Effects of Health Programs on Child Mortality in Sub-Saharan Africa* (Washington, 1993). Zoe Matthews and Ian Diamond, "The Expanded Programme on Immunisation: Mortality Consequences and Demographic Impact in Developing Countries," *Genus* 55 (1999): 73–100, estimate that deaths deferred by the EPI will average about 5.5 million a year across the period 1980–2025. Stan Becker and Robert E. Black, "A Model of Child Morbidity, Mortality, and Health Interventions," *Population and Development Review* 22 (1996): 431–56, explain how to think simultaneously about all the problems involved in reducing child mortality in developing countries.

[28] E.g., Debabar Banerji, "Crash of the Immunization Program: Consequences of a To-

authority to persuade people to comply. Others point to diseases and conditions not addressed by EPI: diarrhea, low-birth-weight infants, and acute respiratory infections.[29]

From smallpox forward in time to the hepatitis B program, vaccination campaigns have regularly fallen short of what is possible in protecting people from immunizable diseases. Much of the most effective effort to devise successful programs has focused on providing inexpensive vaccine material in a form easily administered to people in remote areas lacking electricity or refrigeration and on training the health workers needed to administer vaccines. Less effort has been invested in providing a convincing rationale for vaccination to people who are not literate, who are unfamiliar with the germ theory of disease, or who refuse to accept that theory.[30]

Antimicrobials

The idea that substances can be found that kill harmful material without damaging tissue circulated before germ theory was developed. It was promoted by Ignaz Semmelweis's 1848 use of sulfuric acid and chlorine washings to cleanse equipment and the hands of medical students delivering infants at the Allgemeines Krankenhaus in Vienna. Childbed fever

talitarian Approach," *International Journal of Health Services* 20 (1990): 501–10. There is also an anti-immunization argument, represented by books such as Walene James, *Immunization: The Reality behind the Myth*, 2nd ed. (Westport, Conn., 1995). She argues that immunizations have many harmful side effects. She also argues for some unaccepted ideas, such as the transmission of smallpox by bedbugs.

[29] Michael A. Koenig, Vincent Fauveau, and Bogdan Wojtyniak, "Mortality Reductions from Health Interventions: The Case of Immunization in Bangladesh," *Population and Development Review* 17 (1991): 87–104.

[30] The people most in need of vaccination programs have often proved the most resistant to them. T. Stephen Jones, Ronald J. Waldman, and William H. Foege, "The Role of Immunization Programmes," in Jacques Vallin and Alan D. Lopez, eds., *Health Policy, Social Policy and Mortality Prospects* (Liège, 1985), pp. 45–55.

became less common, although Semmelweis could not explain why. Laboratory findings, such as D. L. Romanovskii's discovery that quinine introduced into the blood of a person with malaria damaged specifically the asexual forms of the malaria parasite, also helped clarify the concept of antimicrobials. The search for particular agents, pressed aggressively during the 1890s, showed that chemicals could be used to disinfect diseased patients and raised hopes for chemical therapy. The search also showed how tedious and hazardous the process of finding chemical agents would be. The German chemist Paul Ehrlich introduced an arsenic derivative in 1909, marketed under the name Salvarsan, which in one form or another proved useful in treating syphilis and relapsing fever. Ehrlich hoped but failed to find a single substance that would destroy all pathogenic microbes, as well as one with fewer toxic side effects than his arsenic compound. Wilhelm Roehl's Germanin, discovered in 1916 as a treatment for sleeping sickness, and Fritz Schöfer's Plasmoquine, which worked against malaria much more effectively than traditional quinine treatments, confirmed that chemical therapies without disabling side effects could be found. But most compounds tested had no useful effects and many had harmful effects, leading scientists to the view that the most promising path to follow was to try to bolster the immune response.

In 1931, however, Gerhard Domagk and Philipp Klee discovered that a commonplace compound produced in making chemical dyes, designated prontosil, worked against streptococcus bacteria. Precursor to a series of sulfa drugs, prontosil inhibited the growth of bacteria by interfering with their capacity to synthesize folic acid. A brief golden age of sulfonamides followed, but it lasted only until 1942, when the first antibiotic, penicillin, was introduced into more general use after testing with human patients the year before. Antibiotics kill bacteria by disrupting their metabolism. Penicillin destroyed several types of pathogens yet showed few toxic side effects. In 1943 Selman Waksman, an agricultural microbiologist who had identified soil microorganisms he called actinomycetes, isolated streptomycin from one such organism. Effective against many pathogens, streptomycin had the particular value of curing tuberculosis.

The new drugs, beginning with Salvarsan and culminating with the antibiotics, vastly augmented the power of medicine to abbreviate the course of many diseases and reduce the likelihood of death. They put chemotherapy into a position of leadership over immunotherapy. In 1900 medical science possessed only a few drugs of unambiguous efficacy, such as quinine, digitalis, and opium; many of the drugs in use had unwanted and serious side effects. Moreover, although used against a wide range of maladies, they appear to have been effective against only a few diseases. The new drugs sharply increased the range of diseases that could be treated successfully. Aspirin, introduced in 1899, relieved pain and fever. Insulin (1921) controlled diabetes, an endocrine disorder, far more effectively than the dietary regimes previously used, providing markedly longer survival for people with the disease. But it was the antibiotics that transformed medicine's capacity to treat disease by putting most bacterial agents of disease at the mercy of chemicals capable of killing them and by further modifying the public's expectations about treatment. Whereas earlier patients had expected doctors to treat disease symptoms, with antibiotics patients came to expect treatments that dealt with underlying causes.[31]

Ironically, the sulfa drugs and antibiotics appeared at a time when the diseases against which they are effective had already lost their role as the leading causes of death in the West. In some cases antibiotics hastened the decline of death rates from these diseases; in other cases they merely maintained the rate of decline that already existed.[32] Strains of disease re-

---

[31] Beeson, "Changes in Medical Therapy."

[32] See Elina Hemminki and Anneli Paakkulainen, "The Effect of Antibiotics on Mortality from Infectious Diseases in Sweden and Finland," *American Journal of Public Health* 66 (1976): 1180–84; and, for the opposing finding, Johan P. Mackenbach and

sistant to the new drugs appeared in some patients only a short time after the drug began to be used. (Penicillin-resistant staphylococci were observed in 1947; streptomycin-resistant tuberculosis bacilli appeared in 1946, only two years after the drug's introduction.) But it was not until the late 1980s, with the spread of drug-resistant tuberculosis, that new research orientations appeared. One sought to replace blind screening as the leading means of identifying new antibiotics with more efficacious methods; another searched for ways to disarm rather than kill bacteria.[33]

Germ theory led to specific scientific discoveries that improved means of disease control. Its appearance also inaugurated a debate about the origins of disease, a debate pitting a microscopic view enhanced by laboratory research against a macroscopic view enhanced by sociological investigation. Proponents of the microscopic view argued that germs are a necessary and often also a sufficient cause of disease. It is enough to combat them by preventive or therapeutic means. This line of reasoning leads to investment in medical services, research laboratories, vaccinations, and medications. The historical form of this argument celebrates the role of medicine in disease control and treatment, in saving lives and in deferring death.[34] Against this stands the macroscopic argument, which holds that

Caspar W. N. Looman, "Secular Trends of Infectious Disease Mortality in the Netherlands, 1911–1978: Quantitative Estimates of Changes Coinciding with the Introduction of Antibiotics," *International Journal of Epidemiology* 17 (1988): 618–24.

[33] See the section titled "Resistance to Antibiotics" in *Science* 264 (1994): 359–93; and Hans Zähner and Hans-Peter Fiedler, "The Need for New Antibiotics: Possible Ways Forward," in P. A. Hunter et al., eds., *Fifty Years of Antimicrobials: Past Perspectives and Future Trends* (Cambridge, 1995), pp. 67–84.

[34] Walsh McDermott has been one of the most effective proponents of the good effect of medicine. See, e.g., his "Absence of Indicators of the Influence of Its Physicians on a Society's Health: Impact of Physician Care on Society," *American Journal of Medicine* 70 (1981): 833–43. See also J. Rogers Hollingsworth et al., *State Intervention in Medical Care: Consequences for Britain, France, Sweden, and the United States, 1890–1970* (Ithaca, 1990), esp. pp. 87–88; and Eliot Freidson, *Profession of Medicine: A Study of the Sociology of Applied Knowledge* (New York, 1971), p. 16, where Freidson makes the argument about curative power, a keystone of his case about professionalization.

the origins of disease are "to be found in the patterns of human society and of people's lives."[35] This other line of reasoning leads to attempts to protect people from behaviors that put them at risk to disease and to counteract environmental allies of disease such as poverty, inadequate housing, unbalanced diet, limited access to medical services, and defective information about disease prevention. The historical form of this argument denies that medicine played much of a role in the health transition, emphasizing instead diet, public health improvements, and other modifications of the human relationship with the environment.[36] Sometimes its proponents question or reject germ theory because of its association with Western science.

Except for smallpox, the diseases most susceptible to control through immunizations or antibiotics began to retreat in the West before either means of control had been deployed. Biomedical remedies helped in the continued reduction of morbidity and mortality from infectious diseases. In most of the remainder of the world, however, immunization and antibiotics appeared before or in the early stages of the health transition. Although those remedies were not always widely deployed (witness China,

---

[35] Roy M. Acheson and Spencer Hagard, *Health, Society and Medicine: An Introduction to Community Medicine* (Oxford, 1984), p. 6. This text revises Thomas McKeown's *An Introduction to Social Medicine*.

[36] Thomas McKeown, *The Modern Rise of Population* (London, 1976), has become the standard exposition of the view that medicine contributed little to the mortality decline. See also René Dubos, *Mirage of Health: Utopias, Progress, and Biological Change* (New York, 1959), esp. p. 19; Thomas McKeown, *The Role of Medicine: Dream, Mirage or Nemesis?* (Oxford, 1979); John B. McKinlay and Sonja M. McKinlay, "The Questionable Contribution of Medical Measures to the Decline of Mortality in the United States in the Twentieth Century," *Milbank Memorial Fund Quarterly/Health and Society* 55 (1977): 405–28; and J.H.R. Brotherston, *Observations on the Early Public Health Movement in Scotland* (London, 1952). Ivan Illich, *Medical Nemesis: The Expropriation of Health* (New York, 1976), remains a classic statement of this position, formulated more as an attack on medicine than a demonstration of the effectiveness of managing the environment and behavior. And for skepticism about the value of posing this question, see Kunitz, "The Personal Physician and the Decline of Mortality."

discussed above), aggressive deployment made it possible to limit infectious disease morbidity and mortality much more effectively and in a much shorter period of time than had been required in the West. In the 1950s and thereafter, death rates from infectious diseases decreased much more rapidly in developing countries than they had earlier in developed countries. In Nigeria, for example, biomedicine led an advance of fourteen years in life expectancy between 1963 and 1980.[37] The developing world benefited more from these elements of biomedicine than did the West. But biomedicine has often proved unable to cope with tropical diseases, and pharmaceutical companies, which sponsor research, have sometimes been discouraged from research on tropical diseases by the meager profits they can hope for.[38]

Survival Without Recovery and the Rise of Technomedicine

Germ theory enhanced survival prospects by showing how to protect people from many infectious diseases and by resolving diseases earlier and more often favorably. Thus biomedicine had the coincidental effect of reducing three things: mortality, the incidence of new episodes of disease, and (in certain circumstances) sickness time. In other forms modern medicine has contributed more to the prolongation of life without recovery. Some of the means of this have been technological, others mechanical, and still others biochemical. All of them build on the central contribution

---

[37] For the context, see Olukunle Adegbola, "The Impact of Urbanization and Industrialization on Health Conditions: The Case of Nigeria," *World Health Statistics Quarterly* 40 (1987): 74–83.

[38] John F. Ryder, "Who Needs New Antimicrobials?," in P. A. Hunter et al., eds., *Fifty Years of Antimicrobials: Past Perspectives and Future Trends* (Cambridge, 1995), pp. 165–77.

of medical practice to survival, which is to advise people about how to cope with their diseases and injuries. Thus the modern capacity to prolong life for the sick has added significantly to medicine's power to ease the lot of patients who have what for the moment at least are incurable maladies. In this way modern medicine has reduced mortality by adding months or years of life for people who, in earlier times, would have died from intractable ailments.[39] That effect adds to sickness time. The prevalence of morbidity increases because more people survive their diseases for longer periods. In some cases the added survival time occurs when the malady is still active and disabling. But in many cases modern medicine has found ways to manage disease, restoring a person to an active life.

Diabetes provides a classic case of such an effect. Before the introduction of insulin, patients and physicians tried to manage diabetes through diet but were able to do little to decrease suffering or to slow the development of the disease. The discovery of insulin by Frederick Banting during the winter of 1921-22 and its commercial introduction in 1923 allowed diabetics to live much longer and more active lives by controlling the disease. But the disease remained uncured.

Surgery transformed its focus from the removal of diseased matter to the repair and replacement of diseased or worn-out body parts. Open-heart surgery, introduced in the 1950s, and bypass surgery added years to the life of people whose hearts were damaged or whose arteries were clogged. The pacemaker regulated heart rhythm. Transplant surgery, made possible by the development of immunosupressant drugs, led to the replacement of diseased organs, including hearts and kidneys. Surgery repaired joints or replaced them with substitutes. Microsurgery reduced

---

[39] On the implications of this, see Ernest M. Gruenberg, "The Failures of Success," *Milbank Memorial Fund Quarterly/Health and Society* 55 (1977): 3–24; and Eliot S. Valenstein, *Great and Desperate Cures: The Rise and Decline of Psychosurgery and Other Medical Treatments for Mental Illness* (New York, 1986).

trauma. These therapies, too, extended the lives of people whose diseases or injuries were managed more often than cured.

Germ theory promoted the importance of laboratory study of body fluids, aiding diagnosis. In the modern era technological equipment – computerized axial tomography, magnetic resonance imaging, ultrasound, and other devices – has enhanced the physician's capacity to understand disease processes without invading a patient's body. These measures and the advent of general population testing, which dates from tuberculosis testing in the 1920s, led to earlier diagnosis of many ailments. Medical people had long argued that they find it easier to manage disease when it is discovered early in its course. The new technology often reduced by leaps and bounds the period of time between the onset of disease and its recognition by a patient or a doctor.

Although these mechanical, technological, and biochemical innovations prolonged life for people at all ages, much of the effect was concentrated among people in their fifties or above who were showing signs of organ deterioration. Thus the advances suggest a model of replacement of worn-out or misused body parts. Although patients treated by these means often enjoy many additional years of active life, the necessarily piecemeal repair or replacement of body parts does not restore them to new life.

The cost of medical services in this form far surpassed prior experience, leading to a rapid escalation in spending. The United States, where free market forces held sway, led the world: spending on health increased from 5.3 percent of GDP in 1960 to 13.3 percent in 1991. Many candidates for technomedicine could not afford it.[40] It is difficult to imagine future circumstances in which such technology can be made readily available to all the people of the world.

---

[40] David J. Rothman, *Beginnings Count: The Technological Imperative in American Health Care* (New York, 1997).

Primary Health Care

Primary health care (PHC) describes a strategy for taking basic health services to the people, especially to mothers and children.[41] It is a particular form of a longstanding idea, the idea being to promote community health and nutrition services and to supply a larger quantity rather than a higher quality of medical practitioners.[42] Under Fidel Castro, Cuba emerged as one of the most aggressive practitioners of popular health care. The Cuban model stressed free and accessible health services delivered by well-trained physicians and nurses who had studied not just medicine but also how to deal with educational and class differences between doctors and patients. Put into effect in Cuba in the 1960s, Castro sought during the 1970s and 1980s to make Cuba into a world medical power by sending doctors and nurses to sixty countries, most in Africa.[43]

Taken up by the WHO in 1978, PHC was meant to redress the deficiencies of an earlier strategy followed in many developing countries, which built hospitals, acquired Western medical technology, and tried to provide high-quality care for people who could gain access to it. In many countries 70 to 80 percent of the population could not gain access to such facilities. Even if people lived close enough to visit them, the hospitals

[41] Leonardo J. Mata, *The Children of Santa María Caugué: A Prospective Field Study of Health and Growth* (Cambridge, Mass., 1978), drew attention to child morbidity rates five to fifty times higher in his study population than in industrial societies.
[42] The oversupply of surgeon-general practitioners and apothecaries in much of nineteenth-century Western Europe, partly stimulated by insurance programs, represents an early example of an unplanned experiment in quantity over quality. R. Paul Shaw and Charles C. Griffin, *Financing Health Care in Sub-Saharan Africa through User Fees and Insurance* (Washington, 1995), describe similar hopes for modern Africa. On the many planned programs active in the 1940s and 1950s, see the articles in Benjamin D. Paul, ed., *Health, Culture, and Community: Case Studies of Public Reactions to Health Programs* (New York, 1955). For one testament to their successes, see Robert A. LeVine et al., *Child Care and Culture: Lessons from Africa* (Cambridge, 1994), pp. 170–71.
[43] Julia Margot Feinsilver, *Healing the Masses: Cuban Health Politics at Home and Abroad* (Berkeley, 1993).

were expensive and could accommodate only a fraction of the people needing care.[44] Hence the shift toward grass-roots basic health care. PHC focuses on prevention rather than treatment. For developed countries PHC has meant greater community involvement and more stress on preventive health care. For developing countries it has meant those things plus a much greater provision of health services, often by local people trained, albeit briefly, to give basic health care.

After World War II, buoyed by the miracle drugs, medical providers hoped to improve health by taking these drugs (and later also immunizations) to the people. Such aspirations guided health providers in colonial areas, and they stand behind the Chinese plan of the 1950s to train barefoot doctors. Thus the theory of primary health care arose from the optimism of postwar medicine, which had two specific elements. First, it promoted an efficacious medicine, able to treat and prevent many diseases. Second, it favored the democratization of medical care on the conviction that such care offered the best way for ordinary people to improve their health. Both elements can be seen in developed and developing countries alike.

For developing countries this approach displaced an older tropical medicine that often lacked confidence in the capacity of Western medicine to prevent or cure most tropical diseases and thereby focused on trying to protect Europeans from local diseases. PHC aimed to reach everyone at the village level, employing traveling clinics staffed by nurses and university-trained physicians or village clinics staffed by people with more rudimentary training, such as the aid post orderlies of Papua New Guinea or volunteer workers.[45] Like the old tropical medicine, PHC rep-

[44] Stewart MacPherson, *Social Policy in the Third World: The Social Dilemmas of Underdevelopment* (Brighton, 1982), esp. pp. 91–114, gives a good synthesis of the assessment of health problems in developing countries when PHC promotion was adopted as a policy objective. Maurice King, ed., *Medical Care in Developing Countries* (Nairobi, 1966), was influential in alerting Western agencies to defective access to health services in poor countries.
[45] Donald Denoon, Kathleen Dugan, and Leslie Marshall, *Public Health in Papua New*

resented a plan designed by medical authorities with little or no consultation with the people to be served. Nevertheless, comparisons of health experience between sites that had access to health services and those that did not registered a strong advantage for the former group. Thus I. O. Orubuloye and John C. Caldwell, in an important article published in 1975, showed that the residents of Ido in Nigeria enjoyed much lower death rates than those of Isinbode. Both sites enjoyed similar public health facilities; the key difference between them lay in the access of Ido residents to medical services.[46]

The WHO gave PHC a boost in 1978 by adopting it as a goal and as the key element of a strategy intended to provide "health for all by the year 2000." At that time some 2.6 billion people living chiefly in developing countries relied on self-help or traditional medicine. PHC would give them access to biomedicine in the form of immunizations, medications, and advice centered on germ theory. Although itself expensive – early estimates suggested that initial costs would range from $40 to $85 billion – PHC was seen as the most cost-effective way of providing health care, measured either as the cost of supplying it or according to its effects on mortality and morbidity.[47]

It proved easy enough to set up pilot programs, which demonstrated that effective care could be given to people who had not previously had it, and that the community in which a center was situated could be drawn into the public health effort.[48] But, as had been discovered in earlier pro-

---

Guinea: Medical Possibility and Social Constraint, 1884–1984 (Cambridge, 1989), pp. 93–94.

[46] I. O. Orubuloye and J. C. Caldwell, "The Impact of Public Health Services on Mortality: A Study of Mortality Differentials in a Rural Area of Nigeria," *Population Studies* 29 (1975): 259–72.

[47] David R. Phillips, *Health and Health Care in the Third World* (New York, 1990), p. 156.

[48] E.g., E. A. Afari et al., "Impact of Primary Health Care on Childhood and Mortality in Rural Ghana: The Gomoa Experience," *Central African Journal of Medicine* 41 (1995): 148–53.

posals of the same sort, such as Rockefeller Foundation clinics set up in Sri Lanka and Kerala in the 1920s and 1930s, it proved far more difficult to expand these pilot projects into regional or national networks. Most developing countries lacked the resources, either financial or in the form of trained doctors and nurses, to build and staff centers on the required scale. Even a large share of a small national budget could not buy enough centers and staff. Donor countries did not provide aid on anything close to the necessary level. Even so, individual units were often effective in providing health services, drawing community members into organized programs for identifying and responding to health problems, and promoting social and environmental improvements.

The pledge of health for all by the year 2000 raised expectations that could not be met. In an attempt to set more realistic goals, a redefinition was suggested around 1980 in favor of Selective Primary Health Care (SPHC). Western experts, informed chiefly by the means of disease treatment and prevention then available and much less so by knowledge of the disease problems of poor countries, selected four tactics: the six or seven immunizations discussed above in the Expanded Program on Immunization, oral rehydration therapy, the promotion of breastfeeding, and antimalarial drugs.[49] To many critics in developing countries, the very adoption of these limited means seemed to testify to an almost immediate collapse of commitment to the pledge made in 1978.

Although the immunization program reached large numbers and proportions of the children at risk, other features of the SPHC program had a more questionable effect. Oral rehydration therapy proved difficult to explain to mothers in unambiguous ways, so that some mothers expected it to control diarrhea when its effect, preventing dehydration, initially in-

[49] Julia A. Walsh and Kenneth S. Warren, "Selective Primary Health Care: An Interim Strategy for Disease Control in Developing Countries," *New England Journal of Medicine* 301 (1979): 967–74; and Kenneth S. Warren, "The Evolution of Selective Primary Health Care," *Social Science and Medicine* 20 (1988): 891–98.

duces more diarrhea. Breastfeeding campaigns, meant to increase the proportion of infants partially protected for their first four to six months by their mother's immune system through breastfeeding, ran into effective advertising from companies making infant formula, which urged mothers to forgo breastfeeding. Critics pointed up the shortcomings of SPHC, but they rarely identified substitute measures that would be better but also practical.

The introduction of basic medical services, therapeutic and preventive, maternity care, and health education to new areas continued into the 1990s to play an important role in the reduction of mortality.[50] Areas where basic health services had been available for some years often began during the 1990s to upgrade services by setting standards for medical training for clinic workers and evaluating performance.

Maternal Mortality

When mothers die in childbirth, they do so usually because infections develop or because of hemorrhaging. High rates of maternal death during or soon after, and for reasons related to, childbirth are estimated for Western countries in the seventeenth century, when the earliest grounds for such estimates appear. In England those rates seem to have declined from as many as 160 deaths per 10,000 births around 1650 to about 105 by 1700–1750, to 75 by 1750–1800, and to 55 by 1800–1870. In some Western countries asepsis and antisepsis were applied usefully to reduce maternal mortality in the period 1880–1910. But in many countries the maternal death rate failed to decline in that period, and in the West in general it failed to decline between 1910 and the mid-1930s. Wider use of caesarian sections in the early decades of the twentieth century reduced the risk

---

[50] G. Pison et al., "Rapid Decline in Child Mortality in a Rural Area of Senegal," *International Journal of Epidemiology* 22 (1993): 72–80.

of maternal death, but further decline of maternal mortality awaited the appearance of sulfonamides and antibiotics, which made it possible to control puerperal fever and other infections. The displacement of home by hospital deliveries during the twentieth century may also have helped reduce maternal mortality.[51]

The more surprising part of this story deals with the long period before asepsis and antisepsis. Then maternal mortality rates declined in some countries because midwives, who were usually women without formal medical education, were trained more effectively in coping with certain birthing problems, such as postpartum hemorrhages, and because the provision of midwifing services was increasingly limited to trained practitioners. Women who before had trained only as apprentices acquired some formal schooling. It also seems to have mattered that birth attendance received more respect as a medical service, and perhaps also that books explaining midwifery made up one of the more popular of eighteenth-century medical texts. Thus some measure of training was not difficult to acquire. By the 1870s Sweden's maternal mortality rate had dropped to about 50 per 10,000 and by the 1890s to 23, a threshold maintained until the late 1930s.[52] During the 1950s and 1960s marked differences in maternal mortality rates among Western countries disappeared, and by the 1980s the rate fell to less than one death per 10,000 births in many rich countries. After the 1880s declining fertility assisted in lowering maternal mortality to the degree that births in high-risk groups di-

---

[51] Irvine Loudon, *Death in Childbirth: An International Study of Maternal Care and Maternal Mortality, 1800–1950* (Oxford, 1992); and Jacques Gélis, *La sage-femme ou le médecin: Une nouvelle conception de la vie* (Paris, 1988). On the period before 1800, see the essays in Hilary Marland, ed., *The Art of Midwifery: Early Modern Midwives in Europe* (London, 1993). On abortion mortality, see World Health Organization, *Unsafe Abortion: Global and Regional Estimates of Incidence of and Mortality Due to Unsafe Abortion* (Geneva, 1998).

[52] In some Western countries maternal mortality rates actually increased in the early twentieth century, in part because of rising numbers of illegal abortions performed by unskilled and untrained people.

minished (women at particularly young or old ages and those who had already given birth to more than three children).

Those advantages had reached developing countries only in piecemeal form by the 1980s. As of 1983 one estimate suggested that about 500,000 women died each year in childbirth, 494,000 of them in developing countries. The highest rates occurred in Africa (70 per 10,000 births in Western Africa) and Southern Asia (65 per 10,000). Continued high fertility, with its age and parity hazards, the low status of women in some developing countries, and the continuing use of untrained or poorly trained birth attendants seem to be the leading factors behind these high levels.[53]

Maternal mortality emerges as an area where possibly the least progress has been made either in applying Western methods of limiting risk or in finding substitutes for them. Even though medical services requiring only limited training seem to have played the largest role in controlling maternal mortality in the West, comparable services remain unavailable to many women. Their lack is only partly compensated for by access to antibiotics.

Spending on Health

Two great surges in health spending have so far occurred in the health transition. In the first, the public sector made unprecedented investments in sanitary improvements in order to provide safe water and to dispose of human waste. European cities inaugurated these investments in the 1850s; on a global scale they remain incomplete.

The second surge involved private and public spending on health services. At the beginning of the twentieth century medical services ac-

[53] Carla Abou Zahr and Erica Royston, *Maternal Mortality: A Global Factbook* (Geneva, 1991), p. 3; and Nahid M. Kamel, "Determinants and Patterns of Female Mortality Associated with Women's Reproductive Role," in Alan D. Lopez and Lado T. Ruzicka, eds., *Sex Differentials in Mortality* (Canberra, 1983), pp. 179–91.

counted for less than 1 percent of gross domestic product, and spending on health in all forms, including public health improvements, less than 2 percent. By 1990, amidst a continuing rise, health spending in developed countries ranged from a low of 6.2 percent of gross domestic product in the United Kingdom, which had a national health scheme, to a high of 12.1 percent in the United States, which did not.[54] Such sharp differences in levels of investment invite comparisons between health spending and life expectancy. On one hand, Japan seems to get big returns from a small investment, spending only 6.5 percent of its GDP on health but, at eighty years in 1997, achieving the highest life expectancy at birth. On the other hand, the United States seems to get much less for its investment, spending 12.1 percent of GDP on health services, 2.8 percent above Canada, the next highest case, yet reporting a life expectancy that ranked twenty-third among all countries. In a still larger paradox, health spending as a proportion of income has advanced even while mortality has declined.

Health spending grew rapidly during the twentieth century in all developed countries. Lay people and experts alike often assumed that the number of physicians and the quantity of medical research play a large role in survival time and the quality of health. Yet no direct association is evident. Statistical examination of the association between health spending, numbers of physicians, or investments in medical research, on one hand, and life expectancy or other measures of health, on the other, produces variable answers. In some countries it appears that a larger investment in health in the existing form would produce a higher life expectancy, but in other countries that does not seem to be the case.[55]

---

[54] George J. Schieber, Jean-Pierre Poullier, and Leslie M. Greenwald, "U.S. Health Expenditure Performance: An International Comparison and Data Update," *Health Care Financing Review* 13 (1992): 1–87.

[55] Also Milton M. Chen and Douglas P. Wagner, "Gains in Mortality from Biomedical Research, 1930–1975: An Initial Assessment," *Social Science and Medicine* 12C (1978): 73–81, find that increased biomedical research accounted for about 25 percent of U.S.

Moreover, some countries got more for their investment than did others, at least in added survival time.

What is more, a number of poor countries achieved life expectancy equal to that of developed countries by making basic health services widely available rather than by spending more on health. Thus by 1990 Dominica, Cyprus, and Greece all reached life expectancy levels higher than the United States with much smaller investments in health services. And a number of other countries, among them Costa Rica, Jamaica, and Cuba, reported life expectancy nearly as high as in the United States on modest investments. Health spending generally shows a closer association with income than with life expectancy or other health targets. Table 3.2 explores this relationship in thirty-seven countries during 1990–94: life expectancy rises with per capita GDP, but the association between health spending and life expectancy is much weaker. Per capita GDP plays a bigger role in driving health spending than health spending does in driving life expectancy. Thus the United States derives little advantage in life expectancy from its high level of spending on health.

Conclusion

Traditional medicine offered and continues to offer social, emotional, and spiritual benefits, which help the sick; some useful therapies; and time-worn but helpful advice about rest and recuperation. Biomedicine added some spectacularly effective chemical and biological agents to the doctor's repertoire, sharply augmenting the capacity to abbreviate and ameliorate some maladies, and laboratory and technological agents, which improved diagnosis. It also added an explanation for why many diseases occur that

gains in life expectancy. Kari Poikolainen and Juhahi Eskola, "The Effect of Health Services on Mortality: Decline in Death Rates from Amenable and Non-Amenable Causes in Finland, 1969–81," *Lancet*, no. 8474 (1986): 199–202, argue that health care accounted for about half the decline in mortality in Finland in the period studied.

Table 3.2. *Life Expectancy, Per Capita Gross Domestic Product, and Health Spending in Thirty-Seven Countries*

	Life expectancy (years)	GDP per capita (1994 PPP $)	Health spending as a share of GDP (%)
Zimbabwe	49	2,196	3.2
Senegal	49.9	1,596	2.3
Nigeria	51	1,351	1.2
Kenya	53.6	1,404	2.7
India	61.3	1,348	1.3
Pakistan	62.3	2,154	1.8
Indonesia	63.5	3,740	0.7
Russian Federation	65.7	4,828	3.0
Vietnam	66	1,208	1.1
Brazil	66.4	5,362	2.8
Nicaragua	67.3	1,580	6.7
China	68.9	2,604	2.1
Thailand	69.5	7,104	1.1
Saudi Arabia	70.3	9,338	3.1
Poland	71.2	5,002	6.0
Malaysia	71.2	8,865	1.3
Republic of Korea	71.5	10,656	2.7
Sri Lanka	72.2	3,277	1.8
Czech Republic	72.2	9,201	5.9
Argentina	72.4	8,937	2.5
Chile	75.1	9,129	3.4
United States	76.2	26,397	13.3
Germany	76.3	19,675	9.1
United Kingdom	76.7	18,620	6.6
Belgium	76.8	20,985	8.1
Netherlands	77.3	19,268	8.7
Norway	77.5	21,346	8.4
Spain	77.6	14,324	6.5
Italy	77.8	19,363	8.3
Greece	77.8	11,265	4.8
Switzerland	78.1	24,967	8
Australia	78.1	19,285	8.6
Sweden	78.3	18,540	8.8

(continued)

Table 3.2. *Continued*

	Life expectancy (years)	GDP per capita (1994 PPP $)	Health spending as a share of GDP (%)
France	78.7	20,510	9.1
Canada	79	21,459	9.9
Iceland	79.1	20,566	8.3
Japan	79.8	21,581	6.8

Source: United Nations Development Programme, *Human Development Report: 1997* (New York, 1997), pp. 146–48, 176–77, and 207.

allows people to take more useful steps toward disease avoidance. Before the appearance of biomedicine, people suffering sickness hoped that their doctors could point them toward recovery. Europeans saw humoral treatments as part of the process of recovery. After biomedicine's appearance patients expected also that the doctor would identify the specific malady, shorten its course and moderate its symptoms, and point them toward recovery. Technomedicine added the promise of replacing defective, diseased, or worn-out body parts.

If we take traditional medicine out of the balance of forces affecting human survival, in the past or the present, we can surmise that sicknesses would be more unsettling and stressful. They would lead to death more often and probably also sooner. If we take biomedicine out of the balance of medical forces in the last century or so, we can surmise that many more people – especially children in poor countries – would have suffered diseases and died. Immunizations and chemical medications are not the only means to prevent disease, but they are the means on which people have relied, to an increasing degree. Thus medicine has contributed to the mortality decline in three leading ways. First, traditional medicine drew more people into its ambit, familiarizing them with medical advice and with the notion of submitting to such advice. The decline of maternal mortality before the appearance of biomedicine gives a forceful example of the efficacy of traditional medical expertise. Second, biomedicine contributed in an important way to reducing mortality from infectious diseases, especially those of childhood. Its effects were felt in developed countries, but they were felt more strongly still in poor countries where a sanitary revolution did not precede the appearance of biomedicine. Third, technomedicine found ways to prolong life for patients whose diseases could not be cured.

Like public health, medicine gives and it takes away. Biomedicine and technomedicine demand an expensive medical infrastructure comprised of laboratories and researchers, hospitals, training facilities, doctors and pharmacists, pharmaceutical researchers and makers, diagnostic equipment, surgeons and operating rooms, and other things. This investment, too, is troubled by inefficiencies, which are especially noticeable in a demographic appraisal that compares life expectancy with spending levels. Poor countries, which invest on a much smaller scale and invest more on improving patient access to doctors and nurses than they do on technical medicine, seem to get more for their investment. Indeed, some of them report survival rates that surpass those in rich countries even though the rich countries pay vastly more for medicine. In the long run it may be difficult for even the richest countries to sustain an investment of 8 to 12 percent of GDP in health services, much less to continue to add to that investment.

Suggestions for Further Reading

Michael Bliss. *The Discovery of Insulin.* Chicago, 1982.

W. F. Bynum and Roy Porter, eds. *Companion Encyclopedia of the History of Medicine,* 2 vols. London, 1993.

Daniel Callahan. *False Hopes: Why America's Quest for Perfect Health Is a Recipe for Failure.* New York, 1998.

Patrice Debré. *Louis Pasteur.* Trans. Elborg Forster. Baltimore, 1998.

Daniel De Moulin. *A History of Surgery.* Dordrecht, 1988.

Medicine

Paul Ewald. *Evolution of Infectious Diseases.* New York, 1994.

Horacio Fábrega, Jr. *Evolution of Sickness and Healing.* Berkeley, 1997.

Kris Heggenhougen et al. *Community Health Workers: The Tanzanian Experience.* Oxford, 1987.

Ivan Illich. *Limits to Medicine: The Expropriation of Health.* London, 1976.

John M. Janzen. *The Quest for Therapy in Lower Zaire.* Berkeley, 1978.

Kenneth F. Kiple et al. *The Cambridge World History of Human Disease.* Cambridge, 1993.

Jonathan Liebenau. *Medical Science and Medical Industry: The Formation of the American Pharmaceutical Industry.* Baltimore, 1987.

C.J.L. Murray, R. Govindaraj, and P. Musgrove. "National Health Expenditures: A Global Analysis." *Bulletin of the World Health Organization* 72 (1994): 623-37.

Lynn Payer. *Disease-Mongers: How Doctors, Drug Companies, and Insurers Are Making You Feel Sick.* New York, 1992.

Roy Porter. *The Greatest Benefit to Mankind: A Medical History of Humanity.* New York, 1997.

Roy Porter, ed. *The Cambridge Illustrated History of Medicine.* Cambridge, 1996.

A. Ramesh and B. Hyma. "Traditional Indian Medicine in Practice in an Indian Metropolitan City." *Social Science and Medicine* 15D (1981): 69–81.

Stanley Joel Reiser. *Medicine and the Reign of Technology.* Cambridge, 1978.

William B. Schwartz. *Life Without Disease: The Pursuit of Medical Utopia.* Berkeley, 1998.

Milton Wainwright. *Miracle Cure: The Story of Penicillin and the Golden Age of Antibiotics.* Oxford, 1991.

4

Wealth, Income,
and Economic Development

Income is an unsatisfactory measure of the quality of the human condition.[1] People living in high-income countries certainly enjoy advantages over their counterparts in low-income countries, but the advantages have a particularly uncertain relationship to life expectancy. Jamaica and Belize had 1997 life expectancies of 74.8 and 74.7 years, versus 76.7 in the United States. Yet per capita GDP in Jamaica totaled only $3,440 and in Belize $4,300, compared with $29,010 in the United States. Neither countries nor individuals have sought to gain higher incomes as a way to improve their survival prospects. Nor will anyone confuse generous wealth or income with longevity. The relationship is mediated.

Recent research suggests that there may be three routes of mediation. On the first route income is an enabling tool, the compensation from which varies according to the choices made by individuals and public institutions. At the individual level higher income may lead to more command over important proximate factors of survival, such as food and

---

[1] This point is developed in Richard A. Easterlin, *Growth Triumphant: The Twenty-First Century in Historical Perspective* (Ann Arbor, 1996), esp. pp. 131–44.

health care. And at the level of a society higher average income may lead to a better provision of services important to survival, such as clean water, immunizations, sanitary facilities, education, and health institutions such as hospitals. On the second route, higher average income may make it easier to reduce poverty and thereby diminish the share of the population whose prospects of escaping premature death are especially fragile. Even though per capita income estimates, by their very nature, fail to capture differences among countries in income distribution, they should be considered because higher average incomes are associated with less poverty. Poor countries often have higher infant mortality, which may be the strongest link between per capita income and life expectancy. On the third route, political and civic institutions, specifically, a higher degree of either political and civil liberty or of civic engagement, may promote gains in income and life expectancy at the same time. Thus both higher income and life expectancy may be effects.[2] The initial question to be addressed is this: did nineteenth-century countries with higher mean incomes per capita command an advantage in life expectancy?

Are Rich Nations Also Long-Lived Nations?

Reliable estimates of both life expectancy and income in Europe are first available for the early nineteenth century. By that point several countries had learned how to promote ongoing economic growth, after a history in which, from one year to the next, growth had been no likelier than con-

---

[2] These avenues of mediation are discussed in Sudhir Anand and Martin Ravallion, "Human Development in Poor Countries: On the Role of Private Incomes and Public Services," *Journal of Economic Perspectives* 7 (1993): 133–50, which stresses the capacity of a better provision of public services to elevate survivorship, and Partha Dasgupta and Martin Weale, "On Measuring the Quality of Life," *World Development* 20 (1992): 119–31, which stresses the association of political liberties and gains in life expectancy. Amartya Sen, *Development as Freedom* (New York, 1999), makes a still bolder argument for freedom broadly construed.

traction. The initiation of sustained economic growth in Britain, the Low Countries, and France in the second half of the eighteenth century coincided with the beginning of sustained gains in longevity. As time passed other countries joined this simultaneous march toward higher income and rising life expectancy. By the end of the nineteenth century most of the countries in Western and Central Europe enjoyed high income and survival. This congruence in change over time, which is rough rather than precise, has often been taken to show that economic growth – specifically, an improved standard of living – promoted the health transition.

But the congruence did not exist across the continent. Some locales, such as the Norwegian parish of Rendelen, some countries, such as Norway, and some regions, especially the Nordic lands, had both low incomes and low death rates. Britain, in contrast, had a high income and low death rates. The Dutch Republic, the Southern Low Countries, and France all had high death rates and high incomes, compared with their European neighbors. Figure 4.1 examines the relationship between per capita GDP and crude death rates in ten countries around 1820. There is only a weak association between income and mortality.[3] Most of these ten countries had quite similar levels of per capita income but quite dissimilar mortality. England stands out, having a high income and low mortality. But the beginning of the mortality decline in England did not coincide with the beginning of ongoing economic growth, and its beginning elsewhere did not await a country's arrival at a position of high income. In this cross-sectional approach, income does not seem to have been a determinant of survivorship.[4]

[3] Italian mortality is represented by Lombardy and Tuscany alone, and the United Kingdom's by England alone. Crude death rates bear comparison in this way because of the similarity in age structures among these countries.

[4] George J. Stolnitz, "A Century of International Mortality Trends," *Population Studies* 9 (1955): 24–55, and 10 (1956): 17–42, points out that mortality differences among European countries diminished before economic differences. E. A. Wrigley et al., *English Population History from Family Reconstitution, 1580–1837* (Cambridge, 1997), p. 552,

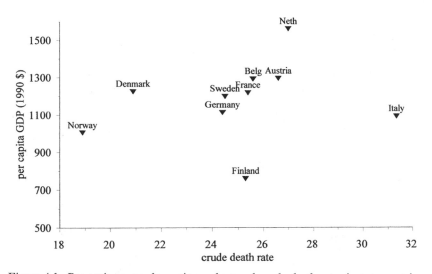

Figure 4.1. Per capita gross domestic product and crude death rates in ten countries, 1820. *Source:* Angus Maddison, *Monitoring the World Economy, 1820–1992* (Paris, 1995), p. 23; B. R. Mitchell, *European Historical Statistics 1750–1975* (New York, 1981), pp. 114–17; and E. A. Wrigley et al., *English Population History from Family Reconstitution, 1580–1837* (Cambridge, 1997), p. 614. The crude death rate is for England and the GDP per capita estimate is for the United Kingdom. The Belgian crude death rate estimate is for 1830.

Much the same conclusion arises from examining the experience of six countries across the period 1830 to 1910, as shown in Figure 4.2. Each country's position has been plotted by per capita output and crude death rates, without aligning the positions chronologically. In Belgium and Sweden death rates decreased as income increased. Given the sharply different income rankings of these two countries, what seems to have mattered is not the level of output but its pace of improvement. In contrast, French and German output rose rapidly from the 1830s up to the 1870s without coinciding with lower crude death rates. And in Spain and Italy,

conclude that "mortality changes were not closely linked to economic factors such as changes in real incomes per head."

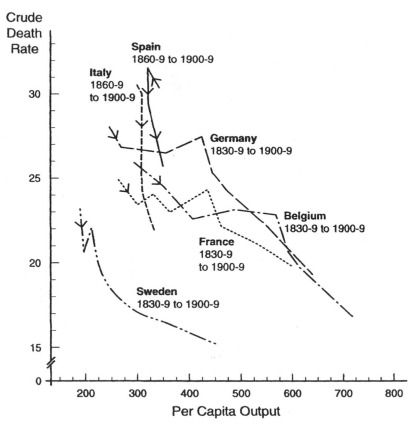

Figure 4.2. Per capita output and crude death rates in six countries, 1830–1910. *Source:* See Fig. 4.1.

which enter observation only from the 1860s, death rates decreased without any significant gains in output.

Nor do the data assembled in Figure 4.2 suggest the existence of a threshold above which output gained the power to push mortality down. Not until the 1890s did Sweden's per capita output surpass that in Spain or Italy. But Sweden's death rates had long been much lower than death rates in those two countries. As of 1901–10 Sweden and the United Kingdom had achieved virtually identical crude and age-standardized death rates, but per capita income in the United Kingdom was nearly twice that in Sweden. Finally, there is nothing in the time series approach to suggest that the germ theory or any other innovation in understanding disease or survival hazards transformed the relationship between income and survival prospects. Thus in nineteenth-century Europe neither the cross-sectional nor the time series analysis suggests a consistent or strong association between income and survivorship.

Studying mortality patterns in the twentieth century, Samuel Preston found noteworthy similarities in the hierarchy of income and life expectancy, but concluded that income growth has had limited effect on mortality trends. Specifically, income growth accounted for some 10 to 25 percent of growth in life expectancy between the 1930s and 1960s, in the sense meant by regression analysis. Preston suggested that improvements in medical knowledge and sanitary practice came in a form that made mortality reductions available at progressively lower levels of development.[5] The developed countries considered alone do not show much correlation between mortality and income. But developing and developed countries, taken together, suggest that it is much easier for rich than poor countries to achieve low mortality. Administrators at the WHO consider this relationship so compelling that they have identified extreme poverty as the leading underlying cause of premature death and suffering from disease across the globe.

Putting the several analyses together, two conclusions seem to be warranted. First, modern countries are likely, much likelier than their counterparts around 1820, to rank in a similar order in survivorship and in-

---

[5] Samuel H. Preston, *Mortality Patterns in National Populations with Special Reference to Recorded Causes of Death* (New York, 1976), pp. 72–77; and Preston, "The Changing Relation between Mortality and Level of Economic Development," *Population Studies* 29 (1975): 231–48. See also G. B. Rodgers, "Income and Inequality as Determinants of Mortality: An International Cross-Section Analysis," *Population Studies* 33 (1979): 343–51; and Easterlin, *Growth Triumphant,* esp. pp. 69–82.

come. This stands to reason to the degree that it was more difficult in 1800 or 1850 to invest higher incomes in things that paid off handsomely in higher life expectancy. Sanitation and clean water provided the first unambiguous opportunity to use higher income in service of survival, mostly after 1850. Even in 1900, however, sanitary improvements remained incomplete in Britain, which built them the most aggressively and led Europe in income. Second, gains in income may not drive up life expectancy in all countries or all circumstances.

The weak relationship observed between income growth and higher survivorship in nineteenth-century Europe may run in both directions or, more often, from higher survivorship to higher income, rather than the other way, as most researchers have supposed. Rising survival rates for children in the nineteenth century changed the proportions between people of working ages, roughly fifteen to sixty-five, and nonworking ages. Thus the form the health transition took in nineteenth-century Europe initially promoted higher per capita levels of productivity for the entire population, even though some countries, such as Sweden, apparently failed to capture those advantages. There may also be an association between the freedom of a country's political and civic institutions and its gains in income or life expectancy.

Rich Nations and Life Expectancy in the Twentieth Century

During the twentieth century differentiation in income among countries expanded. Differentiation in life expectancy probably grew in the early century, but it diminished in the second half of the century. These movements alone suggest that, at the national level, income and life expectancy do not have a fixed relationship. Figures 4.3 to 4.6 explore this issue further. In each figure the countries considered appear twice in the same column, with life expectancy represented by a triangle pointing upward and GDP per capita by a triangle pointing down.

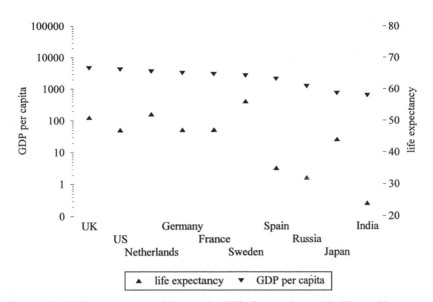

Figure 4.3. Life expectancy and income in 1900. *Source:* Angus Maddison, *Monitoring the World Economy, 1820–1992* (Paris, 1995), p. 27.

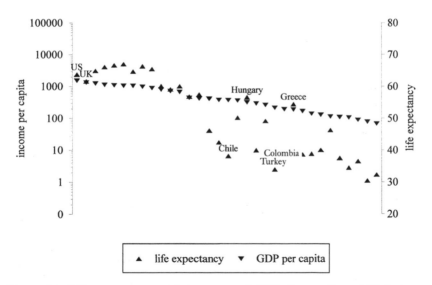

Figure 4.4. Life expectancy and income around 1940. *Source:* Samuel H. Preston, "Causes and Consequences of Mortality Declines in Less Developed Countries during the Twentieth Century," in R. A. Easterlin, ed., *Population and Economic Change in Developing Countries* (Chicago, 1980), pp. 289–360.

129

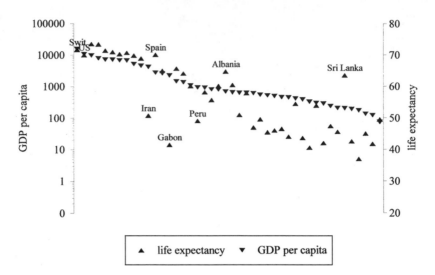

Figure 4.5. Life expectancy and income in 1960. *Source:* United Nations Development Programme, *Human Development Report 1997* (New York, 1997), pp. 161–63, and *Human Development Report 1999* (New York, 1999), pp. 134–37; and United Nations Secretariat, Department of Economic and Social Affairs, Population Division, *World Population Prospects: The 1998 Revision*, 2 vols. (New York, 1998), I: 546–73.

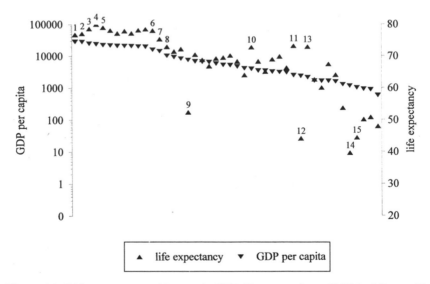

Figure 4.6. Life expectancy and income in 1997. Key to numbers: (1) United States, (2) Singapore, (3) Switzerland, (4) Japan, (5) Canada, (6) Spain, (7) Portugal, (8) Argentina, (9) Gabon, (10) Fiji, (11) Sri Lanka, (12) Zimbabwe, (13) Albania, (14) Uganda, (15) Burkina Faso. *Source:* See Fig. 4.5.

130

Figure 4.3 shows life expectancy and GDP per capita in ten countries in 1900, and Figure 4.4 shows income per capita and life expectancy in 33 countries around 1940. Figure 4.5 reports these factors for 48 countries in 1960, and Figure 4.6 reports these factors for the same 48 countries in 1997.[6] In terms of what levels of income imply about life expectancy some countries can be described as overachievers or underachievers in each period.

Sweden and Japan stand out as overachievers in 1900 (Fig. 4.3); their life expectancy levels were much above what would be estimated on the basis of the relationship between GDP per capita and life expectancy in all countries. The U.S. position most closely approaches an under-achiever; its income level implies a higher life expectancy.

In 1940 the income curve extends from a high of $1,549 in 1970 dollars in the United States to a low of $67 per capita in India. The United States and the United Kingdom underachieved, among high-income countries, and Chile, Turkey, and Colombia all underachieved among low-income countries. Hungary and Greece led the overachievers.

In 1960 the income curve extends from a high GDP per capita of $15,779 in Switzerland to a low of $75 in China. Switzerland and the United States might be deemed underachievers, but Iran, Gabon, and Peru unambiguously earn that characterization. Spain, Albania, and Sri Lanka attained much higher levels of life expectancy than other countries at their levels of per capita income.

In 1997 the GDP per capita curve extends from $29,010 in the United States to $580 in Tanzania. The United States, Singapore, and Switzerland qualify as modest underachievers, and Gabon, Zimbabwe, Uganda, and Burkina Faso as gross underachievers, compared with other countries at their levels of per capita income. Japan, Canada, Spain, Portugal, and

[6] The 48 countries include nine of the ten countries in Figure 4.3, excluding Russia; the largest countries in population; and a random sample of remaining countries.

Argentina qualify as modest overachievers, and Fiji, Sri Lanka, and Albania as robust overachievers. In both 1960 and 1997 the association between income and life expectancy tends to break down in lower-income countries.[7]

The most interesting relationship between income and life expectancy is represented by countries that under- or overachieve. John Caldwell explored this issue in the 1980s. The countries and regions he designated as superior achievers had low levels of per capita income, but also low infant mortality and high life expectancy relative to income. Thus Sri Lanka, with a 1982 per capita gross national product (GNP) of $320, reported an infant mortality rate of 32 deaths per 1,000 live births and a life expectancy of sixty-nine years; Saudi Arabia with a per capita GNP of $16,000 reported infant mortality of 108 per 1,000 and a life expectancy of fifty-six.[8]

It is possible, Caldwell argued, "to break the economic shackles." Greater female autonomy; high investments in education; broadly accessible schooling and health care; and the provision of a nutritional floor characterized the superior achievers. The combination of these selected policies emphasizing social justice plus a more even distribution of resources allowed high survivorship amidst poverty. Perhaps grass–roots political activism, even radical activism, which influences the way policies are selected and resources are allocated, accentuated the effect of those policies. But there does not seem to be any particular form of education, health care, or even political activism that makes the difference.

---

[7] The 1900 GDP estimates are expressed in 1990 dollars, the 1940 estimates in 1970 dollars, the 1960 estimates in 1987 dollars, and the 1997 estimates in 1997 dollars.

[8] John C. Caldwell, "Routes to Low Mortality in Poor Countries," *Population and Development Review* 12 (1986): 171–220, the quote from p. 174. See also Alberto Palloni, "Health Conditions in Latin America," in Jacques Vallin and Alan D. Lopez, eds., *Health Policy, Social Policy and Mortality Prospects* (Liège, 1985), pp. 465–92; and Ermelinda Meksi and Gianpiero Dalla Zuanna, "La mortalité générale en Albanie (1950–1990)," *Population* 49 (1994): 607–36, who associate Albania's gains with Soviet aid.

The southwestern coastal state of Kerala, one of the poorest states in India, provides a dramatic example of overachievement. That region entered the modern era with an advantage in life expectancy, compared with all of India. Survivorship began to improve earlier than in the country as a whole and by means of a distinctive strategy that has come to be known as the Keralan model. This model features social rather than economic development. It promotes male and female literacy; greater female participation in the labor force; later marriage and earlier family planning, thus lower fertility; a health policy of readily accessible clinics; and fair-price food shops. Although Kerala is densely populated, poor, rural, and its people poorly nourished, compared with the remainder of India, it has the lowest fertility and the highest life expectancy in the country.

Some of its advantages are historical. People in the area traditionally boiled drinking water, the dense population was distributed in many small settlements, every village had a school, and females commanded a more nearly secure place in society. Annual runoffs flushed the countryside of refuse. Other advantages were introduced or intensified during the twentieth century. By 1991, 94 percent of males and 87 percent of females aged seven and older were literate in Kerala, compared with 64 and 39 percent, respectively, in India as a whole. Kerala built health centers, staffed them with trained personnel, and situated them to make access easy. Its clinics provide immunizations, maternal and infant care, and treatment of injury and disease. Kerala has fewer doctors than West Bengal, for example, but its health centers are more numerous and more often staffed by doctors. The costs of health care remain modest. Keralan women are not only more often literate than their counterparts elsewhere in India, but they also have more years of schooling. This translates into a greater frequency of use of health centers, high immunization rates, and medically supervised childbirth.[9]

[9] Moni Nag, "Impact of Social Development and Economic Development on Mortality:

Lower mortality in Kerala has been accompanied by a continuing heavy burden of disease among children and adults. Keralans report more sickness episodes and more sickness time than do their counterparts elsewhere in India. Gopalakrishna Kumar attributes this in part to a greater awareness of health, assisted by ready access to health centers, and in part to a rising real burden of illness associated with the transition from brief infectious to more often protracted degenerative diseases. In Kerala, heart disease, neoplasms, and diabetes among adults coexist with a heavy burden of diarrheal diseases, worm infestations, and acute respiratory infections among children.[10] The first characteristic makes Kerala resemble developed regions, and the second makes it resemble developing regions. But Kerala stands just as squarely among the developed regions in its life expectancy as it stands among developing regions in its per capita income.

Since 1982, when the rankings Caldwell used were constructed, few countries have retained their relative positions.[11] Saudi Arabia's life ex-

Comparative Study of Kerala and West Bengal," *Economic and Political Weekly* 18 (1983): 877–900; P. N. Suchama, "Social Context of Health Behavior in Kerala," in John Caldwell et al., eds., *What We Know about the Health Transition: The Cultural, Social, and Behavioural Determinants of Health*, 2 vols. (Canberra, 1990), II: 777–87; Mari Padaru Bhat, "Mortality in India: Levels, Trends and Patterns," Ph.D. thesis, University of Pennsylvania, 1987; and P.K.B. Nayar, "The Case of Kerala, India," in Jacques Vallin and Alan D. Lopez, eds., *Health Policy, Social Policy and Mortality Prospects* (Liège, 1985), pp. 371–81.

10 B. Gopalakrishna Kumar, "Low Mortality and High Morbidity in Kerala Reconsidered," *Population and Development Review* 19 (1993): 103–21; and S. Irudaya Rajan and K. S. James, "Kerala's Health Status: Some Issues," *Economic and Political Weekly* 28 (1993): 1889–92.

11 Short-run economic downturns seem, in some historical circumstances, to have slowed the rate at which death rates decline, at least in the economic groups most seriously affected. M. Harvey Brenner, "Mortality and the National Economy: A Review, and the Experience of England and Wales, 1936–1976," *Lancet* (Sept. 15, 1979): 568–73. Perhaps recoveries promote compensatory growth for those same groups. In modern developing countries evidence for a strong effect is lacking. Economic downturns have coincided with somewhat higher infant mortality, but they have had little effect at higher ages. People seemed to adjust, even during the serious downturns of the 1970s and 1980s. Kenneth Hill and Alberto Palloni, "Demographic Responses and Economic

pectancy improved to 70.7 years in 1995 even though its per capita GDP diminished to $8,516, a victim of plunging oil revenues. Costa Rica, Sri Lanka, and Kerala, which Caldwell studied most closely, have all remained overachievers. That category has been expanded, adding not just Fiji and Albania, which appear in the sample of forty-eight countries considered in Figure 4.5, but also a number of countries in Latin America and the Caribbean. In 1997 a total of thirty-eight countries with GDP per capita below $10,000 had life expectancies of seventy or above.[12] It is difficult to associate the superior achievers of 1960, 1982, and 1997 with political and civic freedoms; they represent countries from across the political spectrum.

Whether the factors that Caldwell distinguished have played a strong role in breaking economic shackles among this growing group of overachievers remains to be discovered. Additional research has been done on a more general version of one of the factors he considered, which is the limitation of poverty. A more egalitarian distribution of income within a country may promote higher life expectancy. Richard Wilkinson offers one way to understand this effect: in many populations survivorship is strongly differentiated between low- and middle-income groups and individuals, but weakly differentiated between middle- and high-income groups and individuals. Being poorer makes a big difference in survival prospects, but being richer makes less difference. Societies in which few people stand far below the modal level of income have a higher average life expectancy because they benefit from a more favorable income distribution. For concrete illustration Wilkinson compares survivorship and income in Japan and Britain between 1970 and 1990. Both countries started the period with similar distributions of income and similar levels

Shocks: The Case of Latin America," *Proceedings of a Conference on Peopling of the Americas*, 4 vols. (Liège, 1993), III: 411–37.

[12] United Nations Development Programme, *Human Development Report 1999* (New York, 1999), pp. 134–37.

of life expectancy. Over time Japan's survival jumped ahead of Britain's, the inequality of income distribution in Britain widened, but Japan maintained its egalitarian position of income distribution.[13]

It is not difficult to understand why the limitation of poverty in a rich country might improve life expectancy. People who struggle to make ends meet find it difficult to obtain many of the things that influence survivorship, relative to their favored compatriots. What is more surprising is that this relationship seems to exist also in poor countries. This suggests that, in longevity, both relative and absolute poverty matter.

Between 1950 and the 1980s most countries within the Sino-Soviet orbit managed to achieve survivorship levels higher than would be expected on the basis of levels of per capita income. Those countries overtly pursued a strategy of investing in public services – education, clinics, hospitals, medical services, sanitary improvements, mass immunizations – calculated to improve the length of life, and they succeeded. It may be that a weaker differentiation in standards of living across the population plus a floor of public services well above a subsistence level helped elevate life expectancy.

In sum, life expectancy varies across countries for many reasons. Each nation, sometimes each region within a nation, varies in life expectancy performance for reasons that are peculiar to its own development and the choices its people have made and for reasons that are best understood by comparing that country with others. A first approach toward understanding this calls for scholars to write thorough national and regional histories of the health transition. A second approach suggests the possibility of building a theory of national performance, albeit

---

[13] R. G. Wilkinson, "Income Distribution and Life Expectancy," *British Medical Journal* 304 (1992): 165–68; and Wilkinson, *Unhealthy Societies: The Afflictions of Inequality* (London, 1996). Also Rogers, "Income and Inequality as Determinants of Mortality"; and Harriet Orcutt Duleep, "Mortality and Income Inequality among Economically Developed Countries," *Social Security Bulletin* 52 (1995): 34–50.

one that is likely to be more effective at showing effects than causes. This latter approach has been pursued by a World Bank team of researchers led by Jia Wang.[14] Their aim was to describe how 115 countries, none high income, rank in the mortality of children, adults, and overall life expectancy. Since comparisons with other countries that are similar in basic ways reveal more than do global comparisons, the World Bank team elected to control for education, income, and region (i.e., to make comparisons net of these factors). The results identify under- and over-achievers between 1960 and 1990, but the team purposely avoided the attempt to explain why particular countries achieved the positions observed. They limited interpretation to an overall assessment of factors contributing to the eleven-year gain in life expectancy that they observed and a country-level analysis. Technical progress contributed the most, followed by female education and income.[15] Their analysis suggests that factors that may come from inside or outside a country, which embody technical progress, mattered more in that period than did policies followed within the country, except of course for the adoption of new knowledge.

Both education and income have changing rather than fixed associations with survival. The survivorship associated with any given level of GDP per capita has improved over time. Hence poor countries have gained on rich countries in life expectancy. The World Bank team's results, which report a status for every five years, show country perfor-

[14] Jia Wang et al., *Measuring Country Performance on Health: Selected Indicators for 115 Countries* (Washington, 1999). For the intellectual antecedents of this approach, see, esp., Jacques Vallin, "La mortalité dans les pays du tiers monde: Evolution et perspectives," *Population* 23 (1968): 845–68; and Samuel H. Preston, "Causes and Consequences of Mortality Declines in Less Developed Countries during the Twentieth Century," in R. A. Easterlin, ed., *Population and Economic Change in Developing Countries* (Chicago, 1980), pp. 289–360.

[15] But in this analysis income and education are measured directly, whereas technical progress is proxied by time effects. The level of detail is meager.

mance has varied over time and across the 115 countries studied, even holding income and education constant. Thus, for example, Bolivia fell short on both female and male life expectancy, standing out in 1960 as the poorest performer on both gauges. Between 1960 and 1990, however, Bolivia reduced its deficit from a shortfall of 13.8 years to one of 3.1 years in female life expectancy and from 15.2 to 1.5 years in male. In contrast Zambia's position deteriorated on both gauges.[16] It is difficult to reduce the team's findings to a few numbers. Nevertheless, the results identify countries worthy of study in any attempt to discover ways that things go wrong or right. So far, attention has been focused on the overachievers, but the World Bank study suggests that it may be equally revealing to study the improving underachievers.

Since 1960, life expectancy has been democratized across countries while differences in per capita income have grown. Table 4.1 gives values for GDP per capita in 1987 dollars and life expectancy, distinguishing developing countries from industrial countries. Even though there is no obvious way to make a comparison on the same terms, differences in life expectancy have shrunk much more than differences in per capita GDP. The utility of higher income as a means of enhancing survival declined across those years. For rich countries the health transition to date has been accomplished by capital-intensive means. Those are especially noticeable in the huge investments that the industrial countries made in sanitary systems, medical education and research, the development of drugs and vaccines, better housing, and modifications of the environment that promote health, such as drainage projects. As Figure 3.1 shows, rich countries differentiate themselves sharply from poor countries in the share of national GDP they spend on health. For the developing countries a health transition in the capital-intensive form was not in prospect in 1960 and has not since become possible. Without looking into this issue in detail, it is evi-

---

[16] Ibid., pp. 39–42.

Table 4.1. *A Comparison of Per Capita Gross Domestic Product and Life Expectancy, 1960 and 1995*

	GDP per capita (1987 U.S. $)	Life expectancy at birth
Developing countries, 1960	330	46.0
Industrial countries, 1960	7,097	68.6
Developing countries, 1995	867	62.2
Industrial countries, 1995	12,764	74.2

Source: United Nations Development Programme, *Human Development Report 1998* (New York, 1998), pp. 142 and 149.

dent that poor- and medium-income countries have turned increasingly to non-capital-intensive modes of health transition. In the past the countries that pioneered the health transition and reached high levels of survivorship early have seemed to be the most important models to be studied by countries lagging them. In the future the countries likeliest to command such close scrutiny will be those that have achieved the most at the least cost.

Do Rich Individuals Live Longer?

T. H. Hollingsworth used genealogical information to reconstruct survival among English peers in the preindustrial era. He found, for the highest ranks of England's aristocracy, that life expectancy was low and that it waxed and waned over time. Many years later Wrigley and Schofield reconstructed fertility and mortality in the English population during the era of the parish registers. Assuming that the structure of mortality by age had long matched that of the mid-nineteenth century, they also estimated life expectancy. Like Hollingsworth, they found that life expectancy waxed and waned over time. But their estimates suggest that the general population of England outlived the peerage up to the late seventeenth century. Then the peerage drew even and began to draw ahead. By the mid-nineteenth century life expectancy in the peerage was well ahead of that in the general population. In other countries the picture is less clear. In some the evidence suggests that elites outlived the general population or the common people early on, in others that they did not.[17]

Even for the very rich it was a difficult matter to find ways to control survival hazards before 1800. Then, for reasons that remain unexplained, they began to control those hazards more successfully than the general population. Elites showed some advantage in the eighteenth century, but during the nineteenth century that advantage rose sharply. By the mid-twentieth century survival prospects in Britain were arrayed in a socio-economic hierarchy showing the advantages of income and status. Many observers expected the introduction of the National Health Service in 1948 to allow less-favored groups to catch up. But the Black Report of 1980 revealed, for both mortality and sickness prevalence, that higher classes retained their advantage.[18] Indeed, between 1931 and 1981 the survival difference between the highest (professional) and the lowest (un-

[17] T. H. Hollingsworth, *The Demography of the British Peerage, Population Studies*, 18, Supplement (1965); and E. A. Wrigley and R. S. Schofield, *The Population History of England, 1541–1871: A Reconstruction* (Cambridge, 1989), pp. 528–29. Alfred Perrenoud found a class structure in seventeenth-century Genevan life expectancy, which suggests that socioeconomic differences appeared in cities. Alfred Perrenoud, "L'inégalité sociale devant la mort à Genève au XVIIe siècle," *Population* 30, Special Number (1975): 233 and 236. Also Sigismund Peller, "Births and Deaths among Europe's Ruling Families since 1500," in David V. Glass and D.E.C. Eversley, eds., *Population in History* (London, 1965), pp. 87–100; Aaron Antonovsky, "Social Class, Life Expectancy and Overall Mortality," *Milbank Memorial Fund Quarterly* 45 (1967): 31–73; and Alain Blum, Jacques Houdaille, and Marc Lamouche, "Eléments sur la mortalité differentielle à la fin du XVIIIe et au début du XIXe siècle," *Population* 44 (1989): 29–53.
[18] Peter Townsend and Nick Davidson, eds., *Inequalities in Health: The Black Report* (London, 1992).

skilled) occupational classes rose sharply. Survival improved in both groups, but much more rapidly in the favored group.

Pioneer students of nineteenth-century economic growth, including Karl Marx, Gustav Schmoller, and Simon Kuznets, suspected that the early stages of industrial modernization aggravated inequality in income and quality of life. In the "standard of living" debates, historians have considered whether and when inequality may have risen.[19] Newly gained evidence about heights, which shows social differentiation more effectively than older evidence about wages and prices had done, suggests that inequality did increase. Youths examined for military service, who seem to represent the unemployed and underemployed poor, showed declining stature as time passed in the early nineteenth century. Thus the peerage and other favored groups drew ahead in life expectancy in the first half of the nineteenth century also because urban unskilled laborers and their family members fared so badly.

Another part of the explanation lies with tuberculosis, a disease often termed "undemocratic" because of its strong association with socioeconomic status, mediated by crowding, poor nutrition, poorly ventilated and dank housing, and perhaps also overwork.[20] (In contrast, influenza is a "democratic" disease because it does not exhibit these differences.) Tuberculosis, the leading cause of death in cities and, excluding infants, probably in the overall nineteenth-century British population, aggravated differentiation by status. Furthermore, in the second half of the century childhood mortality declined earlier and more rapidly in favored social

[19] For recent discussions of this long and active debate, see Peter Lindert, "Unequal Living Standards," in Roderick Floud and Donald McCloskey, eds., *The Economic History of Britain since 1700*, 2 vols. (Cambridge, 1994), I: 357–86; and N.F.R. Crafts, "Some Dimensions of the 'Quality of Life' during the British Industrial Revolution," *Economic History Review* 50 (1997): 617–39.

[20] Milton Terris, "Relation of Economic Status to Tuberculosis Mortality by Age and Sex," *American Journal of Public Health* 38 (1948): 1061–70.

groups.[21] Sanitary reforms, introduced first in neighborhoods where elites lived, protected wealthier people first. Thus the socioeconomic differential has been preserved across major shifts in the disease profile, the level of income, the effectiveness of medicine, access to health services, and individual health behavior.[22]

Britain receives close scrutiny here because so much more attention has been given to the issue of socioeconomic differentiation in survival there than in most other countries. Comparisons among developed countries at the end of the twentieth century suggest that Britain occupies a middle position in its degree of differentiation, having more than the Nordic lands, about the same amount as the United States on many indicators, and less than France. In the 1980s U.S. black males living in Harlem, a depressed neighborhood in New York City, had a smaller chance of surviving to age sixty-five than did males in Bangladesh.[23] Differentiation increased after 1980 within many Western countries. It is more evident for males than females and for majority than for minority populations.[24] Many factors have been identified as potential contributors to these patterns, but the mechanisms are not yet well understood. Very little has been learned

[21] Michael R. Haines, "Socio-Economic Differentials in Infant and Child Mortality during Mortality Decline: England and Wales, 1890–1911," *Population Studies* 49 (1995): 297–315.

[22] Elsebeth Lynge, *Socio-Economic Differences in Mortality in Europe: Newly Emerging Trends in Mortality* (Strasbourg, 1984); John Fox, ed., *Health Inequalities in European Countries* (Aldershot, 1989); and Richard G. Wilkinson, "Equity, Social Cohesion and Health," in S. S. Strickland and P. S. Shetty, eds., *Human Biology and Social Inequality* (Cambridge, 1998), pp. 58–75.
   For another attempt to conceptualize the problem, see Robert G. Evans, Morris L. Barer, and Theodore R. Marmor, eds., *Why Are Some People Healthy and Others Not? The Determinants of Health of Populations* (New York, 1994).

[23] Colin McCord and Harold P. Freeman, "Excess Mortality in Harlem," *New England Journal of Medicine* 322 (1990): 173–77.

[24] Sally Macintyre, "Social Inequalities and Health in the Contemporary World: Comparative Overview," in Strickland and Shetty, eds., *Human Biology and Social Inequality*, pp. 20–35.

about the association between socioeconomic inequality and survivorship in developing countries. But it appears to be the case that the so-called diseases of affluence – especially heart disease – occur more often among the less than among the more affluent in rich countries.

Conclusion

Income is an enabling factor, which boosts or diminishes life expectancy, depending on how it is spent. The high-income countries achieved most of their high survivorship by capital-intensive investments in public health, medicine, and other things. These countries show that, in the circumstances of the end of the twentieth century, it is difficult not to elevate life expectancy at birth to seventy years or more when a country is rich. Beside them stand a rising number of poor and middle-income countries that have pursued strategies of social development. These countries show that it is possible to elevate life expectancy to seventy years or more without first becoming rich. And there is a third group of countries where incomes remain low and life expectancy has risen but has not approached seventy years.

In each category there are overachievers and underachievers, considering income alone as a correlate of survivorship. Important questions about the other characteristics of under- and overachievement await exploration. Countries where people engage actively in discussion of health policies and policies about factors proximate to health seem to have an advantage. But it is difficult to associate this engagement with particular political institutions, such as democracy. Also interesting is this question: how did social elites with higher incomes gain a stronger advantage in life expectancy in Europe in the nineteenth century and hold on to that in the second half of the twentieth century even in many countries that attempted to equalize access to education, public health, and medical care?

Poverty denies people the options that allow them to escape premature death. Even though many low- and middle-income countries have found ways to compensate for the effects of national poverty on survivorship, many more countries have not. Especially in South Asia and Africa, the costs of poverty in years not survived are huge. With the exception of only a few countries, where the distribution of income is the least skew, poverty within countries shows up boldly in life expectancy and survivorship at most ages. Within countries, too, the costs of poverty are obvious and large.

Suggestions for Further Reading

Mel Bartley, David Blane, and George Davey Smith, eds. *The Sociology of Health Inequalities.* Oxford, 1998.

Veena Bhasin. *People, Health and Disease: The Indian Scenario.* Delhi, 1994.

John C. Caldwell. "Routes to Low Mortality in Poor Countries." *Population and Development Review* 12 (1986): 171–220.

Richard W. Franke. *Life Is a Little Better: Redistribution as a Development Strategy in Nadur Village, Kerala.* Boulder, 1993.

Hartmut Kaelble. *Industrialisation and Social Inequality in 19th-Century Europe.* Trans. Bruce Little. New York, 1986.

Jim Yong Kim et al., eds. *Dying for Growth: Global Inequality and the Health of the Poor.* Monroe, Me., 2000.

Stephen J. Kunitz and Stanley L. Engerman. "The Ranks of Death: Secular Trends in Income and Mortality." *Health Transition Review* 2 (1992, supplementary issue): 29–46.

P.G.K. Panikar and C. R. Soman. *Health Status of Kerala: The Paradox of Economic Backwardness and Health Development.* Trivandrum, 1984.

S. S. Strickland and P. S. Shetty, eds. *Human Biology and Social Inequality.* Cambridge, 1998.

5

Famine, Malnutrition, and Diet

Undernutrition and overnutrition both elevate mortality.[1] For most of the history of the health transition, undernutrition posed the more serious threat. Food supplies failed, causing famine; some people ate too little so often that they were chronically undernourished; many people consumed diets deficient in particular nutrients. Many of the economic and geographic trends of the last 200 years have also favored overnutrition, with resulting obesity and degenerative diseases. At the end of the twentieth century the two problems coexist. Poorer people, especially in developing countries, are likelier to face malnutrition than other populations. But many people in poorer countries are also showing signs of obesity.

The relationship between nutrition and good health is not yet fully understood. On one hand, a deficiency of specific nutritional elements may damage the immune system (zinc deficiency) or expose a person to a particular disease (iodine deficiency). Deprivation in the prenatal period or in infancy adds to adult vulnerability to chronic disease. A deficit of calo-

---

[1] Body mass index values below 20 and above 30 are especially dangerous. For an illustration of the point, see Hans Th. Waaler, "Height, Weight, and Mortality: The Norwegian Experience," *Acta Medica Scandinavica, Supplementum* 679 (Stockholm, 1984).

ries during growth grave enough to result in stunting may place an individual at serious risk to sickness and death. Population-level malnutrition, especially protracted malnutrition, may provoke actions that make it easier for communicable diseases to spread.[2] On the other hand, pathogens generally require the same nutrients as do human hosts, so that they often find it difficult to live and reproduce in poorly nourished hosts. Experiments with animal models suggest that undernutrition can extend survival and elongate reproductive years.[3] Similarly, while overnutrition elevates the risk of certain degenerative adult diseases, it may also protect against other diseases. Nutrition furnishes us with tactics of disease avoidance, prevention, treatment, and management, but its principal promise lies in avoidance. People who eat too much can avoid disease by moderating their diets; people who eat too little or who eat unbalanced diets can protect themselves against disease if they can secure adequate diets.

Famine

In 1798 Thomas Malthus described famine as the ultimate positive check on population growth, arguing that rapidly growing populations would outrun their food resources. To many authorities Malthus seems to have been better at summing up the past than at predicting the future. There is some evidence that a regime in which people lived close to the limit of food resources existed in England into the sixteenth century, in France into the seventeenth, and in Ireland and Finland even into the nineteenth

---

[2] D.J.P. Barker, *Mothers, Babies, and Disease in Later Life* (London, 1994), and Diana Kuh and Yoav Ben-Shlomo, eds., *A Life Course Approach to Chronic Disease Epidemiology* (Oxford, 1997), present opposing explanations for chronic disease in adulthood; both emphasize nutrition.

[3] Based on rodent models. Among the recent replications of findings about dietary restriction, see Rita B. Effros et al., "Influence of Dietary Restriction on Immunity to Influenza in Aged Mice," *Journal of Gerontology: Biological Sciences* 46 (1991): B142–B147.

century.[4] When Malthus wrote, the last European food shortage had taken place in the 1740s, when in most countries famine had been averted.[5]

On the global scale famine did not disappear in the preindustrial era. Large-scale famines continued to occur in the nineteenth century, and in the twentieth century they have affected still broader regions and populations. The second half of the twentieth century has known famines of previously unsurpassed scale. The total effect has been so great that it is the twentieth century, rather than any other recent historical period, in which famine deaths have accumulated to the largest numbers.

This recurrent experience with famine has led to a more subtle interpretation of causes. Malthus believed that famine results from an absolute shortage of food: the growing population that presses against its food resources runs the risk that a harvest failure will result in widespread starvation. A population may even overwhelm its food supplies. Under the influence of this idea, historians discovered subsistence crises in preindustrial Europe, occasions when a sharp rise in food prices, indicating harvest failure, coincided with an increase in mortality. But why did death rates increase so quickly? A food shortage would, in an ordinarily well-nourished population, lead to a gradual but not an abrupt transition into malnutrition. How much time would pass until people actually starved would depend on how much of nutritional needs people had to forgo. Some authorities have suggested that preindustrial Europeans were chronically undernourished and thereby suffered immediately from any shortfall in food resources. That interpretation has been countered by the argument that people monitored harvests closely and that the anticipation

---

[4] E. A. Wrigley maintains that England was not prey to subsistence crises, in which death prompted a rise in mortality, in the seventeenth or eighteenth century. E. A. Wrigley, "Mortality and the European Marriage System," in Catherine Geissler and Derek J. Oddy, eds., *Food, Diet and Economic Change Past and Present* (Leicester, 1993), pp. 35–49.

[5] John D. Post, *Food Shortage, Climatic Variability, and Epidemic Disease in Preindustrial Europe: The Mortality Peak in the Early 1740s* (Ithaca, 1985).

of harvest failure mobilized them to search for food and jobs and also activated speculation and food hoarding. Food shortages provoked migrations, the disruption of sanitary practices, and a more efficient spread of communicable diseases.[6] Mortality escalated especially when rural people, who had not been exposed to many diseases, moved to cities searching for food and jobs and there encountered smallpox, typhoid fever, and other diseases endemic in cities. Mortality crises continued to recur as long as public authorities could do so little to move food from areas of surplus into areas of dearth. Improvements in grain storage facilities, in the capacity of public authorities to anticipate food shortage, and in the movement of grain to markets, which developed in the seventeenth and eighteenth centuries, all dampened European subsistence crises. So, too, did a more varied group of food plants. Adding the potato and beans to diets based on grain improved nutrition and supplemented the agriculturalist's defenses against the effects of cold and wet summers on food plants. This is nonetheless a Malthusian model, albeit modified. A food shortage provokes higher mortality, if indirectly, through migration rather than starvation, and the effect is especially intense in dense rural populations.[7]

Market mechanisms, which are expected to maintain a proportion between prices and supply, break down at moments of food shortage, and people often lose their jobs. Food prices often seem to rise faster than the degree of shortage would explain, led by speculators and hoarders, who

---

[6] John Walter and Roger Schofield, "Famine, Disease and Crisis Mortality in Early Modern Society," in Walter and Schofield, eds., *Famine, Disease and the Social Order in Early Modern Society* (Cambridge, 1989), pp. 1–73.

[7] Thomas Robert Malthus, *An Essay on Population,* 2 vols. (London, 1958); Pierre Goubert, *Beauvais et le Beauvaisis de 1600 à 1730,* 2 vols. (Paris, 1960); Kari J. Pitkänen, *Deprivation and Disease: Mortality during the Great Finnish Famine of the 1860s* (Helsinki, 1993); John D. Post, "Nutritional Status and Mortality in Eighteenth-Century Europe," in Lucile F. Newman et al., eds., *Hunger in History: Food Storage, Poverty, and Deprivation* (Cambridge, Mass., 1990), pp. 241–80; and Karl Gunnar Persson, "The Seven Lean Years, Elasticity Traps, and Intervention in Grain Markets in Pre-industrial Europe," *Economic History Review* 49 (1996): 692–714.

see a chance to hold food off the market early in a crisis in anticipation of huge profits later on. If dearth develops in this way, does famine result from a shortage of food, a failure of market mechanisms, or from yet another source? The economist Amartya Sen argues that famines take place when entitlements fail. Sen uses that term to describe the economic and political capacity of people to acquire food, suggesting that a sudden and disproportionate increase in food prices leads to a loss of entitlement. His example of an entitlement failure is the Bengal famine of 1943, in which ordinary channels for food imports were cut off by World War II. British colonial authorities in India failed to foresee the problem and failed also, once the shortage existed, to find alternative sources of food or to make food available at prices that the poor could afford. Between 1.5 and 3 million people died.[8]

The Dutch hunger winter of 1944–45, during World War II, assumes importance in the history of nutrition as a famine averted. German occupation forces seized food to send to Germany. The Dutch responded by controlling the distribution of the remaining food supply, rationing short supplies to adults and children. Everyone suffered, the poor more than most. Because of rationing, however, no one lost his or her entitlement to food. Mortality from tuberculosis increased during the famine, as did malnutrition.[9] But the Dutch survived a famine lasting about six months with few intermediate or long-term effects.[10] The Dutch hunger winter suggests that even a serious and sustained food shortage will not neces-

[8] Amartya Sen, *Poverty and Famines: An Essay on Entitlement and Deprivation* (Oxford, 1981). On the history of famine in India, see Arup Maharatna, *The Demography of Famines: An Indian Historical Perspective* (Delhi, 1996).

[9] Tuberculosis develops more readily in people lacking some nutritional values. See Ancel Keys et al., *The Biology of Human Starvation*, 2 vols. (Minneapolis, 1950), esp. II: 1002–56.

[10] L. H. Lumey and F.W.A. van Poppel, "The Dutch Famine of 1944–45: Mortality and Morbidity in Past and Future Generations," *Social History of Medicine* 7 (1994): 226–46.

sarily lead to famine or higher mortality if food resources are divided fairly and if groups at particular risk, such as pregnant women and infants, receive extra food.

Famines of two types have occurred repeatedly in the twentieth century, and this capacity to survive has not characterized either of them. First, and easier to explain, the Soviets blundered into famine in 1932–34, and other Marxist countries have repeated Soviet experience. Hoping to squeeze the agricultural sector in order to create resources for industrialization, Soviet authorities forced the collectivization of farms. They tried also to control farming practice, dictating which crops should be planted and how they should be cultivated. The result was a sudden, sharp drop in output, produced in part by mismanagement and in part by the antagonistic reaction of farmers to collectivization. China duplicated this horrible blunder in 1958–59, suffering the largest famine, measured by the loss of life, in human history. Up to 26 million people died, over and above ordinary mortality, and another 33 million births were forgone because of the famine. North Vietnam followed the Soviet example in 1956, and Ethiopia repeated this disaster in 1980.

Thus in one category twentieth-century famines have been created by public policy. Soviet authorities in the 1930s planned to export food and continued to execute those plans even after the famine had begun. But they also controlled market mechanisms, so that it is difficult to apply entitlement theory to the Soviet famine. Much less is known about the distribution of food within China and North Vietnam during famine, but there, too, entitlement theory seems to have less explanatory power than the sheer arrogance of state authorities in causing a shortage of food.

The second type of famine has usually been made, or at least provoked, by natural disaster and, less often, by civil conflict. An arid period in Africa pushed the Sahara southward, reduced grazing lands, and cut crop size in much of the continent during 1968–74 and again in the early 1980s. The inundation of low-lying cropland, whether caused by cyclones or severe monsoon flooding, has repeatedly threatened famine in Bangladesh. Nigeria's civil war of 1967–68 brought famine.[11]

Across this period the meaning of the term "public authority" expanded to include leaders of international agencies, some intergovernmental, such as the United Nations, and some private, such as Oxfam and the Red Cross. National authorities in sub-Saharan Africa and South Asia often proved unable to avert or temper famines, so that international authorities increasingly assumed the task of formulating policy and taking action. During the 1970s and 1980s they organized shipments of food, usually rough grains, such as millet, the reallocation of which would have little effect on food prices in the countries supplying assistance. Donors counted on recipient states to organize the receipt and distribution of this food.

The human story of famine in Africa and South Asia contains many familiar elements. When local food shortages threatened or developed, people left their homes in search of food and jobs. Whereas in preindustrial Europe people turned first to cities, African authorities directed migrants to relief camps, set up at sites where food was to be distributed. Time and again camp populations outran the supply of water and food, so that hungry people, often exhausted from weeks of walking in search of assistance, faced not just a shortage of food but also ineffective sanitation and unclean water. Measles and diarrhea epidemics broke out in the camps, intensifying the effects of food shortage and dislocation. Moreover, the primary relief tactic, moving grain into the famine area, took months to organize. Recipient governments often proved incapable of distributing relief food. Much of it was diverted from the stomachs of the hungry onto the black market, which the hungry could not afford to patronize.[12]

---

[11] John C. Caldwell and Pat Caldwell, "Famine in Africa: A Global Perspective," in Etienne van de Walle, Gilles Pison, and Mpembele Sala-Diakanda, eds., *Mortality and Society in Sub-Saharan Africa* (Oxford, 1992), pp. 367–90.

[12] Alexander de Waal, *Famine That Kills: Darfur, Sudan, 1984–1985* (Oxford, 1989), esp. pp. 172–226.

Relief agencies meant to distribute free food. Their aims were often perverted by local realities, leading to a tragic position in which food was plentiful but inaccessible to the hungry. This was not the entitlement problem that Sen described in Bengal, but it was a problem of entitlement. The hungry lacked the economic or political resources to command access to the food provided by relief agencies. The famines ended when the hungry people who had not died found their own ways to cope with famine, often assisted by the longer-run effects of food relief and the arrival of a new harvest season.[13] In South Asia and perhaps also in parts of Africa the number of deaths during food shortages created by natural disasters may have been augmented by malaria.[14]

By the late 1990s, in the aftermath of hurricane devastation in Nicaragua and Honduras and earthquake damage in Turkey, relief experts emphasized not the provision of food but of money, hoping to address the problem of entitlements by distributing the means to buy food, housing, and other necessities. Money would be faster mobilized and easier to distribute, and it could be used, following Sen's advice, to restore entitlements by providing jobs for people without them. But it was not clear that it would counteract the market failures associated with crises or be kept safe from diversion into the pockets of local authorities. And it was also not clear whether outsiders who had been generous in supplying food assistance would be as generous in sending cash.

Rapid global population growth and rapid growth in poorer countries contribute to the continuing problem of food supply. The green revolution developed hybrid grains that, from the 1960s to the 1990s, allowed global

[13] These coping strategies remain one of the least well understood aspects of famine.

[14] Tim Dyson, "On the Demography of South Asian Famines," in two parts in *Population Studies* 45 (1991): 5–26 and 279–97; and Maharatna, *Demography of Famines.* Sheila Zurbrigg, "Did Starvation Protect from Malaria? Distinguishing between Severity and Lethality of Infectious Disease in Colonial India," *Social Science History* 21 (1997): 27–58, argues that acute but not chronic hunger leads to higher mortality from malaria.

food output to grow faster than population.[15] India, a food importer at the beginning of that period and, for many 1960s observers, a classic example of the threat of a Malthusian crisis of food shortage, became a food exporter while the calorie intake of its populace improved. Transgenic modifications in other food plants may continue the green revolution. But warnings of future food shortages continue to be given.[16] By 2050 it will be necessary to feed not just the six billion people alive at the end of the twentieth century but an additional three billion or so. As Malthus noticed, the math of population growth always seems threatening.[17]

Malnutrition

Serious nutritional deficiencies have been commonplace in many parts of the twentieth-century world. Perhaps as many as 100 million children under age five showed signs of protein-energy malnutrition in the early 1980s. Of those, perhaps 10 million had serious signs of disease, and one million had clinical symptoms such as found in marasmus or kwashiorkor.[18] Protein-energy malnutrition occurs in young children whose diets

---

[15] Thomas T. Poleman, "Recent Trends in Food Availability and Nutritional Wellbeing," *Population and Environment* 19 (1997): 145–65.

[16] A. J. McMichael et al., eds., *Climate Change and Human Health* (Geneva, 1996), pp. 107–21, who project a net contraction of food supplies from climatic change; and Lester R. Brown, *Tough Choices: Facing the Challenge of Food Scarcity* (New York, 1996), who warns of an impending food crisis.

[17] E.g., Gary Gardner, *Shrinking Fields: Cropland Loss in a World of Eight Billion* (Washington, 1996). Food supply may be monitored in a variety of good sources, including the annual *State of the World,* published by the Worldwatch Institute; and the many reports of the U.N. Food and Agricultural Organization (FAO), such as FAO, Economic and Social Development Paper 116, *Compendium of Food Consumption Statistics from Household Surveys in Developing Countries,* 2 vols. (Rome, 1993); and FAO, *Production Yearbook,* an annual.

[18] Ivan Beghin and Marc Vanderveken, "Nutritional Programmes," in Jacques Vallin and Alan D. Lopez, eds., *Health Policy, Social Policy and Mortality Prospects* (Liège, 1985), p. 81.

lack enough protein and enough calories. It is especially common in children who, upon the arrival of a new infant, can no longer be breastfed. This condition often coincides with disease and may in part be a result of the disease processes, chiefly fever and diarrhea, that deprive a child of nutritional resources. In addition to these clinical signs, protein-energy malnutrition often shows up as atypically high mortality among children aged one to four.

Should children at risk to protein-energy malnutrition be offered supplemental foods, including protein-rich foods? Or should they be given immunizations, antibiotics and antiviral drugs, and medical care with the aim of preventing or treating disease? These questions acquired renewed urgency in the 1970s and 1980s, under the effect of high fertility and the oil price shock. The continuation of high fertility in countries where death rates had begun to diminish increased the share of children in those populations. Population growth put pressure on food output, and the victims of this pressure were overwhelmingly children. Suddenly higher oil prices in the 1970s made it more difficult for most developing countries to supplement domestic food resources by purchases abroad. National governments and the international community mounted nutrition programs, following models introduced in the 1950s. These programs often failed to solve nutritional problems in the beneficiary countries, giving rise to strong criticism. But the evaluation of the programs was often based on the gap between desired and attained levels of nutrition and survivorship, rather than on the more direct issue of how many premature deaths had been avoided.

Even among poor countries, risks to survival differ markedly. Among developing countries in the second half of the twentieth century, attention has focused on infant and child mortality, on maternal nutrition, on devising ways to capture information in the absence of reliable statistics, and on identifying determinants. Figure 5.1 shows the distribution of mortality among children under five years of age in three categories and

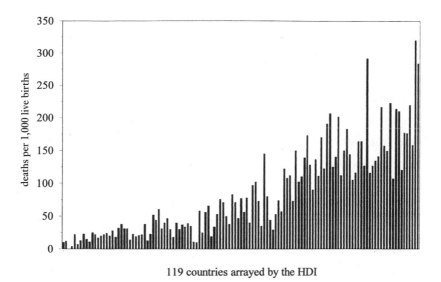

Figure 5.1. Mortality among children under five, 1996. *Source: Human Development Report 1998* (New York, 1998), pp. 156–57.

by the overall level of development measured by the Human Development Index. As expected, there is some general agreement between levels of development and survivorship. What is noteworthy is the degree of variation within each category of countries. Death rates for children under five remain distressingly high in most of the 119 countries represented in this figure.

An international research program on infant and child mortality dates from the 1960s, when analysts incriminated malnutrition as something that made it likelier that a child would get sick or die. The initial assumption was that undernutrition or the graver status of malnutrition made it likelier that a person would contract a disease. Subsequent research has replaced this claim with the argument that poor nutrition affects the outcome of disease more than the risk of contracting most diseases. Because poor nutrition often impairs the immune system, poorly nourished children have more severe episodes of disease and are likelier

155

to die.[19] For people in general, tuberculosis, other respiratory diseases, and some diarrheal diseases are made more lethal by poor nutritional status.[20] Food supplement programs seem to reduce infant and child mortality more by lowering the lethality of disease episodes than by preventing disease. Diseases, especially repeated episodes of diarrhea, also promote malnutrition. Around 1970 the number of people suffering chronic malnutrition was estimated to be about 950 million. By 1990 the figure had declined, but some 800 million people, mostly children, still suffered chronic malnutrition.

A new search for the factors behind high child mortality in developing countries began in the 1980s, assisted by the World Fertility Survey and the Demographic and Health Survey. This search has developed along two paths, one asking how to grade the efficacy of specific interventions and the other exploring a more complex hypothesis, which is that sociocultural factors have particular importance in infant and child survival.[21] Both approaches raise substantial problems in differentiating effects because both hypothesize that effects are at once direct and mediated.

On the first path the factors that have been considered include income,

[19] Nevin S. Scrimshaw, Carl E. Taylor, and John E. Gordon, *Interactions of Nutrition and Infection* (Geneva, 1968); and, for recent revisions, Reynaldo Martorell and Dirk G. Schroeder, "The Morbidity and Mortality Effects of Nutrition Interventions," in Hoda Rashad, Ronald Gray, and Ties Boerma, eds., *Evaluation of the Impact of Health Interventions* (Liège, 1995), pp. 75–94; and Leonardo Mata, "The Fight against Diarrhoeal Diseases: The Case of Costa Rica," in Vallin and Lopez, eds., *Health Policy, Social Policy and Mortality Prospects*, pp. 57–79. For a literature review on malnutrition and the immune system, see David N. McMurray, "Cell-Mediated Immunity in Nutritional Deficiency," *Progress in Food and Nutrition Science* 8 (1984): 193–228; and for a review on nutrition and infection, see Gerald T. Keusch and Michael J. G. Farthing, "Nutrition and Infection," *Annual Reviews in Nutrition* 6 (1986): 131–54.
[20] Stephen J. Kunitz, "Mortality since Malthus," in David Coleman and Roger Schofield, eds., *The State of Population Theory: Forward from Malthus* (Oxford, 1986), p. 279. Also "The Relationship of Nutrition, Disease, and Social Conditions: A Graphical Presentation," *Journal of Interdisciplinary History* 14 (1983): 503–6.
[21] Barbara Mensch, Harold Lentzer, and Samuel Preston, *Socio-Economic Differentials in Child Mortality in Developing Countries* (New York, 1985).

the maternal environment, water supply and waste disposal, access to health care, use of oral rehydration to treat diarrheal disease, vaccinations, health education, and food supplements. Researchers have sought to discover which intervention may have the greatest effect in which circumstances and to identify affordable forms of intervention. The problem was initially approached by comparing national experiences, using statistical analysis to test the apparent efficacy of individual factors across countries. More recently, research has shifted to the local level and to studies using individual-level data. Both approaches show that interventions may have much value, depending on local circumstances. No single mode of intervention trumps the others across the developing world; the strategy used in any setting must be tailored to that setting.

Along the second path more attention has been given to the issue of women's status and authority. Some mothers seem prone to lose children; some families seem to be vulnerable.[22] In societies where women's status is seriously abridged, infants and children die at higher rates.

Taking both strands together, this search has affirmed the importance of maternal education, access to health services and to knowledge about such specific therapies as oral rehydration, and socioeconomic status. Another result has been to point up the importance of women as participants in decision making at various levels: the household and the family, the community, and the nation. Where women are impoverished and powerless, relative to men, high risks to survivorship make up one of a group of undesirable demographic characteristics. Those include not so much high fertility as a big gap between the size of the family that women hope to have and the size they actually have. And they may include a son prefer-

---

[22] Katherine A. Lynch and Joel B. Greenhouse, "Risk Factors for Infant Mortality in Nineteenth-Century Sweden," *Population Studies* 48 (1994): 117–33; and Olle Lundberg, "The Impact of Childhood Living Conditions on Illness and Mortality in Adulthood," *Social Science and Medicine* 36 (1993): 1047–52.

ence, accompanied by discrimination against female children in nutrition and the provision of health services.[23]

This approach seems to have recognized two separate strands of development. On one hand, markedly in developed countries in the West, the feminization of decision making about reproduction and child care has been promoted by political movements that, since the French Revolution, have fostered sexual equality and the legal rights of women. On the other hand, markedly in some developing countries, the feminization of decision making has been promoted by cultural movements that foster the idea that women should shoulder heavier responsibilities without breaking all traditional political and legal restrictions. Whereas the middle class has led Western feminization, in developing countries feminization has often been a popular movement.

Two things seem to be evident. First, the search to understand high child mortality has identified a number of tactics of greater or lesser merit, depending on local circumstances. Among those, cultural interventions seem promising. Second, while it has been comparatively easy to identify factors that matter, such as maternal status and education, little progress has been made at learning how to modify them. Infant and child survival has benefited from the feminization of decisions about child care across much of the world and from close parental attentiveness. Most authorities have counted on broadcasting these insights into the link between women's status and child survival more than on trying directly to reshape the values that people have. Even though the medical and public health

---

[23] John Caldwell and Pat Caldwell, "Women's Position and Child Mortality and Morbidity in Less Developed Countries," in Nora Federici, Karen Oppenheim Mason, and Sølvi Sogner, eds., *Women's Position and Demographic Change* (Oxford, 1993), pp. 122–39; van de Walle, Pison, and Sala-Diakanda, eds., *Mortality and Society in Sub-Saharan Africa;* and Eliwo Akoto, *Déterminants socio-culturels de la mortalité des enfants en Afrique noire: Hypothèses et recherche d'explication* (Louvain-la-Neuve, 1993). Christopher P. Howson et al., eds., *In Her Lifetime: Female Morbidity and Mortality in Sub-Saharan Africa* (Washington, 1996), pp. 54–79, surveys literature on female nutrition.

interventions seem, in most cases, to have less power to curtail mortality, they often remain a preferred approach because they pose less of a threat to prevailing values, which are more sensitive.

More recently still, attention has turned back to socioeconomic differentiation, specifically, to the problem of absolute poverty (sometimes defined as a per capita income below one purchasing power parity U.S. dollar per day). In 1993, 1.3 billion people shared this characteristic. The proportion of people in absolute poverty has declined, but, since dire poverty is concentrated in countries where population growth has been rapid, in South Asia and Africa, the scale of the problem has failed to shrink. The very poor are more exposed to famine, malnutrition, low-birth-weight infants, children stunted in growth, and high mortality.[24]

Thus at the end of the twentieth century three strategies seeking to reduce infant and child mortality in developing countries vied for resources: specific medical and public health interventions, such as primary health care; cultural modifications that favor female education and women's status; and the reduction of absolute poverty. All promise good effects. All pose major costs at least in the scale of resources needed and some also in the degree to which attitudes and behaviors must be altered. Collectively, the challenge of high infant and child mortality surpasses any other modification of the global health infrastructure yet accomplished.

Nutrition and the Decline of Mortality in Europe

Widespread undernutrition in the modern world intensified the suspicion that historical populations were poorly nourished, in the sense of having had too little to eat. Thomas McKeown, a pediatrician skeptical about the

---

[24] See the papers in *Nutrition and Poverty: Papers from the ACC/SCN 24th Session Symposium, Kathmandu, March 1997* (Geneva, 1998). Also T. Paul Schultz, "Mortality Decline in the Low-Income World: Causes and Consequences," *American Economic Review* 83 (1993): 337–42.

capacity of medicine to improve population-level health, examined cause-of-death data in England and Wales from the mid-nineteenth century forward, searching for an explanation of the decline of mortality. In a fashion reminiscent of Sherlock Holmes, McKeown tested the two leading explanations, medicine and public health. Because medicine possessed, in his judgment, little explanatory power before the mid-twentieth century and because sanitary reforms possessed too little to explain the overall effect, McKeown concluded that the answer must lie in general with socioeconomic gains, specifically with diets richer in calories. That is, he posited that, even in England and Wales, ordinary people had too little to eat before the health transition began. Mortality declined because their standard of living improved and especially because they ate more.[25]

These arguments appealed to Robert Fogel, who has added some specifications. Arguing that European populations were chronically undernourished, Fogel hypothesizes a nutrition schedule in which 10 percent of the population in preindustrial and pre–health transition Europe was immobilized by the sheer lack of energy in its diet. An additional 10 percent had so little to eat that they could barely engage in activities such as work. Those malnourished people, and the generally undernourished working classes, began during the nineteenth century to eat enough to

---

[25] Thomas McKeown, *The Modern Rise of Population* (London, 1976). Also Roderick Floud, Kenneth Wachter, and Annabel Gregory, *Height, Health and History: Nutritional Status in the United Kingdom, 1750–1980* (Cambridge, 1990). Simon Szreter and Sumit Guha have debated the relative importance of nutrition as a factor in England's mortality decline: Simon Szreter, "The Importance of Social Intervention in Britain's Mortality Decline c. 1850–1914: A Re-interpretation of the Role of Public Health," *Social History of Medicine* 1 (1988): 1–37; and Sumit Guha, "The Importance of Social Intervention in England's Mortality Decline: The Evidence Reviewed," *Social History of Medicine* 7 (1994): 89–113. For evidence about a deprived area, see Susan Scott and Christopher J. Duncan, *Human Demography and Disease* (Cambridge, 1998).

survive. From such a distribution Fogel has argued that survival chances improved as people's basic dietary needs were met.[26]

Evidence about dietary change derives from the study of human stature, a subject to which many historians and economists have devoted themselves in recent years.[27] These investigations show that average heights advanced by several centimeters in many nineteenth-century European populations and that they continued to rise in the twentieth century. Stature – the final height achieved – is determined by a combination of factors, including genetic endowment, the supply and composition of diet, disease history, and the energy demands of work, play, and growth itself. The finding that adult heights rose can be explained in several ways. The anthropometric historians have usually interpreted it as an effect of a larger food intake, allowing people's physiological systems to allocate more energy for growth. It may also be interpreted as an effect of a diet changing to include more growth-assisting foods, especially meat protein. It may be related to the increasing reliance on machines to perform or assist work previously done by humans and therefore to the diminishing physical and energy demands of work. The withdrawal of children from the informal work force, which rural children in the eighteenth century entered as early as age six by taking on

[26] R. W. Fogel, "Second Thoughts on the European Escape from Hunger: Famines, Chronic Malnutrition, and Mortality Rates," in S. R. Osmani, ed., *Nutrition and Poverty* (Oxford, 1992), pp. 243–86; and Fogel, "The Contribution of Improved Nutrition to the Decline in Mortality Rates in Europe and America," in Julian L. Simon, ed., *The State of Humanity* (Oxford, 1995), pp. 61–71. Other essays in the Osmani volume provide much useful insight into controversies in interpreting evidence about undernutrition.

[27] See the review essay: Bernard Harris, "Growing Taller, Living Longer? Anthropometric History and the Future of Old Age," *Ageing and Society* 17 (1997): 491–512; plus Floud, Wachter, and Gregory, *Height, Health and History;* and Richard H. Steckel, "Stature and the Standard of Living," *Journal of Economic Literature* 33 (1995): 1903–40.

farm tasks and urban children entered around age fourteen by being apprenticed, may have assisted human growth. By sending children to school, nineteenth-century parents unwittingly reduced their children's energy requirements. And, last, rising stature may be an effect of fewer episodes of disease and less competition from disease for nutrients.

That is, along one line of thinking, rising stature may be an effect of better diets, so that the key element of change lies in how much and what types of food people ate. Along another line of thinking, however, rising stature may be an effect of whatever factors reduced the number of disease episodes a person experienced, especially during growth spurts.

The historical evidence suggests that Europeans were often poorly nourished on the eve of the health transition, lacking diets containing all the vitamins and minerals later found to be essential. Poorer people were usually shorter. But there is little evidence to show that Europeans were malnourished, which is a degree of undernourishment serious enough to show up in such symptoms as malaise or edema, or that they were chronically malnourished.[28] England's peers enjoyed a decided advantage in nutrition and were taller, but they held those advantages long before they began to outlive the general population. In an important study of food supply in the manufacturing city of Manchester during the industrial revolution, Roger Scola attributes continuing high mortality in the city to endemic diseases, crowded housing, poor sanitation, and adulterated food, but not to a deficient supply of food.[29] The timing of gains in stature

---

[28] See Massimo Livi-Bacci, *Population and Nutrition: An Essay on European Demographic History*, trans. Tania Croft-Murray (Cambridge, 1991); and Anne Hardy, *The Epidemic Streets: Infectious Disease and the Rise of Preventive Medicine, 1856–1900* (Oxford, 1993), pp. 280–82. These sources, the debate between Szreter and Guha (n. 25 above), and research into stature all relate to the standard of living debate discussed in the previous chapter.

[29] Roger Scola, *Feeding the Victorian City: The Food Supply of Manchester, 1770–1870* (Manchester, 1992), esp. pp. 270–80. For more general expressions of doubt, see Livi-Bacci, *Population and Nutrition;* and, for a reexamination of the dismal case of Russian

sometimes coincided with improvements in survival, as it has in the twentieth century, and sometimes did not. In other cases, however, mortality declined without any improvement in height or early life conditions.[30] Stature rose, but what meaning should be attached to that?[31]

Food research in the late nineteenth and early twentieth centuries showed the existence of vitamins and minerals and their importance for good health. Such knowledge, plus research showing which foods contain which elements, has made it possible to design diets that meet minimal requirements. Scurvy, a dietary disease of some importance in the eighteenth century, could be treated successfully by that century's end. The discovery of vitamins and minerals and of deficiency diseases revealed much about how to improve diets to maximize energy, growth, and well-being, but it revealed only a few associations to diseases prominent in the cause-of-death profile of the nineteenth century. Pellagra, a major cause of disease in Italy, the American South, the Middle East, and parts of Asia and Africa in the nineteenth and early twentieth centuries, could be prevented by enriching bread with niacin. Rickets, a disease common among children in many nineteenth-century European cities, could be cured by more exposure to sunlight and adding foods rich in vitamin D to the diet. Goiter, prominent in East Asia and a cause of endemic cretinism, was linked to iodine deficiency. Nineteenth-century health authorities also worried about the adulteration of foods and devised chemical tests to dis-

serfs, see Steven L. Hoch, "Famine, Disease, and Mortality Patterns in the Parish of Borshevka, Russia, 1830–1912," *Population Studies* 52 (1998): 357–68.

[30] See George Alter and Michel Oris, "Early Life Conditions and the Decline of Adult Mortality in the Belgian Ardennes, 1812–1890," Working Paper, August 21, 1999.

[31] A similar problem arises in using gains in nutrition to explain rising scores on intelligence tests. See the discussion by Marian Sigman and Shannon E. Whaley, "The Role of Nutrition in the Development of Intelligence," pp. 155–82, and Reynaldo Martorell, "Nutrition and the Worldwide Rise in IQ Scores," pp. 183–206, both in Ulric Neisser, ed., *The Rising Curve: Long-Term Gains in IQ and Related Measures* (Washington, 1998).

cover when food contained bacteria, toxins, or fillers.[32] Nineteenth-century science made major progress in establishing standards of growth by measuring height, weight, upper-arm fat, and other indicators. And science worked out the measurement of energy intake and expenditure by the human machine.

Nineteenth-century critics of the European diet, who drew a link between protein and energy, called for more animal protein. In response, adults, especially males, tried to add animal protein to their diets, believing that they needed beef, mutton, pork, or another meat to work. Later research showed that the association was erroneous, leading, by the 1960s, to sharply reduced recommendations for adult protein intake. On one hand, the added protein is recognized as unnecessary and, since animal meat is more expensive than most other food items, too costly. On the other hand, diets high in saturated fats damage the circulatory system and promote obesity. From that point of view the European diets preferred in the period roughly 1850–1960 contained so much protein that they aided the development of degenerative diseases. Thus the diets of the eighteenth century, which were monotonous but rich in bread and other foods made from grains and in beer or wine, have come to seem less dangerous.[33]

In the European health transition well-balanced diets replaced diets usually sufficient in bulk but sometimes unbalanced in minerals and vitamins. That makes it easier to understand how some European (Greece) and non-European societies (Japan, Kerala) achieved important gains in

[32] J. C. Drummond and Anne Wilbraham, *The Englishman's Food: Five Centuries of English Diet*, rev. ed. (1957; London, 1991), provide much detailed information; and K. J. Carpenter, *The History of Scurvy and Vitamin C* (Cambridge, 1986).

[33] S. Boyd Eaton, Majorie Shostak, and Melvin Konner, *The Paleolithic Prescription: A Program of Diet and Exercise and a Design for Living* (New York, 1988), argue for a return to hunter-gatherer fat levels, exercise, and dietary patterns. But see also B. K. Armstrong and A. J. McMichael, "Overnutrition," in N. F. Stanley and R. A. Joske, eds., *Changing Disease Patterns and Human Behavior* (London, 1980), 491–506.

life expectancy before achieving much greater stature. The nutritional problems evident in many poorer countries in the second half of the twentieth century do not seem closely similar to the nutritional problems of Europe before or during the early stages of the health transition.[34]

Overnutrition

Economic development coincided with, and often assisted, a dietary transition with two elements. First, almost by definition, economic development meant labor-saving technology, a growing reliance on machine power, and a diminishing reliance on physical labor. The result has been a sustained decline in the energy expenditure associated with work. Over time people have needed to eat progressively fewer calories. In many cases this shift has been gradual, so gradual indeed that people hardly noticed they were expending so much less energy than they had or than their parents had. In other cases – for example, in China between 1989 and 1993 – the transition was abrupt.

Second, as people acquired higher incomes their food preferences changed. Whereas formerly they had eaten grain-based diets high in fiber and low in fat content, they began to eat more fats, more sweeteners, and more refined carbohydrates. Urbanization pushed both developments along, since city dwellers typically expend less energy and more often demand diets high in fats and refined carbohydrates and low in fiber. The result has been rising body mass and a rising share of people whose weight classifies them as obese. The particular element of this process leading to more commonplace obesity and to the development of diseases associated with obesity – diabetes and heart disease – is sometimes called the nutri-

---

[34] Post, *Food Shortage*, pp. 271–72; and Walter and Schofield, "Famine, Disease and Crisis Mortality."

tion transition.[35] While obesity is usually condemned for its negative effects on health, rising obesity in the United States has not prevented the decline, since the 1960s, of cardiovascular disease mortality. Thus the specific hazards associated with obesity remain elusive.

Initially a problem faced by higher-income groups in rich countries, who in the late nineteenth century began to exhibit many of the diseases of affluence, the move toward population obesity has undergone two shifts. In the first, many people in higher-income groups in rich countries modified their diet and exercise patterns to avoid obesity, but many people in lower-income groups began to eat the diets of obesity. In the second, populations in lower-income countries began in the 1980s to exhibit sharply rising levels of obesity as they, too, began to eat higher-fat diets. For example, in Brazil in 1974 underweight adults outnumbered overweight adults by one and a half to one; but by 1989 overweight outnumbered underweight people by two to one, with the largest increase occurring in the poorest families.[36] This pattern is a matter of particular concern if it is true, as has been suggested, that people who are undernourished early in life compensate in ways that exaggerate the ill effects of overnutrition later in life.[37]

Some authorities warn that a global epidemic of obesity is developing. Its worst effects will be felt among poorer members of society.

Conclusion

Famine remains a serious problem, as does also the efficacious relief of famine. Much more needs to be learned about how to distribute relief,

[35] Barry M. Popkin, "The Nutrition Transition and Its Health Implications in Lower-Income Countries," *Public Health Nutrition* 1 (1998): 5–21.
[36] Ibid. Also, Andrew Peter Flood, "Nutrition and the Epidemiologic Transition in Indonesia," *Journal of Population* 3 (1997): 67–96.
[37] Barker, *Mothers, Babies, and Disease in Later Life.*

how to use relief resources to protect people's entitlements, and how to temper the effect of shocks to food supplies. Undernourishment is a still larger problem because it is so commonplace, especially in poor countries, and because it affects young children so strongly. At the same time increasing numbers of people confront the problems of overeating, which reveal themselves in degenerative diseases of late adulthood.

Poor nutrition has been both diminished and aggravated during the health transition. Europeans fell shorter of their potential stature in 1800 than in 2000, and poor nutrition contributed to the high disease risks of childhood. A child's life lost is more important, at least in demographic terms, than an adult's life lost, and it is unambiguously the case that Western children were better nourished in 2000. But by then the diseases of overeating had become endemic among adults. During the health transition deficiency diseases were discovered, along with the dietary supplements required to avoid them. But the role of poor nutrition as a proximate factor in morbidity and mortality mattered more than deficiency diseases in the number of people affected.

In developing countries not much is known about nutrition around 1800. There the leading problems of the twentieth century have been famine and the undernutrition or malnutrition of children. The diseases of overnutrition joined these threats more recently. At the end of the twentieth century, famine, the undernutrition of many children, and the overnutrition of many adults coexisted.

Suggestions for Further Reading

S. Boyd Eaton and Stanley B. Eaton. "The Evolutionary Context of Chronic Degenerative Diseases." In Stephen C. Stearns, ed., *Evolution in Health and Disease* (Oxford, 1999), pp. 251–59.

R. W. Fogel. "The Contribution of Improved Nutrition to the Decline in Mortality Rates in Europe and America." In Julian L. Simon, ed., *The State of Humanity* (Oxford, 1995), pp. 61–71.

Penny Kane. *Famine in China: Demographic and Social Implications.* New York, 1988.

Massimo Livi-Bacci. *Population and Nutrition: An Essay on European Demographic History.* Trans. Tania Croft-Murray. Cambridge, 1991.

Amartya Sen. *Poverty and Famines: An Essay on Entitlement and Deprivation.* Oxford, 1981.

Richard H. Steckel and Roderick Floud, eds. *Health and Welfare during Industrialization.* Chicago, 1997.

6

Households and Individuals

Neither the human environment at its most intimate, in the household, nor individual behavior seem to have allowed many opportunities for extending survival around 1800, on the eve of the health transition. In both the Indian ayurvedic and the Western humoral traditions of medicine the path to good health lay in the maintenance of a balance of humors within a person's body. Western authorities urged moderation in diet, exercise, exposure to air, bathing, and emotion, on grounds that, in extreme or violent forms, these things often led to sickness or death. In Europe good health practice required some preventive measures, such as periodically drawing blood and, by the eighteenth century, avoiding contact with decomposing organic matter. Germ theory added measures meant to avoid or defeat germs: washing hands after using the toilet, cleaning a sick room with antiseptic chemicals, pasteurizing milk, and immunizing against pathogens. In the late twentieth century risk factor theory added the idea that life-long experiences and habits may cause disease, and it revived the idea that the delayed effects of earlier life stimuli may do the same thing. Under risk factor theory, good health practice stressed the avoidance of things toxic or harmful or that might later turn out to have ill effects.

Figure 6.1. The French impressionist Renoir captures a new sentimentalism toward mother and child and a new attentiveness to their health (Pierre Auguste Renoir, *Claude et Renée* (1903), courtesy of National Gallery of Canada, Ottawa).

The agents of health have also changed over time. More hope has come to be vested in the value of things we can do for ourselves. Health education classes in school and public service advertisements reflect growing confidence in the individual's capacity to make useful choices about health and survival and sometimes also the power of advertisers to insert messages into putatively objective forums. The physician's role, too, has been enlarged by the medicalization of many conditions that were not previously defined as health issues, such as alcoholism. And the household has emerged as an agent of health. The idea that the household can be reorganized around health-attaining goals can be traced, in the West, to the oft-republished advice manuals that appeared in the second half of the seventeenth century. They proffered rules of healthy behavior and sought to arm householders with the information they needed to cope with the demands of life.[1] The middle-class Western householder became a leading actor in the attempt to ensure good health during the nineteenth century. By the late twentieth century good health could be described as something achieved not just by medicine and public health but also by the attentive household alerted by the medical and social sciences to threats to health and survival and their avoidance, prevention, and management.[2]

It is difficult to disentangle this element of the health transition from the middle class, which first became numerous and socially powerful in the nineteenth-century West. Every culture has its ideas about health behavior and child care and can be studied for the effectiveness its members

---

[1] See, e.g., the health articles in Noel Chomel, *Dictionaire oeconomique; or, The Family Dictionary Containing the Most Experienced Methods of Improving Estates and Preserving Health* . . . , trans. and revised by R. Bradley, 2 vols. (London, 1725), which first appeared in 1709.

[2] Peter Berman, Carl Kendall, and Karabi Bhattacharyya, "The Household Production of Health: Integrating Social Science Perspectives on Micro-Level Health Determinants," *Social Science and Medicine* 38 (1994): 205–15, show how to organize one's thoughts about this approach.

display in carrying out those ideas.[3] This chapter treats the emergence of the middle class as a cultural group often transcending national boundaries. One characteristic of this class was to welcome and use expert advice about health and its many determinants and about the health and welfare of infants, children, and adults. Another characteristic has been to emphasize all of these agents of health, from the individual and the householder to the physician. Until the emergence of growing middle classes in many developing countries in the late twentieth century, developed countries still possessed the largest populations of middle-class people; this chapter focuses on those middle classes.

Housing

For ordinary people the history of housing is a history of small and often crowded, damp and dirty, poorly built and therefore temporary structures. The rich, in contrast, have usually lived in spacious and well-built dwellings maintained by servants. The contrast is shocking, but it does not appear to have been enough to produce different life expectancies. In England such differences appeared in the eighteenth century and became noticeable and a matter of public attention and investigation in the nineteenth century. At that moment one of the best hypotheses for explaining the differential seemed to lie in the housing of the urban poor.[4] In cities single men and women lived, sometimes 20 or 30 to a room, in barracks-like structures, and families lived in tenements crowded six, eight, or ten people to a room. In a lodging-house quarter of Leeds in 1851, 2,500 peo-

---

[3] One good example of this point exists in the comparison of the Gusii in Kenya with middle-class Americans, especially regarding child care and health. See Robert A. LeVine et al., *Child Care and Culture: Lessons from Africa* (Cambridge, 1994), esp. pp. 169–95.

[4] Among the most effective presentations of this case is James Burn Russell, *Public Health Administration in Glasgow* (Glasgow, 1905).

ple occupied 222 houses, 4.5 to a room and 2.5 to a bed. In Paris the physician Bayard visited a patient in a room 25 meters square where 23 adults and children lived, sharing five beds. The housing of the urban poor, especially unemployed and unskilled workers, deteriorated in the early nineteenth century in Britain, the Low Countries, France, and Germany. In German cities people with lower incomes spent a larger share of their income on housing and, per square meter, paid more for living space than did higher-income groups.[5] Rural housing improved earlier, assisted by a nineteenth-century shift in the terms of trade favoring people who had food to sell.[6] But the gap in space and housing quality between rich and poor remained vast, obvious, and a leading candidate for explaining the higher mortality of the poor in the nineteenth century. In 1990 about a billion people across the world occupied housing deemed grossly inadequate.[7]

Nineteenth-century observers incriminated crowding and filth as the leading factors behind the great mortality of the European poor. They might also have pointed to the social differentiation of the city by neighborhood, thus the concentration of health problems in poorer neighborhoods. Moreover, those neighborhoods were regularly the last to obtain public services, including water, sewage disposal, clinics and hospitals, transport, and paved roads.

By the 1960s across Europe the standard urban dwelling had become

[5] Enid Gauldie, *Cruel Habitations: A History of Working-Class Housing, 1780–1918* (New York, 1974); A. S. Wohl, *The Eternal Slum: Housing and Social Policy in Victorian London* (London, 1977); Hartmut Kaelble, *Industrialisation and Social Inequality in 19th-Century Europe*, trans. Bruce Little (New York, 1986), pp. 108–10 and 113–27; Elsie Canfora-Argandoña and Roger-Henri Guerrand, *La répartition de la population: Les conditions de logement des classes ouvrières à Paris au 19e siècle* (Paris, 1976); and Nigel Morgan, *Deadly Dwellings: Housing and Health in a Lancashire Cotton Town: Preston from 1840 to 1914* (Preston, 1993).

[6] Roman Sandgrüber, *Die Anfänge des Konsumgesellschaft* (Munich, 1982), pp. 327–30.

[7] Sandy Cairncross, Jorge E. Hardoy, and David Satterthwaite, eds., *The Poor Die Young: Housing and Health in Third World Cities* (London, 1990), p. xviii.

a high-rise apartment of several rooms, equipped with labor-saving devices to combat filth and to dispose of human waste. Crowding had diminished as families spent a share of growing discretionary resources on living space and because families themselves had become smaller. In the new form of housing, individuals could gain privacy for sleeping and bathing. Heating systems provided warmth and promoted air circulation. In some countries, such as The Netherlands, flats were built to expose one side to sunlight. Ever larger numbers of people were housed more spaciously in the same area by building upward. Such housing reduced or eliminated whatever contribution housing had made to poor health.

For European cities the transition to satisfactory housing began in the late nineteenth century in another shift in the terms of trade, in which building materials became cheaper relative to food and manufactured goods. Householders began to use natural gas to heat and light their homes in the 1890s and gradually added piped water, toilets, and waterborne sewage disposal. Public and private action jointly promoted the transition to safer housing: local government invested more aggressively in housing for low-income groups, and prosperous groups spent a significant part of their growing wealth on more spacious, airy, sunlit, and solidly constructed housing.[8]

What had bad housing contributed to poor health? Sewerage systems, in Europe built chiefly between the 1850s and the 1950s, removed the most dangerous forms of filth. But dirty housing also harbored insect vectors, flies and cockroaches, which transmitted some diarrheal diseases. By the 1920s screens, higher standards of household cleanliness, and a

---

[8] M. J. Daunton, *House and Home in the Victorian City: Working-Class Housing, 1850–1914* (London, 1983). For a comparative history of housing in Europe, see Anne Power, *Hovels to High Rise: State Housing in Europe since 1850* (London, 1993). Roger Burridge and David Ormandy, eds., *Unhealthy Housing: Research, Remedies and Reform* (London, 1993), assesses health problems associated with poor housing in modern Britain.

stronger aversion to insects reduced the role that houseflies played in disease transmission. Otherwise the leading problem was crowding. Grandparents and parents transmitted tuberculosis to their children, guaranteeing the nearly complete infection of each new generation. Children transmitted other airborne diseases, such as measles and respiratory infections, to one another and to their parents. In retrospect it is apparent that housing of this form and quality did not offer the means for isolating the sick at home or for the air circulation, sunlight, or ventilation necessary to impede communication of such diseases. Thus airborne diseases, including tuberculosis, scarlet fever, and diphtheria, played a large role in nineteenth-century morbidity and mortality.

The pattern found in nineteenth-century Europe, in which urbanization and modernization brought deteriorating housing and health for the poor, has been repeated many times and is still being repeated. In Russia's Donets Basin, miners lived in filthy dugouts, shallow trenches lined with boards supporting wooden frames topped by earth or mine tailings. In Tianjin, the port city near Beijing, less prosperous industrial workers of the 1920s and 1930s lived in one room of 23 cubic meters per family in houses with walls of mud, bitterly hot in summer and freezing in winter. In Nigeria the Lagos slum clearance scheme initiated in 1955 proved ineffective, leaving the slum area of the city overcrowded, congested, and lacking sanitary facilities. Repeated studies of other Nigerian cities have produced similar conclusions regarding Ibadan, Aba, Calabar, and elsewhere. Because the city has grown so rapidly, about half of Kinshasa households have piped water and most of the rest buy water from vendors. In Bombay, the Indian city under the most intensive housing pressure, censuses of 1971 and 1981 showed 37 percent of the populace living in slums or *Jhuggies;* the modal housing unit was one room accommodating 5.3 people. In some cities bad housing rallied working-class demands for political power, sometimes leading to legislative efforts, halfhearted or not, to improve housing quality or reduce cost. In the West, urbanization

175

coincided with economic growth, freeing private and public resources to be spent on housing in the late nineteenth and twentieth century. But in developing countries, urbanization has usually proceeded without much economic growth.[9]

Makeshift dwellings – temporary, usually lacking running water or sanitary facilities, with earthen floors, without screens, crowded, on the whole worse than the bad housing of nineteenth-century European cities – have appeared again and again in rapidly expanding industrial or mining areas and, above all, in cities. Sometimes they evolve into urban slums. Although these settlement patterns make it difficult to gather statistics, the evidence points to much higher mortality and morbidity in such districts.

Hong Kong's rapid growth after World War II forced many people to live in squatter and slum housing. City authorities and builders reacted to the extraordinary demand for housing by building high-rise apartment blocks, increasing the density of housing units but reducing crowding within housing. The city also invested in water and sewerage connections in all neighborhoods. Although population density continued to rise, life expectancy increased, reaching seventy-nine years in 1995. Few countries have been as fortunate as Hong Kong in how much private individuals and

---

[9] Theodore H. Friedgut, *Iuzovka and Revolution* (Princeton, 1989), pp. 89–91 and passim; Gail Hershatter, *The Workers of Tianjin, 1900–1949* (Stanford, 1986), pp. 69–70; Tade Akin Aina, *Health, Habitat and Underdevelopment in Nigeria* (London, 1990), esp. pp. 18–19; Jorge E. Hardoy and David Satterthwaite, *Squatter Citizen: Life in the Urban Third World* (1989; rpt., London, 1995); and Cedric Pugh, *Housing and Urbanisation: A Study of India* (New Delhi, 1990), p. 259. On bad housing as a stimulus to working-class activism, see, e.g., Ronn Pineo and James A. Baer, eds., *Cities of Hope: People, Protests, and Progress in Urbanizing Latin America, 1870–1930* (Boulder, 1998). And for an example of urbanization in Europe, see Johan Söderberg, Ulf Jonsson, and Christer Persson, *A Stagnating Metropolis: The Economy and Demography of Stockholm, 1750–1850* (Cambridge, 1990). But consider also the striking counterexample of Shanghai where housing and living space deteriorated sharply during a period of improving survivorship: R.J.R. Kirkby, *Urbanization in China: Town and Country in a Developing Economy, 1949–2000 AD* (New York, 1985), pp. 164–68.

the public sector could spend on housing. More typical is the story of merely intermittent attempts to accommodate growing populations and the maintenance, even the growth, of squatter and slum dwellings. Bad housing provides one of the leading explanations for low survival rates in developing countries and for marked socioeconomic differentials in survival in some rich countries, such as the United States. Although attention has more often been drawn to the problem a rising global population faces in finding food, the problems people face in finding housing are also serious. Projections into the future suggest continuing rapid growth of cities and of the share of populations housed in slums and squatter settlements.[10]

Domesticity; or, the Well-Ordered Bourgeois Life

Beginning in the eighteenth century in Europe the home and the family acquired new importance as the center of individual development. Immanuel Kant argued that the home is the foundation of social order. Similar ideas guided, or more probably reflected, social interest in family life and in improving the survival prospects of infants and children. The bourgeoisie devised a distinctive form of family life that accentuated activities centered on the home: dining *en famille;* domesticity and extended maternal responsibility for raising the children; an ideal of male leadership, especially outside the household; and a reality of feminized family life, in which key decisions about reproduction, the education of children, and the allocation of household resources were mostly made by women. Before Marx, socialists, too, placed their hopes for regeneration in the family, as opposed to the state. These ideas came to fruition in the nineteenth century in focusing hope for individual development on the home and the family.

[10] Leslie Kilmartin and Harjinder Singh, *Housing in the Third World: Analyses and Solutions* (New Delhi, 1992).

The bourgeois ideology of family life existed on two planes. It was, first, a set of ideas about behavior, which emphasized the importance of the individual. But it was also a taste for amenities that simplified life and made it more convenient. Thus the impetus around 1900 to outfit homes with running water, baths, toilets, and other hygienic instruments derived less from ideas about health than from the importance in bourgeois culture of the well-appointed home. Many of the consumer goods democratized in the eighteenth-century consumer revolution in Europe and North America had health implications without having been designed for reasons of health. The mirror, a rare household item in 1600, became commonplace. Like photography in the second half of the nineteenth century, the mirror made personal appearance and cleanliness an issue.

Bourgeois ideas and ideals accentuated domesticity, allocating new economic and intellectual resources to family life and revising the sexual division of labor to put women more firmly in charge of home life. Enlightenment-era thinkers favored the education of women for roles as wives and mothers and as householders, the people in charge of household management.[11] Women acquired responsibility for understanding cleanliness and for encouraging it. By 1850 the ideal and often, too, the reality of bourgeois and working-class family life emphasized the well-ordered household led by a woman. It is necessary to see this development as a major step in the subordination of women: they controlled the domestic sphere, which was less important. But it is also necessary to see this development as a seizure of power by women, who gained control over home and family life and whose specialization in that sphere transformed home life. Women took the initiative from public health authorities, who aimed to clean the milieu, and to a large degree also from professional advice givers, such as physicians. They played a major role in the ideology

---

[11] E.g., J. Burton, *Lectures on Female Education and Manners,* 2nd ed., 2 vols. (London, 1793), esp. I: 75–90 and 107–22.

of home and family health in the period 1850–1950 and probably also in the reality of health.[12] To assess the impact of this female specialization in household health on mortality, however, historians need to learn more about how women interpreted and applied filth theory, germ theory, and nutritional advice.[13]

In the meantime there are many suggestive indexes of the effects of domesticity. In the seventeenth and eighteenth centuries, pewter dishes, which could be cleaned, replaced the slab of bread and the wooden bowl as the standard table implements of working-class families in Western Europe. Next, ceramic plateware replaced wooden and pewter implements; it could be cleansed with soup and water much more effectively than the earlier utensils had been cleansed with sand or grit. Washable cotton garments took the place of woolens, simplifying control of body lice and fleas. The consumption of soap rose, driven first by the demand to wash clothing and somewhat later by interest in washing the body. In England soap output increased from 3.5 pounds a person in the early nineteenth century to 8 pounds in 1861; the 1878 Leblanc process of soda making reduced the price of soap. Legislation limiting child labor and, later in the century, compulsory schooling protected children, cultivated literacy, and urged the adoption of bourgeois ideas about the child-centered family by the working classes.[14] The number of books owned by a household rose, and the mixture more often included tracts on medicine and child care.

---

[12] Joel Mokyr, "Why 'More Work for Mother?' Knowledge and Household Behavior, 1870–1945," *Journal of Economic History* 60 (2000): 1–41.

[13] And perhaps also about the beneficent role played by fathers. See Stephen M. Frank, *Life with Father: Parenthood and Masculinity in the Nineteenth-Century American North* (Baltimore, 1999).

[14] E.g., Colin Heywood, *Childhood in Nineteenth-Century France: Work, Health and Education among the "Classes populaires"* (New York, 1988), esp. pp. 217–86; and Lee Shai Weissbach, *Child Labor Reform in Nineteenth Century France: Assuring the Future Harvest* (Baton Rouge, 1989).

Both filth and germ theory influenced the advice that colonial health authorities gave Kenyan and Ugandan housewives about safeguarding family health. The site for a house should be selected with an eye to ventilation, sunlight, and well-drained soils. Authorities explained how to design a water filter, to control mosquitoes and other pests, to treat injuries and sicknesses, to select clothing and foods.[15] They assumed that African women would adopt a European model of householding and that they would have enough resources to implement European ideas.[16]

Personal Hygiene

Some peoples, the Japanese and orthodox Ashkenazi Jews, for example, long bathed regularly as a part of cultural norms.[17] Across the world at the beginning of the nineteenth century most people did not. Eighteenth-century Europeans regarded bathing the entire body as dangerous: it opened a person to the harmful properties of air. They had come, over time, to wash their hands, arms, and faces more often, and in France and Italy in some social classes also to wash their genitals. But they did not bathe.

In Europe the idea of bathing gained currency during the nineteenth century, apparently parallel to spread of the filth theory of disease. Municipalities built public baths, since almost no one had the equipment, the running water, or the space to bathe at home. Gradually the baths drew clients. Schools and the army indoctrinated children and recruits in bathing, and in France Napoleon III mounted a systematic campaign to

[15] Esther Koeune, *The African Housewife and Her Home*, rev. ed. (Nairobi, 1961).
[16] M. K. Jinadu et al., "Childhood Diarrhea in Rural Nigeria: I. Studies on Prevalence, Mortality and Socio-Economic Factors," *Journal of Diarrhoeal Diseases Research* 9 (1991): 323–27, assesses risk factors in households where children more often suffer diarrheal diseases.
[17] Alan Macfarlane, *The Savage Wars of Peace: England, Japan and the Malthusian Trap* (Oxford, 1997), pp. 256–64.

promote bodily cleanliness. In 1852 Parisians took 2.8 million public baths, which is about 3.7 baths a year per adult. By century's end washing had been added to the elements of propriety, which bulked so large in bourgeois society. Proponents argued that bathing prevents disease and assures personal development. A 1983 French survey showed that 38 percent of women and 22 percent of men bathed their entire bodies each day.[18]

Bathing protected people from louse-borne typhus. Typhus epidemics are associated with military campaigns, sieges, and other occasions when even dry cleansing of the body, an older tactic, was difficult to practice. It may have remained a significant threat into the nineteenth century. Typhus and typhoid fever have similar symptoms and were not differentiated from one another until the late nineteenth century. Germ theory added to the force behind the advice to bathe. But it was the aversion to unpleasant odors, cultivated by filth theory, that prompted the argument that personal cleanliness is a device of good health.

Despite the possibility that bathing diminished typhus, the most substantial effect probably came from washing hands, something encouraged by both filth and germ theories. At the beginning of the nineteenth century people washed their hands regularly, perhaps as often as once a day. But they washed as part of a daily ritual of grooming rather than before eating or after urinating or defecating. Physicians did not wash their hands before touching a patient, a thing they were increasingly likely to

---

[18] Jacques Leonard, *Archives du corps: La santé au XIXe siècle* (n.p., 1986), pp. 115–16 and 128–29; Jean-Pierre Goubert, *The Conquest of Water: The Advent of Health in the Industrial Age*, trans. Andrew Wilson (Princeton, 1989), p. 87; Georges Vigarello, *Concepts of Cleanliness: Changing Attitudes in France since the Middle Ages*, trans. Jean Birell (Cambridge, 1988); Annik Pardailhé-Galabrun, *The Birth of Intimacy: Privacy and Domestic Life in Early Modern Paris*, trans. Jocelyn Phelps (Philadelphia, 1991), pp. 130–44; and Julia Csergo, *Liberté, egalité, propreté: La morale de l'hygiène au XIXe siècle* (Paris, 1988). See also Jonas Frykman and Orvar Löfgren, *Culture Builders: A Historical Anthropology of Middle-Class Life*, trans. Alan Crozier (New Brunswick, 1987).

do in the course of an examination, and surgeons did not wash before an operation or assisting in the delivery of a child. The novel thing promoted by both filth and germ theories was an idea about when and why to wash one's hands.

Mothercraft

Around 1900 observers in the West explained high mortality, especially the mortality of infants, which in most countries had not declined since the eighteenth century, by pointing to the effects of poverty: poor housing, poor diets, poor environment. One might imagine many different responses to these circumstances. The one settled on across Europe and North America was an adaptive response. Mothers, especially poor mothers, would be taught to be fit. It was a leap of faith remarkable both for the confidence that mothercraft could be taught and that teaching mothercraft could overcome the effects of poverty. Mothers could be taught to clean their houses, and that would be enough; the houses could remain small, crowded, ill heated and ventilated, and defective on other points. Even more remarkable, the campaign enjoyed many successes.

An urgent interest in infant and child care appeared around 1900, stimulated by the promise that medical science could improve infant care, by anxiety about declining fertility but continuing high infant mortality, and by humanitarian concerns. The campaign advised mothers how to care for their sick children, sometimes by doctors and sometimes by mothers themselves; provided medical and nursing services; and created a role for state authorities in judging the quality of family life while taking some responsibility for its improvement. Legislators tried to compel milk pasteurization, smallpox vaccination, and other remedies meant to protect infants.[19] Another successful tactic was the milk depot organized

[19] Catherine Rollet-Echalier, *La politique à l'égard de la petite enfance sous la IIIe République*, 2 vols. (Paris, 1990), pp. 166–200 on milk sterilization and passim.

to distribute pasteurized milk. Appearing first in France, milk depots underwrote the cost of milk for mothers who could not afford it and supervised milk quality. The promotion of breastfeeding, prenatal health care, well-baby clinics, and, in some countries, state allowances to mothers also expressed an intensive interest in mothers and infants. Although physicians played a part in the mothercraft campaign, the leading role was taken by women, especially bourgeois women, who saw the mobilization of interest in infant and child care as an expression of civic responsibility.[20] World War I provided a rhetoric of patriotism in which to express ideas about how to save the lives of dying infants and to raise cohorts more fit for military service than the ones recruited for the war, which contained many men rejected because of poor health. Eugenics ideas also motivated this campaign, which promised to salvage ethnic groups threatened by depopulation or, in the United States and Canada, by arriving immigrants. But support for the campaign demanded a change in attitude on a key point of genetics. In 1911 the Berlin physician Carl von Behr-Pinnow explained: "We believed that the high mortality rate of children in their first year was the result of natural selection which eliminated the weaker constitutions." "Now we know that it is a great national misfortune."[21]

Britain's health clinics and Germany's infant welfare stations provided medical services and often added preventive and educational activities. In Kensington, then a London neighborhood with pockets of deep

---

[20] Deborah Dwork, *War Is Good for Babies and Other Young Children* (London, 1987); Richard A. Meckel, *Save the Babies: American Public Health Reform and the Prevention of Infant Mortality, 1850–1929* (Baltimore, 1990); Alisa Klaus, *Every Child a Lion: The Origins of Maternal and Infant Health Policy in the United States and France, 1890–1920* (Ithaca, 1993); Lara V. Marks, *Metropolitan Maternity: Maternal and Infant Welfare Services in Early Twentieth Century London* (Amsterdam, 1996); Cynthia R. Comacchio, *"Nations Are Built of Babies": Saving Ontario's Mothers and Children, 1900–1940* (Montreal, 1993); and Lynne Curry, *Modern Mothers in the Heartland: Gender, Health, and Progress in Illinois, 1900–1930* (Columbus, Ohio, 1999).

[21] Quoted by Ann Taylor Allen, *Feminism and Motherhood in Germany, 1800–1914* (New Brunswick, N.J., 1991), p. 177.

poverty, the clinic opened in 1912 offered medical, nursing, and dental services as well as a pharmacist. In their educational services the clinics supplemented schemes of health visitors, such as that set up in Britain in 1892. Funded chiefly by taxation, Britain's health visitors advised mothers about hygiene and the feeding and clothing of infants.

In most countries infant mortality remained high to the end of the nineteenth century and declined rapidly in the first decade of the twentieth century, about twenty years after families in the same countries had begun to limit reproduction.[22] The mothercraft and infant welfare campaigns coincided with the rapid decline of infant mortality in Western Europe and North America in the first decade of the twentieth century, and their expansion coincided with the continued decline of infant and child mortality through the entire twentieth century. The provision of such services did not always lead to a decrease in infant deaths in a locale, especially in the poorest neighborhoods. But these services appear to have played an important part in reducing the death rate of young children, even though the evidence for that conclusion is more inferential than direct.[23]

Before this campaign the mode of feeding had been the major determinant of infant mortality that could be controlled. Thus infants whose mothers died soon after birth and those whose mothers worked outside the home alike suffered much higher mortality, as did infants in regions

---

[22] W. R. Ackroyd and J. P. Kevany, "Mortality in Infancy and Early Childhood in Ireland, Scotland and England and Wales 1871 to 1970," *Ecology of Food and Nutrition* 2 (1973): 11–19.

[23] Jane Lewis, *The Politics of Motherhood: Child and Maternal Welfare in England, 1900–1939* (London, 1980); and Philippa Mein Smith, "Mothers, Babies, and the Mothers and Babies Movement: Australia through Depression and War," *Social History of Medicine* 6 (1993): 51–83, argue against an effect on infant mortality. Gretchen A. Condran and Samuel H. Preston, "Child Mortality Differences, Personal Health Care Practices, and Medical Technology: The United States, 1900–1930," in Lincoln Chen, Arthur Kleinman, and Norma C. Ware, *Health and Social Change in International Perspective* (Boston, 1994), pp. 171–224, argue for such an effect.

or social groups that fed on a substitute, such as cow's milk. Those infants died much more often than did breastfed infants, usually in late summer, which suggests that substitute foods were contaminated or spoiled. Campaigns promoting breastfeeding were organized in the eighteenth and nineteenth centuries, with some good effect.[24] In Sweden parents who worked at iron foundries seem to have been open to advice about better infant care, specifically breastfeeding and smallpox vaccination, but upper-middle-class families led in adopting official advice.[25]

Infant Mortality

In most countries for which death rates are known, infant mortality remained high until 1900.[26] Then, in Western countries, it began a sudden and rapid decline, initiating a long trend that continued to the end of the twentieth century. In France, for example, infant mortality remained above 200 per 1,000 live births throughout the nineteenth century; it dropped to 77 deaths per 1,000 in 1930–32, to fewer than ten deaths per 1,000 by 1977, and to five deaths by 1997. Especially when it is much higher than death

[24] Valerie A. Fildes, *Breasts, Bottles and Babies: A History of Infant Feeding* (Edinburgh, 1986), pp. 79 and 88.

[25] John E. Knodel, *Demographic Behavior in the Past: A Study of Fourteen German Village Populations in the Eighteenth and Nineteenth Centuries* (Cambridge, 1988); Jan Sundin, "Culture, Class and Infant Mortality during the Swedish Mortality Transition, 1750–1850," *Social Science History* 19 (1995): 117–45; and Magdalena Bengtsson, *Det Hotade Barnet: Tre generationers spädbarns- och barnadödlighet i 1800-talets Linköping* (Linköping, 1996). On Johann Peter Frank's insistence on maternal nursing, see Erna Lesky, ed., *A System of Complete Medical Police: Selections from Johann Peter Frank*, trans. E. Vilim (Baltimore, 1976), pp. 112–13.

[26] See Tommy Bengtsson and Christer Lundh, "La mortalité infantile et post-infantile dans les pays nordiques avant 1900," *Annales de démographie historique* (1994): 23–43; Jean-Noël Biraben, "Les aspects médico-écologiques de la mortalité differentielle des enfants aux 18ème et 19ème siècles," *International Population Conference, Manila* (Liège, 1981), II: 307–22; and Carlo A. Corsini and Pier P. Viazzon, eds., *The Decline of Infant and Child Mortality: The European Experience: 1750–1990* (Dordrecht, 1997).

rates at age one, infant mortality has a dramatic impact on life expectancy and perhaps on human behavior. In life expectancy the years lost to survival in infancy make it very difficult to achieve a life expectancy at birth greater than fifty years, even where survival rates after infancy are high. Thus plunging infant death rates have led the twentieth-century rise of life expectancy in developed countries. Milk pasteurization, sterile birthing, preventive health care for mothers and infants, and the development of pediatric expertise lead among factors responsible for the ongoing decline of infant mortality.

The relationship of infant mortality to human behavior is a more complex issue. In the West people began to reduce the number of children they reproduced during the nineteenth century; in most countries the reduction began in the 1880s.[27] At that point child survival had already improved and in a way that was quite noticeable in the 1870s and 1880s, as the urban penalty retreated. But infant mortality remained high. Thus people decided to have smaller families before they could count on the likelier survival of their infants. The continuing retreat of infant and child mortality in the twentieth century may have led families toward progressively lower fertility as they sought to have a certain number of surviving children.

No one has written a history of infant mortality in the twentieth century. Outside the West the decline of infant death rates began somewhat later; by 1960 it was under way in every country. By the end of the twentieth century several Western countries managed to reduce infant mortality to four deaths per 1,000 live births. The world average remained 58, and the average in sub-Saharan Africa 105 and in South Asia 72. The factors responsible for sharply lower infant mortality in the West, which are intimately related to either economic development or the concentration

---

[27] High-birth-order infants typically face higher risks, and the proportion of such children diminished as fertility declined.

of scarce resources on infant and maternal care, were only partly in play outside the West. Nevertheless, the decline of infant death rates also led to rising life expectancy in Asia and Africa.

Germ Theory and Behavior

Whereas the filth theory of disease promoted cleanliness of the milieu, the germ theory offered new ideas about the places where diseases lurk and ways to avoid them. Filth theory urged people to ventilate their homes and work sites, to dispose of waste and befouled water without further human contact, to cleanse the urban environment, to wear clean and dry clothes, and to wash. Germ theory did not quickly supplant that advice, but worked instead by adding ideas about how to avoid disease. It warned against the sneezes, coughing, and spit of people with respiratory sicknesses, especially tuberculosis; against contact with flies, cockroaches, and mosquitoes, which transmitted filth diseases and malaria; against food contaminated by contact with insects; and against eating and drinking with utensils previously used by the sick. The germ theory also gave people additional reasons for washing their hands, especially after toilet use; for removing dirt and dust from the home environment; and for refrigerating food and drink.

Considering applications, filth theory is remarkable chiefly for the dismal failure of individuals and municipal bodies to adopt its measures, according at least to the medical officers who inspected urban spaces and dwellings. Even toward the end of the nineteenth century, filth theorists sought adherents by scorning the failures of municipal authorities and householders to dispose properly of filth. No city street or pathway could be too clean. That same set of expectations developed for the home. Assisted by manufacturers who wanted to sell new products, householders, too, learned that ever more effort was demanded in order to clean the house to a proper standard. The doctrine of household cleanliness – cre-

187

ated by antagonism to filth and refined by the germ theory – stimulated demand for implements of cleanliness: vacuum cleaners, refrigerators, antiseptic soaps and sprays, and, above all else, soap. Its chief actor was the housewife, who adopted the "Victorian gospel of cleanliness" and assumed responsibility for making the home safe from disease.[28]

Germ theorists, however, took another approach. They stressed the training of individuals in specific behaviors. Although germ theory itself had been around since the 1880s, it gained wide public acceptance in the West only around 1900. Between 1900 and the 1920s it was fed by an ongoing series of discoveries about the hiding places of germs and the means of combatting them. Even so, public health manuals still had remarkably little to say about how individuals could apply germ theory to the task of avoiding disease.[29] Milk should be heated before being fed to an infant, sick family members should be isolated from the well, everyone should bathe more often, and the sick room should be thoroughly disinfected: these were the main pieces of advice. In the old filth theory scheme, disinfection usually meant odor-suppressing agents, such as vinegar. In the new germ theory scheme, it meant agents that killed pathogens, such as sulfate of iron dissolved in water.

If, on one hand, filth and germ theories led to a modification of many behaviors that contributed to the disease risks a person faced, on the other hand they invited people to adopt far more elaborate standards of cleanliness than could be justified by disease avoidance alone. People accepted standards of household cleanliness that far surpassed what could, then or later, be shown as efficacious. They vacuumed dust even when tuberculo-

[28] Nancy Tomes, *The Gospel of Germs: Men, Women, and the Microbe in American Life* (Cambridge, Mass., 1998); and Joel Mokyr and Rebecca Stein, "Science, Health, and Household Technology: The Effect of the Pasteur Revolution on Consumer Demand," in Timothy F. Bresnahan and Robert J. Gordon, eds., *The Economics of New Goods* (Chicago, 1997), pp. 143–205.

[29] E.g., Henry Bixby Hemenway, *American Public Health Protection* (Indianapolis, 1916).

sis was no longer a threat and continued doing so long after dust had been recognized as benign. In some countries people washed their bodies and clothing far more often than required for good health.[30] Nevertheless more needs to be learned about the diffusion of ideas across social classes, and about the mixture of good and bad ideas about what should be done before we can evaluate how much the implementation of filth and germ theories at the household level mattered in the health transition.[31]

Excess Female and Male Mortality

Between females and males, mortality has seldom achieved either balance or the modest advantage for females that many authorities regard as natural. In the West, females were at a disadvantage in classical antiquity and the medieval period; between 1500 and 1800 they gained a slight advantage. By 1800 females led at all ages except during reproduction, when the risks stood closer to even. During the nineteenth and early twentieth centuries tuberculosis often put girls and young women, aged about six to twenty-five, at a disadvantage.[32] But in the long run women added to their advantage at those ages and overall until, by 1997, female life expectancy at birth in the developed countries surpassed male expectancy by 6.5 years.[33] Women seem to make better lifestyle decisions than do men; they

---

[30] Suellen Hoy, *Chasing Dirt: The American Pursuit of Cleanliness* (New York, 1995), charts the transition of Americans from people who seemed around 1800, to Europeans, to be dirty into a society "obsessed with cleanliness" (p. xiv).

[31] Mokyr and Stein, "Science, Health, and Household Technology," argue that knowledge about what to do spread quickly across the socioeconomic spectrum, but Samuel H. Preston and Michael R. Haines, *Fatal Years: Child Mortality in Late Nineteenth-Century America* (Princeton, 1991), maintain that this knowledge was initially restricted to upper-income groups.

[32] E.g., Thierry Eggerickx and Dominique Tabutin, "La surmortalité des filles en Belgique vers 1890: Une approche régionale," *Population* 49 (1994): 657–84.

[33] United Nations Development Programme, *Human Development Report 1999* (New York, 1999), p. 138.

also appear to benefit more than men do from marriages based on partnership and companionship.[34]

In the second half of the twentieth century, as repeated studies have shown, women report more sicknesses than do men but live longer.[35] The larger toll of sickness is expressed in more musculoskeletal diseases and other rarely fatal conditions, whereas men have more ischaemic heart disease, cerebrovascular disease, and cancer, a profile suggestive of unwise choices in diet and tobacco use.

In some developing countries, however, females stand at a distinct disadvantage, especially in infancy and early childhood. Judging from the poorer nutrition and medical care provided them in comparison to male children, female children are more often unwanted in Pakistan, Bangladesh, Turkey, and many parts of India. Badly skewed sex ratios among newborns suggest that deaths of female infants are also underreported. A recent study indicates that in India child mortality for girls exceeds that for boys by 43 percent.[36] Sons bring a larger economic advantage, they assure the family line, and they assure that certain religious ceremonies can be performed. Thus the factors that lead to poorer nutrition and medical care for daughters have sources in expectations about the roles that sons and daughters will play when they are adults rather than in conventional public health, medical, physiological, or behavioral health factors.[37]

In the West and much of the developing world male mortality around

---

[34] Judith H. Hibbard and Clyde R. Pope, "The Quality of Social Roles as Predictors of Morbidity and Mortality," *Social Science and Medicine* 36 (1993): 217–25.

[35] L. M. Verbrugge, "Gender and Health: An Update on Hypotheses and Evidence," *Journal of Health and Social Behavior* 26 (1985): 146–82.

[36] Fred Arnold, Minja Kim Choe, and T. K. Roy, "Son Preference, the Family-Building Process and Child Mortality in India," *Population Studies* 52 (1998): 301–15.

[37] Alaka Malwade Basu, *Culture, the Status of Women, and Demographic Behaviour: Illustrated with the Case of India* (Oxford, 1992), esp. pp. 182–224.

age twenty and in middle age is excessive. The surplus of male deaths around age twenty, which has been characteristic of most times past and recent, is associated with risk-taking behavior and often involves alcohol abuse. For middle-aged males the surplus seems to be chiefly an effect of smoking and unhealthy lifestyle choices.

Redesigning the Adult Diet and Behavior

The retreat of infectious and respiratory disease mortality in the West during the nineteenth and first half of the twentieth century exposed heart disease and cancer as leading causes of death among middle-aged people.[38] Across that long period the leading cause of death shifted from smallpox to tuberculosis to heart disease. By 1960 heart disease accounted for the largest share of all deaths in the developed countries.

A new research design sought to identify the factors behind heavy heart disease mortality. The traditional approach emphasized the discovery of pathogens associated with a particular disease and testing antibiotic agents in control groups. The new approach took another tack, proposing to study not a moment in time but the evolution of a study population over time. This prospective approach could consider a wide range of possible disease agents or risk factors, iteratively sampling and resampling a test population. Among the most productive of such studies was the Framingham Heart Study, organized in 1948 among 5,209 mostly white residents of a Massachusetts town. The organizers collected information about eighty variables in the course of providing free medical examina-

---

[38] D. P. Burkitt, "Some Diseases Characteristic of Modern Western Civilization," *British Medical Journal* 848 (1973): 274–78, and others have argued that diseases such as coronary heart disease, obesity, cancer of the bowel, and diabetes were new, or at least newly prevalent, in the industrial West. But medical historians point to the long history of each of these conditions.

tions to participants. Their findings reformulated American thinking about the causes of heart disease. The Framingham study showed that high blood pressure often triggers heart attacks, even for the aged, among whom high blood pressure had been seen as desirable. It also confirmed the dangerous effects of cigarette smoking and of high levels of blood cholesterol, obesity, and a sedentary life. For women the Framingham study pointed up dangers associated with menopause, and for men and women it showed that diabetes often serves as an underlying cause of heart disease. After extracting so much information about the risk factors in heart disease, leaders of the Framingham study planned to add a third generation of subjects in order to examine the genetic origins of disease.

The Framingham results began to appear amidst a growing number of publications criticizing affluence, especially the diets of the affluent, as a factor in disease. Some authorities have labeled certain diseases as Western and as the products of affluence.[39] But it has proved difficult to trace the links, such as those leading from diets deficient in dietary fiber to disease. Moreover, other research suggests that factors present before birth, which show up in gauges such as an infant's birth weight, may also be important.[40] Across the globe, research shows noteworthy statistical associations between diet and several noncommunicable organ diseases and

---

[39] E.g., Norman J. Temple and Denis P. Burkitt, eds., *Western Diseases: Their Dietary Prevention and Reversibility* (Totowa, N.J., 1994).

[40] D.J.P. Barker, *Fetal and Infant Origins of Adult Disease* (London, 1992); and, for context, George Davey Smith and Diana Kuh, "Does Early Nutrition Affect Later Health? Views from the 1930s and 1980s," in David F. Smith, ed., *Nutrition in Britain: Science, Scientists and Politics in the Twentieth Century* (London, 1997), pp. 214–37. However, David A. Leon et al., "Adult Height and Mortality in London: Early Life, Socioeconomic Confounding, or Shrinkage?," *Journal of Epidemiology and Community Health* 49 (1995): 5–9; and Yoav Ben-Shlomo and George Davey-Smith, "Deprivation in Infancy or in Adult Life: Which Is More Important for Mortality Risk?," *Lancet* 337 (March 2, 1991): 530–34, question whether impaired growth in childhood is a marker of adult disease.

perhaps also respiratory disease. But the patterns vary from country to country in ways that make it difficult to isolate additional causal factors or to specify the force of the known factors: obesity, cholesterol, high blood pressure, and smoking.[41]

In the United States, mortality from heart disease began to decline in the 1960s, when results from prospective studies such as that at Framingham were just beginning to appear. The explanation for this downturn remains elusive. It does not seem to be linked to lower rates of tobacco use, diets containing less cholesterol and cholesterol-reducing drugs, or the spread of exercising for physical fitness, all of which began later. Thus these changes help explain the continued reduction of coronary heart disease in some countries since the 1960s, but they do not explain the initiation of this trend.

In the developed world degenerative diseases emerged as communicable diseases waned, so that theorists of the epidemiologic transition can point to successive stages of disease profiles. In developing countries degenerative diseases often emerged when communicable diseases still remain important causes of morbidity and mortality.[42] Since the two types of disease demand substantially different methods of treatment and prevention, their simultaneous existence compounds the problem of disease control in developing countries, adding to the fundamental problem of scarce resources.

---

[41] For recent research summaries and references to this copious literature, see Prakash S. Shetty and Klim McPherson, eds., *Diet, Nutrition and Chronic Disease: Lessons from Contrasting Worlds* (Chichester, 1996); and Vaclav Smil, "Coronary Heart Disease, Diet, and Western Mortality," *Population and Development Review* 15 (1989): 399–424.

[42] See Richard G. A. Feachem et al., eds., *The Health of Adults in the Developing World* (Oxford, 1992); World Bank, *Chile: The Adult Health Policy Challenge* (Washington, 1995); and Andrew Peter Flood, "Nutrition and Epidemiologic Transition in Indonesia," *Journal of Population* 3 (1997): 67–96.

Individual Responsibility

In Western medicine and in many non-Western systems of medical thought, individuals assume an important share of the responsibility for their own sicknesses. European humoral theory held that immoderation in diet, exercise, exposure to air, and other of the so-called non-naturals leads to sickness. In some forms immoderation also carried a moral stigma, so that the person who sinned by violating the norm of moderation might expect an onset of disease in compensation. Individuals could not be certain which action constituted immoderation, but they knew that the burden of responsibility lay with them. Before the health transition began, responsibility for epidemic diseases was often assigned to subordinate groups: the poor, outsiders, members of religious minorities.

Germ theory challenged many aspects of this outlook, but the outlook proved resilient. The non-naturals temporarily lost credibility as an explanation for individual cases of disease, which came to be secularized and depersonalized. The idea nevertheless persisted that epidemic diseases arise among subordinate groups. And the failure of germ theory to account for many diseases, especially the degenerative diseases of middle and old age, revived the idea of individual responsibility. Thus the modern theory of risk factors sees individual behavior as a contributor to disease.

Tobacco use, especially in the form of cigarette smoking, provides the leading model for this line of thinking.[43] Many epidemiological studies have shown that rates of lung cancer, heart disease, emphysema, and other

---

[43] R. T. Ravenholt, "Tobaccosis," in Kenneth F. Kiple, ed., *The Cambridge World History of Human Disease* (Cambridge, 1993), pp. 176–86; Paolo Boffetta et al., "Mortality Patterns and Trends for Lung Cancer and Other Tobacco-Related Cancers in the Americas, 1955–1989," *International Journal of Epidemiology* 22 (1993): 377–84; Richard Peto et al., *Mortality from Smoking in Developed Countries, 1950–2000: Indirect Estimates from National Vital Statistics* (Oxford, 1994); and WHO, *The World Health Report 1999: Making a Difference* (Geneva, 1999), pp. 65–80.

diseases are much higher among people who smoke cigarettes at a certain pace and who have smoked for a certain length of time. Therefore smoking is a risk factor. Just as the germs associated with a disease may be present without causing the disease, a person may smoke without developing any of the diseases associated with smoking. What is merely probabilistic in individuals is deterministic in groups: a certain proportion of the group will bear out the association between smoking and particular diseases, especially lung cancer, chronic bronchitis, and coronary heart disease. Since smoking is a matter of individual choice, it has come to be seen as a voluntary risk. Thus smoking has helped revive the older idea of individual responsibility for good health, recasting it not in terms of immoderation in exposure to the non-naturals but in terms of specific forms of behavior. Neither medicine nor public health but individual behavior seems to provide a key to avoiding these degenerative diseases. The result, since the 1970s, has been added emphasis on exercise and personal fitness,[44] a reappraisal of diet aimed at reducing intake of saturated fat and cholesterol, a more cautious use of alcohol, and, above all, the avoidance of tobacco. Collectively, these behaviors are described as lifestyle choices.[45] The search for these and other risk factors has been one of the principal avenues of scientific inquiry in the late twentieth century.[46]

[44] Arguments favoring fitness are not new in Western thought. But, as the physical demands of work have receded, more people have turned to leisure-time exercise as a means of fitness, using it both to burn off excess calories and to maintain muscle tone and heart function. On nineteenth-century ideas of fitness in Britain and America, see Bruce Haley, *The Healthy Body and Victorian Culture* (Cambridge, Mass., 1978); and James C. Whorton, *Crusaders for Fitness: The History of American Health Reformers* (Princeton, 1982).

[45] Allan M. Brandt, "'Just Say No': Risk, Behavior, and Disease in Twentieth-Century America," in Ronald G. Walters, ed., *Scientific Authority and Twentieth-Century America* (Baltimore, 1997), pp. 82–98.

[46] Stress – consisting of social isolation, suppressed hostility, or disturbing life events – has often been suggested as another risk factor, but its nature and effect remain in dispute. For a recent review emphasizing the effects of stress, see Ben Fletcher, *Work, Stress, Disease and Life Expectancy* (Chichester, 1991). David Armstrong, *Political*

In the humoral theory of individual responsibility the person who behaved immoderately suffered a more or less immediate reaction. In the modern theory of individual responsibility for diseases, however, the disease emerges as an effect of decisions made years, even decades, past: to exercise, watch one's diet, and abstain from alcohol or tobacco, or not. Once more the onset of disease may be evidence of an individual failing, despite the merely probabilistic nature of the risk of disease associated with a personal failure in moral health.

Since the 1970s, when the idea of risk factors entered scientific and popular understanding of disease, two theories have operated at the same time. Beside the germ theory stands the theory of risk factors, which emphasizes behaviors that can be associated with disease. In risk factor theory the behaviors associated with disease seem to be more avoidable than germs.

The Problem of Explanation

On Papua New Guinea after World War I the arrival of Australian government authorities provoked local people to "the panicky digging of haphazard holes in the certain knowledge that they would shortly be required to re-inter people or dig pit latrines."[47] They understood the power of government officials to give orders, but they did not understand the rationale behind their orders. In the West the adoption of behavioral advice about tobacco use, diet, and fitness has been strongly centered on the mid-

Anatomy of the Body: Medical Knowledge in Britain in the Twentieth Century (Cambridge, 1983), argues for another line of development in the origin of individual hygiene in Britain. Richard G. Rogers, Robert A. Hummer, and Charles B. Nam, *Living and Dying in the USA: Behavioral, Health, and Social Differentials of Adult Mortality* (San Diego, 2000), assess the association of a wide range of individual characteristics with mortality.

47 Donald Denoon, Kathleen Dugan, and Leslie Marshall, *Public Health in Papua New Guinea: Medical Possibility and Social Constraint, 1884–1984* (Cambridge, 1989), p. 93.

dle and upper middle class and people with more years of schooling. Other social groups have heard and understood the message, but their members have often elected not to adopt it, even willfully to defy it. They understand the idea of risk factors and appreciate the health risks associated with certain behaviors, but they do not necessarily see themselves individually as being at risk.[48]

The new form of the public health campaign, which seeks to retrain people in the way they lead their lives, has not been accompanied by any profound insight into how to appeal to people across socioeconomic groups within a culture or across cultures. Like the older measures of mass immunization or X-ray examination, it has succeeded best in certain population and cultural strata. Thus smoking has increased among youths in some Western countries and among youths and adults in many Asian countries, and in the West rates of tobacco use have remained high in less favored socioeconomic groups, even amidst aggressive campaigns explaining the health risks associated with smoking.[49]

Conclusion

Eighteenth-century European householders wished to safeguard family members against health hazards and to help them recover when sick. They were limited in what they could do for good effect. Since then much more has been learned about how to safeguard health and care for the sick, and the responsibilities assigned to householders and to the individual have grown. The most dramatically new part of this history deals with the specialization of women as householders. In the eighteenth century women and men worked at many of the same tasks, inside the household and out.

[48] On tobacco use, see Allan M. Brandt, "World Trends in Smoking," in Julian L. Simon, ed., *The State of Humanity* (Oxford, 1995), pp. 106–13.
[49] Lawrence W. Green and Marshall W. Kreuter, "Health Promotion as a Public Health Strategy for the 1990s," *Annual Review of Public Health* 11 (190): 319–34.

If someone in the agrarian village carried the responsibility to know about health hazards and treatments, it was the village's wise woman or its clergyman. During the nineteenth century, often under bourgeois leadership, women took charge of the household, its health, diet, cleanliness, and the education of its members. They took a much larger role in the daily health habits of family members than wise women, clergymen, or medical practitioners had ever done.

Some of the tasks that women were assigned or that they arrogated for themselves were helpful and others not. The mothercraft campaign, based on the idea of child development, protected the lives and health of infants and children. So, too, did disinfecting the sick room, planning a family diet with appropriate vitamins and minerals, and keeping abreast of the family's immunizations. It is more difficult to detect the good health effects of frequent dusting and vacuuming. Space seems to have been a more important factor than cleanliness among the health risks associated with housing. And, curiously, food preparation surfaces remained one of the sites least often disinfected by householders trying to rid domestic life of germs. Householders disinfected toilets far more often than they did sites of food preparation, even though the likelihood of contact with harmful microbes was much greater in the kitchen than the toilet-equipped bathroom.[50]

The individual, too, saw the tasks of health preservation change over time. From moderation in all things, timeworn advice of general efficacy but modest demographic effect, the aim shifted in the twentieth century toward identifying the pathways along which specific defects of diet and behavior elevate risk. The model of tobacco use, in which individuals wait perhaps forty years for the effects to become manifest, has given great power to anxiety about whether the diets and behaviors we adopt in childhood and youth may lead to premature death in adulthood.

---

[50] Margaret Horsfield, *Biting the Dust: The Joys of Housework* (New York, 1998), pp. 160–65.

The West has enjoyed notably little success at sharing the benefits of what has been learned about the individual and household management of health. Two groups especially have been left out. One is comprised of the less favored socioeconomic groups within the West, where the well-ordered bourgeois model of family life, which avoids tobacco use, watches diet, and enjoys spacious housing, often has not been followed. Thus changes in the individual and household management of health have aggravated socioeconomic differences in mortality and morbidity. The other excluded group consists of the non-Western poor. Much more has been done so far to promote pure water, immunizations, and literacy than to promote the housing and the models of individual and household health behavior that have so effectively served favored socioeconomic groups in the West.

Suggestions for Further Reading

Alaka Malwade Basu. *Culture, the Status of Women, and Demographic Behavior.* Oxford, 1992.

Anna Davin. *Growing Up Poor: Home, School and Streets in London 1870–1914.* London, 1996.

Ute Frevert. *Women in German History: From Bourgeois Emancipation to Sexual Liberation.* Trans. Stuart McKinnon-Evans. Oxford, 1989.

Geneviève Heller. *"Propre en ordre": Habitation et vie domestique, 1850–1930: L'exemple vaudois.* Lausanne, 1979.

Christopher Howson et al., eds. *In Her Lifetime: Female Morbidity and Mortality in Sub-Saharan Africa.* Washington, 1996.

S. Ryan Johansson. "Welfare, Mortality, and Gender: Continuity and Change in Explanations for Male/Female Mortality Differences over Three Centuries." *Continuity and Change* 6 (1991): 135–77.

Michelle Perrot, ed. *A History of Private Life: From the Fires of Revolution to the Great War.* Trans. Arthur Goldhammer. Cambridge, Mass., 1990.

R. I. Woods, P. A. Watterson, and J. H. Woodward. "The Causes of Rapid Infant Mortality Decline in England and Wales, 1861–1921." *Population Studies* 42 (1988): 343–66, and 43 (1989): 113–32.

7

Literacy and Education

Ideas about which factors have promoted gains in survivorship change over time. When the question first intrigued them, in the 1950s, scholars usually assumed that medical and public health improvements accounted for the mortality decline. During the 1960s, in the midst of impressive gains in material wealth in developed countries, many began to argue that economic growth had played a large, even a determinant, role. Each explanation, once subjected to the critical scrutiny that is typical of scholarly investigation, proved inadequate. It explained part but not all of the effect. So the search has continued.

In the late 1970s John Caldwell suggested a new idea.[1] It was that the acquisition of literacy played a major role in controlling survival hazards *for the children of parents who had become literate.* The evidence for this explanation derived not from the developed countries, as earlier explanations had, but from developing countries. There, it could be shown, a par-

---

[1] J. C. Caldwell, "Education as a Factor in Mortality Decline: An Examination of Nigerian Data," *Population Studies* 33 (1979): 395–413. See also Susan H. Cochrane, Donald J. O'Hara, and Joanne Leslie, *The Effects of Education on Health*, World Bank Staff Working Paper No. 405 (Washington, 1980).

ent's educational status revealed important things about the likelihood that the children of that family would survive. That effect usually held up even when quantitative and qualitative analyses also considered wealth and occupation, urban-rural residence, access to medical and public health services, and other factors believed to be important. Thus the education of young people to the point of literacy and perhaps to some distance beyond that, emerged as a means of enhancing survival even though the effects showed up more strongly in the next generation than in the current one.[2]

But what does literacy mean? This question, often in debate, continues to draw too little empirical study. The effect of literacy, for the individual and for his or her children, lies in more effective disease avoidance, prevention, treatment, and management. But how do people actualize this effect? Some authorities suggest that literate people have access to information from unfamiliar sources. The literate can obtain advice about life and its hazards not just from relatives, friends, and acquaintances but also from people they do not know, who supply the information in newspapers, pamphlets and journals, books, broadsheets, and other written and printed materials. Other authorities hypothesize that it is less the content of education than its cosmopolitan nature that matters, less the information contained in printed sources than the personal freedom involved in breaking away from customary sources of information and insight. This view implies that literate people take more effective responsibility for the things in their care, including children. Still other commentators see schooling, through which literacy is often acquired, less as a tactic of education and more as a method of socialization, even indoctrination. Schooled people obey instructions better. In their view the important

---

[2] For a recent study of positive effects for people with more years of schooling, see Catherine E. Ross and John Mirowsky, "Refining the Association between Education and Health: The Effects of Quantity, Credential, and Selectivity," *Demography* 36 (1999): 445–60.

point is neither schooling's intellectual content nor its liberation of the individual, but the use of the school as an institution of social homogeneity and sometimes also social control. Finally, there are observers who suspect that literacy and education play their most forthright demographic role by advancing an individual's respectability and prestige. The uneducated person commands less respect, even among intimates. No one of these views excludes another, making it difficult to design a research program that will both determine whether parental education is an important factor and test possible explanations.

The Theory of Literacy and Survivorship

Strong arguments have been made about relationships between literacy and economic development and between literacy and national identity. Human capital theorists maintain that education improves the quality or the productivity of a labor force, even though the relationship seems to operate in both directions rather than only from education to higher productivity. Modernization theorists associate education with personal habits such as time-awareness and punctuality, which are valued in a modern economy. Marxist theorists take a jaundiced view of this relationship in capitalist development, arguing that capitalism requires not so much literate as docile workers and consumers. In the nineteenth century, Marxists argue, European states elected to socialize their populations in state schools, which above all else stressed indoctrination in the service of capitalism.[3]

While Marxists have condemned capitalists for using education as a tool of economic subordination, they have often been willing to try to use

---

[3] The Marxist case is put succinctly in Judith Marshall, *Literacy, Power, and Democracy in Mozambique: The Governance of Learning from Colonization to the Present* (Boulder, 1993), esp. pp. 7–15.

it to build cadres of revolutionaries. Socialization theorists describe schools as the primary institutions for inculcating values prized by state authorities. Academic theorists are more likely to stress the hierarchical nature of schooling, in which progressively more complex skills are taught in higher grades. Studies with all these orientations have typically considered the effects of literacy or higher levels of education on the individual and the social or national progress associated with higher population levels of education. Only rarely do they try to assess health effects even though, in the twentieth century, schools often provide health care and teach health behavior.[4]

Another idea emerged from Caldwell's attempt to explain differing mortality levels in Nigerian villages. Caldwell set out to contrast mortality levels in the presence or absence of health clinics. His research suggested that a factor previously given little attention, maternal education, also mattered: "Most socio-economic factors contributed little to an explanation of mortality differentials. Nevertheless, one factor, mother's education, was of surprising importance." "The chance of a mother without schooling losing a child was two and a half times that of a mother with schooling" in a village with a health clinic and four times that in a village without a health clinic.[5] Other demographers had made similar observations, but Caldwell explained this as an effect of education rather than socioeconomic status. The children of literate mothers more often survived than those of illiterate mothers; increments to education added to survival prospects. So did paternal education, although with much less force. That

[4] E.g., Dov Chernichovsky, "Socioeconomic and Demographic Aspects of School Enrollment and Attendance in Rural Botswana," *Economic Development and Cultural Change* 33 (1985): 319–32.
[5] Caldwell, "Education as a Factor in Mortality Decline," 396. Some authorities suspect that the maternal education variable captures effects actually associated with levels of income. See George T. Bicego and J. Tiers Boerma, "Maternal Education and Child Survival: A Comparative Study of Survey Data from 17 Countries," *Social Science and Medicine* 36 (1993): 1207–27.

is, even in similar circumstances of environment, urban–rural residence, occupation, and other factors, the children of educated mothers fared much better.

Caldwell suggested that the explanation must lie in characteristics of the household and the reaction of its members to illness. That conclusion seems to have appealed to him in part because of the findings of a 1947 English study, which suggests a difference between effective and ineffective mothering. In the Nigerian context, effective mothering seemed to involve steps such as selecting the family diet, choosing hygiene habits, making more forceful or more articulate requests for outside assistance, and knowing more about how to find outside services. But it may also be true that educated mothers, especially mothers with many years of schooling, perhaps even more schooling than their husbands, are likelier to take a larger part in making decisions within the family. Educated people command more respect. In sum, Caldwell posed two general hypotheses: (1) education leads to the acquisition of useful information and the ability to acquire additional information, and (2) education augments a person's ability to persuade others.

Those findings prompted demographers to investigate whether the same things held true outside these Nigerian villages, and in particular to explore the impact of maternal versus paternal education. Paternal education may show a strong association with higher child survival, especially in the absence of differentiation in maternal education. But maternal education seems in most circumstances to play the larger role. The effect, whether expressed in lower rates of disease incidence or lower mortality, applies much more strongly to children than to infants.[6] Even so, the particular benefits associated with schooling have not been specified. Edu-

---

[6] Alberto Palloni, "Mortality in Latin America: Emerging Patterns," *Population and Development Review* 7 (1981): 623–49; and Jürgen Bähr and Rainer Wehrhahn, "Life Expectancy and Infant Mortality in Latin America," *Social Science and Medicine* 36 (1993): 1373–82. T. Paul Schultz, "Returns to Women's Education," in Elizabeth M. King and

cated and uneducated mothers often share similar ideas about disease causation and treatment, but their children survive at sharply different rates.[7]

The research strategy followed so far has sought to identify the mechanisms by which education exerts an influence among the highly varied cultural, social, economic, and political circumstances of South Asia, Africa, and Latin America, where child death rates are high and maternal education may be a key to better survival. But mechanisms or pieces of information that seem to play a significant role in one country often do not appear to have much effect elsewhere. The failure to find such explanations may mean not that the key pathways by which literacy exerts its effect await discovery, but that literacy exerts influence in different ways in different societies and times. Literacy is more of a tool than a storehouse of information.[8]

Literacy before the Health Transition

Europe moved from a position in 1500 in which only a few people were literate to a position in 1800, at the beginning of its health transition, when literacy was much more widespread. England has been studied more closely than other countries, and it is instructive to follow literacy in that country. In 1500 perhaps 10 percent of English males and a still smaller share of females could sign their names. About half the population was

---

M. Anne Hill, eds., *Women's Education in Developing Countries: Barriers, Benefits and Policies* (Baltimore, 1993), pp. 51–99, reviews the literature.

[7] John Cleland, "Maternal Education and Child Survival: Further Evidence and Explanations," in John Caldwell et al., eds., *What We Know about Health Transition: The Cultural, Social, and Behavioural Determinants of Health*, 2 vols. (Canberra, 1990), I: 400–419; and Shirley Lindenbaum, "Maternal Education and Health Care Processes in Bangladesh: The Health and Hygiene of the Middle Classes," in ibid., I: 425–40.

[8] Much of this discussion has taken place in the pages of the *Health Transition Review*. See also the essays in John C. Caldwell and Gigi Santow, eds., *Selected Readings in the Cultural, Social, and Behavioural Determinants of Health* (Canberra, 1991).

literate by 1750: perhaps 70 percent of males versus 30 percent of females. There was little change in the level of literacy between 1750 and 1830. Then literacy expanded sharply, so that by 1900 it was nearly universal among people aged six and above. David Mitch, who studied the period 1830–1900, found that literacy and school attendance grew much faster than did the demand for reading or writing skills in the labor market. Members of the working class used literacy more often in leisure activities than at work. Parents regarded schooling as attractive both because it provided skills that could improve economic opportunities and because it taught orderliness and discipline. Thus working people, who comprised the largest group of illiterates, supported the public policy effort to make schooling universal despite the meager rewards of literacy.[9]

The Enlightenment *philosophe* Helvétius argued "education peut tout" (education makes everything possible), but mere literacy did not achieve much in the way of control over the infectious diseases that posed the leading threat to survival in eighteenth- and early nineteenth-century Europe. Indeed, in none of these phases of England's development is there evidence of an association between national levels of literacy and life expectancy. In the long phase of gradual gains in literacy, 1500 to 1750, life expectancy fluctuated. Between 1750 and 1830 life expectancy improved but literacy did not. After 1830 literacy expanded, but for the nation as a whole life expectancy did not rise until the 1870s and afterward. Although literacy moved apace with economic development, Mitch's investigation leaves little room to explain development as an effect of literacy. England entered industrial modernization with enough literate people to meet its needs. But for many decades further development does not seem to have been driven, or even much advanced, by gains in levels of literacy.

---

[9] David F. Mitch, *The Rise of Popular Literacy in Victorian England: The Influence of Private Choice and Public Policy* (Philadelphia, 1992), esp. pp. 201–6. See also W. B. Stephens, "Literacy in England, Scotland, and Wales, 1500–1900," *History of Education Quarterly* 30 (1990): 545–71.

These inferences rest, however, on a weak foundation. Because the sources they use offer little option, historians have measured changes in the proportion of people able to sign their names. That may not translate into a capacity or a willingness to read or a habit of reading. And it may not translate into a measure of personal freedom. There are other possibilities, too, for explaining why the association between literacy and socioeconomic development seems so weak. Given the patriarchal structure of European society, males were much likelier to be able to sign their names than were females. But modern demographic research suggests that, in child survival, the literacy of the mother usually counts for more than the literacy of the father. Up to 1800 or even 1850, Europeans acquired literacy after no more than a few months' enrollment in schools. Schools did not play a large part in the socialization of people, compared with the home and the community, until the second half of the century, when state authorities began to require school attendance for a certain number of years and to design curriculums.

Local communities invested in schools in ways that drew them together toward a common goal: the education of the children. François Furet and Jacques Ozouf maintain that this deep community interest in schooling was present in France in the eighteenth century as well as the nineteenth.[10] In that sense Robert LeVine and Merry White find schooling, but not formal education, everywhere.[11] Therefore interest in schooling existed long before the nineteenth-century expansion of formal education. Even though illiterate adults often regarded reading and writing skills as having little value for themselves, in the nineteenth and twentieth centuries they have often shared with literate parents the sense that schooling would be a good thing for their children.

[10] François Furet and Jacques Ozouf, *Reading and Writing: Literacy in France from Calvin to Jules Ferry* (Cambridge, 1982), p. 65.
[11] Robert A. LeVine and Merry I. White, *Human Conditions: The Cultural Basis of Educational Development* (New York, 1986), esp. pp. 73–89.

Some other important developments took place in the period between 1450 and 1800. Europeans modified the Asian process of block printing to create the more flexible mode of printing by movable type, vastly reducing the cost of books. In the second half of the seventeenth century they also popularized new kinds of texts, those appealing to a general readership. Almanacs, dictionaries and encyclopedias, and manuals of advice were often published in numbers large enough to suggest that they were being bought and perhaps also read by a general audience. Many ordinary Europeans seem to have acquired the habit of looking to books for information and advice before the health transition began. Among these manuals of advice were many books explaining how to differentiate one disease from another and giving recipes for medicaments.[12] Thus on the eve of the health transition Europeans possessed two important sources of information about diseases and injuries. They could call on an oral tradition of folk wisdom, which identified remedies for particular symptoms, or they could call on formal medicine, represented either by a practitioner or by a book written by a practitioner for a lay audience.

During the nineteenth-century decline of child mortality, European parents invested more household resources, and worked to persuade public authorities to invest more public resources, in children and their education. Nevertheless it is not clear whether literacy or education paid health dividends for the individual or for children. Roger Schofield found that after 1810 in Britain the infants of parents who could sign their own names more often survived, compared with the infants of illiterate parents.[13] But Samuel Preston and Michael Haines, who investigated this

[12] See above, Chapter 3, note 4, for some examples.
[13] Roger Schofield, "Fertility, Nuptiality, and Mortality According to Literacy, 1754–1840," unpublished paper, Social Science History Association, Nov. 17, 1989. See also Marco Breschi and Massimo Livi Bacci, "Saison et climat comme contraintes de la survie des enfants: L'expérience italienne au XIXe siècle," *Population* 41 (1986): 9–36.

208

issue for the United States around 1900, found that literacy explained little of the differences in infant and child mortality.[14] Not until the 1910s or 1920s did either physicians or parents learn how to use the ability to read to protect children. Preston and Haines argue that it was the germ theory that ultimately provided this power.[15]

Literacy as conceived before the twentieth century was not meant to have much to do with survival prospects. Advocates of literacy and education rarely mentioned good health as a possible benefit. Nevertheless, the nineteenth century in Europe is noteworthy as a period when women caught up with men in literacy and as a period in which the survival prospects of females improved faster than those of males. It was also a period of persistent improvement in child but not infant survival. The leading ideas about how to improve survival prospects lay in filth theory, which was disseminated aggressively in the middle decades of the century, often inspiring schoolbook lessons.

Outside the West before the mid-twentieth century, literacy levels varied widely. In Morocco people learned to read chiefly in order to study religious material, and only a few people could read. In China, in contrast, 30 to 45 percent of males could read a few hundred characters by the mid-nineteenth century, and reading served chiefly practical ends: keeping accounts and writing letters.[16] Europeans often had a distinctive advantage in contacts with people elsewhere because more of them could read and write.

---

[14] Samuel H. Preston and Michael R. Haines, *Fatal Years: Child Mortality in Late Nineteenth-Century America* (Princeton, 1991), pp. 171, 175, and passim.

[15] For further discussion of this point, see Chapter 6, and Gretchen A. Condran and Samuel H. Preston, "Child Mortality Differences, Personal Health Practices, and Medical Technology: The United States, 1900–1930," in Lincoln Chen, Arthur Kleinman, and Norma C. Ware, eds., *Health and Social Change in International Perspective* (Boston, 1994), pp. 171–224.

[16] Charles W. Hayford, *To the People: James Yen and Village China* (New York, 1990), p. 6.

Independence, Decolonization, and Literacy

The lands colonized by Europe in the period 1880–1940 often contained small groups of elites that were highly literate in the local language and culture or in a language useful chiefly for reading and interpreting religious texts, such as Arabic. Most of the populace living in the colonized territories of Asia and Africa could not read, had little or no exposure to schools, and depended for the information available to them on local resources. Colonization brought a plan to educate a few people in the language of the colonizing power. The histories of colonial education stress these features of schooling:

1. few children attended either state or missionary schools;
2. both types of schools concentrated on discipline and socialization, emblemized by the missionary school focus on teaching the catechism of the state church;
3. few children moved on to secondary schools;
4. colonial and missionary educators selected children for schooling, favoring families that cooperated with authorities;
5. the curriculum rarely included instruction in hygiene, medical theories, or other information useful for formulating new ideas about the control of risks to health and survival; and
6. children were trained in the colonizer's language.

Nevertheless, the colonial era left people in the areas under European control with a strong sense that education opens doors. Parents skimped in order to send their children to schools, even while they complained about the shortcomings of those schools and even though the schools often failed to open doors in the way that parents had hoped. In many parts of British Africa people seem to have shared the expectation held by the Victorian working class in Britain, which was that schooling would improve their children's lives.

210

In the era after World War II, independence movements often brought ambitious plans to expand education, to promote literacy among children and adults, to reform the curriculum, and, in countries with several or many indigenous languages, to school the population in a common language. Leaders foresaw a curriculum that would promote socialization in the newly independent state and its political and economic ideologies and in personal capabilities. They planned to fashion a secular catechism, using schools and adult campaigns to teach literacy, to promote the interests of the new state, and to arm the individual with useful information. Influenced by modernization theory, they also believed that raising the level of literacy offered the surest way to promote economic development. Arguments for schooling and adult literacy campaigns, which nearly everyone regarded as compelling, were built on the assumption that literacy would assist human capital formation and that sustained economic growth would follow. In many countries the Soviet model had an important influence. The Soviet Union had embarked in 1919 on simultaneous campaigns to improve the literacy level (which rose from 30 percent in 1919 to 87 percent in 1939) and to promote development. Both seemed to have succeeded, and to provide a concrete demonstration of the role of literacy in development.

At the moment of independence, levels of literacy were low in most formerly colonial territories, but literacy proved one of the easier things to provide to a population. Thus literacy rates often rose sharply in the years after independence. Tanzania's literacy rate jumped from 17 percent in 1968 to 63 percent in 1975, under the leadership of a socialist regime, and women nearly caught up with men. World Bank estimates suggest that across Africa literacy rose from an average of 16 percent in 1960 to 34 percent in 1980, with a few countries leading these gains. Besides Tanzania, the largest gains occurred in Mozambique, Tunisia, Zimbabwe, Kenya, Somalia, Zaire, and Rwanda.[17]

[17] E.g., Roy A. Carr-Hill, *The Functioning and Effects of the Tanzanian Literacy Programme* (Paris, 1991).

Outside Africa, too, the period from 1960 to 1980 saw marked gains in literacy and levels of education. Nicaragua elevated literacy from under 50 percent in 1979 to 77 percent at the end of a five-month-long campaign and 87 percent a few years later by teaching people to read phrases and sentences such as "Sandino, leader of the revolution," and "To spend little, save much, and produce a lot – that is making the revolution."[18]

Many campaigns promoted adult and child literacy. In Mozambique successive adult literacy campaigns and the introduction of mass schooling raised literacy from 10 percent of the population in 1975, at independence, to 94 percent by 1991. In only sixteen years Mozambique covered the same territory for which England required the entire period from 1500 to 1900. Large numbers of people joined the pool of individuals to whom written messages could be directed and who possessed other traits of education. Cuba, too, made adult education a centerpiece of a campaign that stressed technical education, literacy, and ideological education.[19]

A few countries lagged. In India literacy rates rose from about 5 percent in 1900 to 17 percent at independence. But population grew rapidly, while both mass schooling and adult education lagged. Thus, in 1981, India, with a literacy rate of 36 percent, claimed far and away the largest number of unlettered people in the world.[20] India's rapid population growth without major gains in literacy meant that, for the world as a whole, the number of illiterate people continued to rise.

Widespread gains in literacy did not translate into economic development. The supply of jobs requiring literacy did not increase nearly as fast as literacy, so that both adults already in the labor force and youths en-

---

[18] Valerie Miller, *Between Struggle and Hope: The Nicaraguan Literacy Crusade* (Boulder, 1985), p. 76; and Robert F. Arnove, *Education and Revolution in Nicaragua* (New York, 1986).

[19] Marshall, *Literacy, Power, and Democracy in Mozambique;* and Theodore MacDonald, *Making a New People: Education in Revolutionary Cuba* (Vancouver, 1985).

[20] See also, on Brazil, Nancy Birdsall and Richard H. Sabot, eds., *Opportunity Foregone: Education in Brazil* (Baltimore, 1996).

tering it found it difficult to translate their new skills into a higher standard of living. In Tanzania the campaign, which had begun amidst high expectations, led some people to a sense of disappointment. A 1991 study suggests that the failure to achieve expected economic and political goals can be attributed either to the overstatement of effective literacy or to the inappropriate content of the reading material used in child and adult schooling. But answers to a survey suggest another interpretation, one pertinent to Caldwell's findings and ideas. When asked a range of questions intended to test the effects of the literacy program, Tanzanians showed little difference between literates and illiterates in political information but big differences in health information. Moreover, women learned more health information than did men.[21]

Although some Tanzanians expressed cynicism about the benefits of literacy, the widespread failure across developing countries to achieve economic goals does not seem to have disturbed the person in the street as much as it did policy makers and politicians. Political leaders could no longer plausibly claim that mass schooling and adult literacy campaigns would lead painlessly to economic development, but observers found other grounds for promoting education. In Kerala, where literacy already surpassed 70 percent in 1981, authorities nevertheless mounted the Total Literacy Campaign in 1989. They aimed to move the Ernakulam district, where literacy rates were low by Keralan but high by Indian standards, to the point of universal literacy. In an elaborate campaign marked by careful mobilization of popular enthusiasm, they raised the literacy level from 73 percent to 96 percent.[22] Besides literacy, the objectives of this campaign centered on personal and economic development. The people leading it wanted to improve the quality of life of Ernakulam illiterates and to promote medical care and immunization. They hoped also to put this poor

---

[21] Carr-Hill, *Functioning and Effects of the Tanzanian Literacy Programme*, esp. p. 261.
[22] K. R. Rajan, *Mass Literacy: The Ernakulam Experiment* (Kalamassery, 1991).

district into a position where it could become the biotechnology center of India. Policy makers continued to draft grand, even grandiose, plans for the effects of literacy campaigns. The failure of those plans to be realized sometimes dampened but did not remove public enthusiasm for literacy and education.

In the meantime, people who acquired literacy found that it did bring important rewards. Socialist countries, which often laid more persistent stress on adult education and invested more heavily in schools, used literacy, schooling, the promotion of national policy through schooling, and the adoption of explicit health objectives to improve the survival prospects of their populations. Cuba, Costa Rica, Kerala, Albania, and China all achieved significantly higher life expectancy than was warranted by their wealth or their investments in medicine and public health, relying in part on mass schooling and adult literacy campaigns.

The Content of Literacy and Its Beneficiaries

Developing countries often set out to provide basic levels of literacy, which could be achieved in a few years of schooling and, for adults, through evening classes. They aimed to make it possible for the people who were instructed to deal with some of the practical demands of everyday life, such as using transport facilities or deciphering an electric bill.[23] The Ernakulam experiment adopted a form of functional literacy as its goal and expressed that in standards: at a minimum, read aloud at thirty words a minute, copy seven words a minute, and read/write the numerals from one to 100. Or, at the highest level, understand the written messages of one's work and living environment, write a short letter, and show

---

[23] See Daniel A. Wagner, *Literacy, Culture, and Development: Becoming Literate in Morocco* (Cambridge, 1993).

a functional understanding of proportions and interest.[24] It is difficult to see how literacy and numeracy at such standards might translate into the human capital needed for a biotechnology center. But it is not difficult to see that such standards could open people to information of importance in their lives, both from the reading material used in literacy instruction and from the newspapers and other written matter to which people acquired access. In sum, the literacy programs set reading goals likely to help people address commonplace problems, including health problems, but unlikely to transform their employment opportunities. Finally, many observers have noticed that the political enthusiasm sometimes found in the early stages of literacy campaigns, often consisting of messages crafted by independence leaders, waned. Literacy programs did not persuade people to adopt a uniform political outlook.

One of the impressive, and most often replicated, findings of research is that additional years of schooling show a robust statistical association with lower mortality. Many studies show that an additional year of mothers' schooling is associated with a reduction of 7 to 9 percent in child mortality. Work by a team of scholars studying literacy and health relationships in Nicaragua suggests that literacy also had a pronounced effect at its most elementary level. Mothers with low measured intelligence who acquired literacy in the Nicaraguan campaign gained more in capacity to safeguard their children than did mothers of high measured intelligence. Moreover, adult literacy had its most pronounced effects among mothers with poor access to health services. In the Nicaraguan case, literacy seems to have led mothers toward coping strategies, even in the least hopeful of circumstances.[25]

---

[24] Rajan, *Mass Literacy*, pp. 31–32.
[25] John G. Cleland and Jerome K. van Ginneken, "Maternal Education and Child Survival in Developing Countries: The Search for Pathways of Influence," in Caldwell and Santow, eds., *Selected Readings*, pp. 79–100. P. Sandiford et al., "Does Intelligence Account for the Link Between Maternal Literacy and Child Survival?," *Social Science and*

What did the mothers learn? In many cases, but not across the board, educated mothers more often protected their children from certain diseases, especially waterborne diarrheal maladies. They also treated diarrhea more successfully, using oral rehydration, took their sick children to clinics, had their children immunized, and acquired prenatal care.[26] In sum, they appear to have used basic ideas about sanitation and medical services more effectively.

Some educational experiments have been built on the idea that women are interested in acquiring literacy less because they expect to use it in their work outside the household and more because they want to learn how to take better care of their children in good health and in sickness.[27] But, as Nelly Stromquist argues, literacy programs have rarely been designed to serve women's needs.[28] Those programs were effective, teaching principles of filth and germ theories, but they were not as effective as they could have been.

At the End of the Twentieth Century

Literacy, further schooling, and adult education seem to promise much as means to maintain gains already achieved in the health transition and to promote further gains. The most obvious area of unrealized promise lies in the schooling of women. Figure 7.1 contrasts female literacy with child survival among 174 countries as of 1995. It shows the close associa-

Medicine 45 (1997): 1231–39; and Sandiford et al., "The Impact of Women's Literacy on Child Health and Its Interaction with Access to Health Services, *Population Studies* 49 (1995): 5–17.

[26] John Hobcraft, "Women's Education, Child Welfare and Child Survival: A Review of the Evidence," *Health Transition Review* 3 (1993): 159–75.

[27] Sylvia van Dijk and Sandra Durón, *Participando una experiencia de educación popular* (Mexico City, 1986).

[28] Nelly P. Stromquist, *Literacy for Citizenship: Gender and Grassroots Dynamics in Brazil* (Albany, 1997), p. 18.

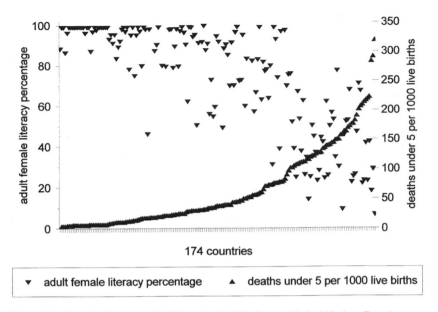

Figure 7.1. Female literacy and child survival, 1995. *Source:* United Nations Development Programme, *Human Development Report 1998* (New York, 1998), pp. 156–57 and 186.

tion between female literacy and child survival, and it shows how many countries had high child death rates in that period. The acquisition of literacy stands out as one of the most promising means to reduce child mortality.

This unmet potential for literacy has not gone unremarked. National governments and international agencies have mounted a number of literacy campaigns, including the 1990 UNESCO International Year of Literacy. Nevertheless, the number of adult illiterates has continued to rise, moving toward a billion in the year 2000. And the affordability of schooling remains a serious problem for developing countries, to the point that perhaps 40 percent of children in the poorest countries do not complete a primary education.

In some ways the very discussion of these issues seems to have curtailed the prospects of successful action. Female education means the empowerment of women, which many people resist. The campaign for female literacy that might seem to be an obvious tool for furthering the health transition has run up against resistance from defenders of traditional culture. The defenders consist of members of those cultures who are often troubled by the role education may play in promoting Western values and attributes and academics, many of whom recognize the close association between education and Westernization and worry that education will violate the integrity of traditional cultures. The case of Taslima Nasrin, the Bangladeshi feminist, is instructive. Nasrin proposed changes in Islamic law giving more rights to women. But those seemed so dangerous to some Islamic faithful that in 1998 they mounted a demonstration against Nasrin and called for her to be executed. Western intellectuals expressed greater alarm about the threat of retaliation against Salmon Rushdie, whose fictional work defamed Islam, than about threats to Nasrin. Even so, there is no consistent pattern of lower survivorship for females in all societies with traditional cultures or all cultures that resist female equality.[29]

Conclusion

Literacy, at least as measured by the capacity to sign one's name or even to read simple texts, held uncertain value for improving health or for economic development up to the early twentieth century. In developing countries literacy or schooling had marked value by the 1950s. Maternal education mattered most. Education leads to the acquisition of particular items of information and attitudes, which unschooled mothers lack, and it enhances the mother's ability to negotiate with those around her. Those gains seem to be incremental. Additional years of schooling add to this quality of personal authority. This effect may be enhanced by the value

---

[29] It would be useful to know more about how women achieve equal or superior survivorship in the face of inequality.

that a culture places on education and by marked differentiation in levels of education within a society. That is, both development and the successful education of most members of a society to a minimum standard may weaken the effect that parental education has on child survival. In the meantime, maternal education and the provision of basic public health and medical services – safe water, immunizations, medications – have played a strong role in reducing death rates among young children living in developing countries during the second half of the twentieth century.

Suggestions for Further Reading

Robert F. Arnove and Harvey J. Graff, eds. *National Literacy Campaigns in Historical and Comparative Perspective.* New York, 1987.

John P. Comings, Christine Smith, and Chij K. Shrestha. "Women's Literacy: The Connection to Health and Family Planning." *Convergence* 27 (1994): 93–101.

Carmen Garcia-Gil et al. "Epidemiological Appraisal of the Active Role of Women in the Decline of Infant Mortality in Spain during the Twentieth Century." *Social Science and Medicine* 29 (1989): 1351–62.

Harvey J. Graff. *The Legacies of Literacy: Continuities and Contradictions in Western Culture and Society.* Bloomington, 1987.

R. A. Houston. *Literacy in Early Modern Europe: Culture and Education, 1500–1800.* London, 1988.

Egil Johansson. *The History of Literacy in Sweden.* Umeå, 1977.

Conclusion

Most people want to live a long life, although some hold out the reservation that the life they want to live should be healthy as well as long. It is not unusual for individual aspirations to conflict with the good of a society. In this case the two things align. Longer lives, especially longer and healthier lives, add much to the well-being of humankind. The individual's emotional life is richer for living long enough to get to know not just the next generation but one or two after it and for grandchildren to know their grandparents. Society benefits from the experience and the wisdom of older people. The rhythms of life are more predictable when the young live to be old. As they age, many people find that each new stage holds its own rewards and pleasures, which are seldom anticipated at younger ages. Living to be old in good or adequate health is, moreover, a form of freedom. It creates the opportunity to think, to read, to work, to love, to enjoy oneself.

The goal of "health for all by the year 2000," set in 1978, could not be achieved. Each year in the early 1990s global deaths totaled some 51 million people. More than half of those deaths occurred in infancy, childhood, or early adulthood, at ages well under the life expectancy in any country. More than 12 million deaths occurred among children under five years of age. The largest single category of causes remained infectious and parasitic diseases, which accounted for 16.4 million deaths. Heart and cerebrovascular diseases plus cancers together caused 15.7 million deaths. It is nevertheless a remarkable thing to have only 51 million deaths a year among about 6 billion people. That equals a crude death rate of 8.5 per 1,000, a figure well under the 30 to 40 per 1,000 that was common across the globe in 1800, before the health transition.

Three topics require further discussion to draw this book to a close. The first looks backward in time, the second looks at today, and the third looks forward.

How Did We Get Where We Are?

No grand hope that humankind has held has come so close to fulfillment as the hope that all people will enjoy a long and healthy life. In 1800 life expectancy at birth surpassed thirty-five years in only a few favored places; in most of the world it certainly fell short of thirty and may not have exceeded twenty-five years. In just 200 years the expectation of a long life has been democratized across the globe. Life expectancy at birth rose to a global average of nearly sixty-seven years in 1997. Never before has such a large share of the human population been able to live long enough for people to frame a mature sense of themselves, to see their children grow up, even to get to know their grandchildren. Never before have so many people been able confidently to anticipate their own survival into old age.

This achievement is a spectacular demonstration of the human capacity to manage itself. It represents the success of efforts to modify human behavior, to reshape the environment, and to invent the means of avoiding, preventing, curing, and meliorating diseases and injuries. Curiously, this is the most covert of achievements. Although people wanted to live to old age, nowhere during the health transition did public institutions pursue this goal with the same directness or intensity that they sought economic, military, or educational goals.

The long lives that people enjoy in most of the world have been achieved by a process akin to the construction, enlargement, reconstruction, and repair of a house. Initially, the Western version of this structure had two rooms, one holding filth theory and the idea of protecting people from disease by cleansing their habitat, the other holding smallpox inoculation and vaccination. Those were the two most efficacious new agents for extending survival around 1800. Over time those rooms were enlarged and reformed, new rooms were added, and repairs were made here and there. The effectiveness of each approach to the problem of controlling hazards to health and survival has changed over time and varied across space. Each country, often each region within a country, has built its own version of this house, with many rooms or few, modernized or not. One of the original rooms remains. People still try to reduce disease risks by cleansing their habitats and avoiding filth. The other was abandoned in 1978 when smallpox was eradicated, existing afterward only in samples of the smallpox virus stored for possible future use, and in the practice of immunization.

Within this building of health the most valuable elements of the health transition fall into two categories. The first consists of contributions from technicians and experts, and it is led by immunization and antibiotics. Jenner's smallpox vaccination stands out, as do also the modern immunizations against childhood diseases, which have had a beneficent effect in rich countries and a stunningly helpful effect in most poor countries. It is more difficult to assess the impact of antibiotics, but they have certainly contributed to the rapid waning of infectious diseases in developing countries since about 1950. Thus medicine, which can be credited with discovering and devising immunotherapy and the miracle drugs, and public health, which is chiefly responsible for the mass application of immunizations and for water purification, preventing the spread of many diarrheal diseases, have led the health transition.

The second category of leading elements has a less heroic nature, consisting, as it does, of the things people have learned to do for themselves. Parenting in the late twentieth-century world was, gauged in terms of the survival prospects of infants and children, superior to what it had ever been before, especially in the capacity parents acquired to protect children from disease and injury and to treat and manage sickness. It is also true that individuals, especially those favored by lengthier education and higher socioeconomic status, have learned and applied many things useful to preserving their own health in diet, exercise, housing, and personal behaviors. Those things have certainly outweighed the negative effects of modern lifestyles.

During the health transition each generation has inherited the rooms already built and added its own, preserving things that worked in the past while adding new technologies, behaviors, and services. By and large this has been done without taking the time and trouble to assess how satisfactory the reformed house is. The result is a house of health that, in the rich countries of the world, is elaborate and expensive, but not necessarily efficient. The achievement of nearly equivalent life expectancies by a number of poor countries, operating with far leaner resources, suggests how much leeway there is for a reappraisal of the health infrastructure in rich countries. It is true that high life expectancy is not the only goal for a health system, which should do many other things, too. Nevertheless, it is important to assess how and whether each element of the system contributes to better survival. This task has been begun, ambitiously enough, at the global level, for which scholars have estimated the annual number of deaths and their causes and used those data to suggest how survivorship can be extended further. It has not yet been done at the national or community level, which is where this approach will teach us most about the identity and the efficacy of the means by which we try to prolong life and improve health.

The comparative study of the health transition indicates that each country should expect to devise its own scheme for advancing good health. Nevertheless, we should all expect to be better informed to the degree that we take into account the successes and failures of other countries.

Where Are We in 2001?

At the beginning of the twentieth-first century we stand not so much toward the end of a long process of epidemiologic transition as we do amidst two epidemiologic regimes, one led by communicable and the other by noncommunicable diseases. It is important, we have discovered through trial and error over the past 200 years, to understand how diseases are transmitted to people and how they are acquired. But the emphasis on causation does not limit us to germ theory and the other explanations of clinical medicine.[1] It alerts us also to the social, behavioral, and cultural circumstances that make disease and injury more or less probable. Each specific disease and injury therefore has come to stand as a code for the things that precede it, causing or allowing it to occur; for the episode itself; and for the effects of the episode. Cause-of-sickness and cause-of-death information has become central to the way we understand sickness and deaths and try to prevent them.

The health transition remains incomplete. For too many people, especially the poor, survivorship has improved, but it has not reached anything approaching its plausible limits. The poor, numerous in the developed countries, make up a large share of the populations of developing countries. For some groups and populations – especially people in AIDS-stricken areas and adult males of the former Soviet bloc – hope has re-

---

[1] Daniel M. Fox, *Power and Illness: The Failure and Future of American Health Policy* (Berkeley, 1995), charges that U.S. health policy fails because it remains oriented toward infectious disease and conceptualized in germ theory.

treated. Life expectancies already achieved are shrinking because of disease and hardship. Everywhere it has proved easier to secure longer lives than to reduce the quantity of sickness time that people accumulate in their lives. Longer sicknesses, especially the protracted last episode, have maintained or added to sickness time and to the expectation of sickness. Thus, at the beginning of the twenty-first century, it is not yet possible to say that any society has achieved its potential for both a long and a healthy life. Humankind still has a considerable distance to travel.

Scholars have lavished talent and attention on questions about mortality's reduction in England, especially in the nineteenth century. Much has been learned. But the English model of sanitary reforms, an important contributor to the control of diarrheal diseases in nineteenth-century cities, explains only a small part of the global reduction of mortality. It is time to reallocate academic talent toward other questions that are also urgent, on which historical research can shed important light. Several have been identified in different parts of this book. Here are a few more:

1. How have so many poor and middle-income countries and regions – Costa Rica, Kerala, Sri Lanka, China, Cuba, and Albania, for example – managed more or less to match the life expectancies achieved in rich countries despite the many handicaps under which those countries operate?

2. Which elements in the existing survivorship strategies of each country have been the most efficacious and which the least efficacious? In particular, how should these strategies be adapted to shed inherited means of mortality control that have lost much of their good effect and to add new, more effective techniques?

3. Each region, oftentimes each country, has devised its own strategy for advancing survivorship, suggesting a kind of comparative advantage. What are the elements of each country's advantage? How much does each element contribute to the sum of health and longevity? Can those

be promoted still more successfully in the country already having that comparative advantage? Can they be adapted to circumstances in other countries?

4. Why has the surplus mortality of female infants and children waxed and waned in some developing regions, especially India, and why has it varied from region to region? Why has the surplus mortality of adult males waxed and waned in the developed countries, and why has it varied so much from country to country? Why has maternal mortality remained so high in so many countries?

There are also some more specific research issues that command attention. What levels and other elements of literacy have been the most valuable for extending human survival? How can the effects of tobaccosis be dampened? How can people who understand the ill effects of certain behaviors, but refuse to change, come to share the highest survival prospects? How can remedies of demonstrated efficacy be explained more effectively to the people who elect whether or not to apply them? What household characteristics have most effectively protected children from communicable diseases in poor societies? How can remedies that need to be applied at the mass population level be evaluated more effectively? What unrecognized advantages or behaviors allow many individuals to escape disease, injury, and premature death when other people with similar recognized characteristics do not?

Where Do We Go from Here?

The total of 51 million deaths is quite low, given historical experience, but unnecessarily high, given what could be achieved. What if global conditions equaled conditions in Japan, the society with the highest life expectancy, or in Costa Rica, one of the poorer countries that has achieved

Table C.1. *Surplus Mortality, 1990–1995 (deaths per 100,000)*[a]

Africa	1,571
(Nigeria)	1,559
Americas	683
(the United States)	520
Eastern Mediterranean	1,161
Europe	576
(Sweden)	452
South East Asia	1,144
(India)	1,145
Western Pacific	709
(China)	699

[a]Standardized by age and sex, and weighted by population size.
Source: Hiroshi Nakajima, *The World Health Report 1995: Bridging the Gaps* (Geneva, 1995), pp. 101–4.

high life expectancy? Japan's standardized death rate in the period 1990–95 was 420 deaths per 100,000 people. Costa Rica's was 479. Table C.1 shows how far World Health Organization member states departed from these figures.[2] If Costa Rica's death rate obtained across the globe, deaths would have totaled 26.3 million rather than 51 million. If Japan's rate obtained, the total would have been 23.1 million.[3] There is much room for improving the survival prospects of today's population.

[2] Hiroshi Nakajima, *The World Health Report 1995: Bridging the Gaps* (Geneva, 1995), pp. 18–19 and 101–4.
[3] Yet another approach would estimate the years of potential life lost, emphasizing in another way the effect of disabilities and deaths among people of less than old age. On this, see Christopher J. L. Murray and Alan D. Lopez, eds., *The Global Burden of Disease: A Comprehensive Assessment of Mortality and Disability from Diseases, Injuries, and Risk Factors in 1990 and Projected to 2020* (Cambridge, Mass., 1996). For a critique of this approach, see Alan Williams, "Calculating the Global Burden of Disease: Time for a Strategic Reappraisal?," *Health Economics* 8 (1999): 1–8.

Which measures promise the most by way of further reductions in mortality that are attainable, given technologies already available?[4] Murray and Lopez listed the leading causes of premature death as of 1990:[5]

diarrheal diseases: 2.9 million deaths, mostly among infants and children in developing countries;

tuberculosis:[6] 2.5 to 2.9 million, mostly adults under fifty living in developing countries;

measles:[7] 2 million, almost entirely among children living in developing countries;

---

[4] See also Daniel E. Bell, "What Policies Will Reduce Death Rates Most Rapidly in Less Developed Countries," in Jacques Vallin and Alan D. Lopez, eds., *Health Policy, Social Policy and Mortality Prospects* (Liège, 1985), pp. 493–505; Milton I. Roemer, "Social Policies and Health Care Systems: Their Effects on Mortality and Morbidity in Developed Countries," in ibid., pp. 541–552; and W. H. Mosley, D. T. Jamison, and D. A. Henderson, "The Health Sector in Developing Countries: Prospects for the 1990s and Beyond," *Annual Review of Public Health* 11 (1990): 335–58.

The periodical *World Health Forum* provides a good way to keep abreast of WHO activities. Important data collections appear in these annuals: WHO, *The World Health Report;* the World Bank, *World Development Report;* UNICEF, *The State of the World's Children;* and in W. W. Holland, ed., *European Community Atlas of "Avoidable Death"* (Oxford, 1988).

[5] Estimates of age- and disease-specific death totals for 1990 may be found in C.J.L. Murray and A. D. Lopez, "Global and Regional Cause-of-Death Patterns in 1990," in Murray and Lopez, eds., *Global Comparative Assessments in the Health Sector* (Geneva, 1994), pp. 21–54. Some of the estimates that follow have been drawn from this source, and some have been taken from specialized studies of individual diseases.

[6] John D. H. Porter and Keith P.W.J. McAdam, eds., *Tuberculosis: Back to the Future* (Chichester, 1993); *TB: A Global Emergency* (Geneva, 1994); Christopher Murray, Karel Styblo, and Annik Rouillon, "Tuberculosis," in Dean T. Jamison et al., eds., *Disease Control Priorities in Developing Countries* (New York, 1993), pp. 233–59; and D.P.S. Spence et al., "Tuberculosis and Poverty," *British Medical Journal* 307 (1993): 359–61.

[7] Andrew Cliff, Peter Haggett, and Matthew Smallman-Raynor, *Measles: An Historical Geography of a Major Human Viral Disease: From Global Expansion to Local Retreat, 1840–1990* (Oxford, 1993); and Peter Aaby, "Measles Immunization and Child Survival: Uncontrolled Experiments," in Hoda Rashad, Ronald Gray, and Ties Boerma, eds., *Evaluation of the Impact of Health Interventions* (Liège, 1995), pp. 11–45.

malaria:[8] about 1 million persons a year, mostly children under five living in developing countries.

AIDS: about 312,000 deaths in 1990, rising to 1.6 million in 1996.

All are communicable diseases.

In the West, diarrheal diseases, tuberculosis, measles, and other communicable diseases causing death especially among the young were brought under control before the introduction of antibiotics. They were controlled using a combination of public health improvements, filth and germ theory advice about behavior, isolation of the sick, more spacious housing, screens, food regulations, and other measures. In developing countries the attempt has been made to control these diseases chiefly by medical means: oral rehydration therapy, antibiotics, immunizations, and antimalarial drugs.[9] This approach has enjoyed noteworthy successes at broadcasting immunizations and modern medications. But many people remain unprotected, and, except for measles vaccine, all of the medical measures now in use provide temporary protection or relief. Oral rehydration therapy reduces the risk of death in the current episode of diarrhea. But it does not affect the chances of future bouts, and in many countries mothers report that their children suffer between three and seven bouts of diarrhea a year. BCG vaccine prevents some forms of tuberculosis, but the main method of tuberculosis control is treatment with a complex and protracted course of medications. Used successfully, those will suppress a current infection, but the damage remains and the infection may reactivate. Measles has been preventable by vaccination since about 1965, and the remaining total of 2 million deaths a year is a measure of

---

[8] L. J. Bruce-Chwatt, "Malaria and Its Control: Present Situations and Future Prospects," *Annual Review of Public Health* 8 (1987): 75–110; and WHO, *The World Health Report 1999: Making a Difference* (Geneva, 1999), pp. 49–63.

[9] E.g., World Bank, *Better Health in Africa: Experience and Lessons Learned* (Washington, 1994).

lack of success in delivering the vaccine. From a biomedical standpoint, malaria remains the most difficult of these diseases to prevent or treat.

Biomedicine paid off handsomely in the short run between about 1950 and 2000. Mortality decline made faster progress where advanced biomedical therapies and vaccines were deployed, as they were in Latin America, Soviet bloc countries, and, to a lesser degree, in Africa and Asia. Biomedicine seems to be the leading factor that allowed developing countries to close the gap separating them from developed countries in life expectancy at birth. Nevertheless, the continuing toll of preventable diseases argues that a system of protection relying on biomedical remedies is unable to control these diseases. Medicine made up only one element in the decline of mortality from communicable diseases in the West. There and in other countries and regions that have achieved a life expectancy at birth over seventy years (see Map 1.1), the health strategy features much more than medicine. It also contains public health improvements, attitudes and behavior conducive to the control of disease hazards, more spacious housing, more years of schooling, democratized access to health clinics, and all the other means that have been discussed in this book. In the short run the immunization of children against disease and treatment of the sick with advanced medications, when they are cheap enough, remains the least expensive course and the most immediately available step to take. But that approach will require the ongoing mobilization of resources for immunization programs and medications delivered from the outside plus the ongoing development of new medications. In the long run it may be less expensive to build the public health, behavioral, and socioeconomic foundations of health appropriate to each culture, preventing disease at a distance rather than with just the immediacy of immunizations.

The resources for implementing this broad spectrum of tactics have become much stronger. Higher levels of education among the world's peoples in the 1990s and the demonstrated association between schooling and better health for the person and for that person's children make it easier to disseminate information. The advantages of retrospective assessment of the efficacy of tactics used previously make it easier to select and tailor tactics that are both effective and well suited to cultural circumstances in a country where life expectancy falls short.

The historical record also suggests that success at reducing deaths before old age to the lowest possible level will require popular engagement rather than obedience. The lively public discussion of a health problem and its possible remedies has been an effective element of public health, which is especially noticeable in countries that have achieved higher levels of life expectancy than their medical, public health, and economic resources seem to warrant. In China (at least before the 1958 famine), Sri Lanka, Costa Rica, and the Indian state of Kerala, public engagement seems to have mattered more than the particular strategy of health improvement. Public argument also has been one of the noteworthy failings of the health transition. Too often, the case for new modes of behavior or action has been made prematurely, before enough information was available to determine what should be done and how it should be done. That was true of sanitary improvements, for which the claim was initially made that they would control all communicable diseases, not just some waterborne diseases. Too often people were obliged to do things against their will, which undermined the effectiveness of the measures taken.

This broad spectrum of remedies needs quick action because the capacity to allot resources to them will soon be challenged by the demands of an aging population for health care and probably also by the extraordinary costs of gene therapy. In 1997 people aged sixty and over accounted for just under 10 percent of global population, and the share aged eighty and over for about 1.1 percent. Those proportions are expected to rise by 2025 to 15 percent and 2 percent, respectively, and to continue to rise throughout the twenty-first century.[10] For women death rates are declining even at extremely high ages around 110.[11] Sickness rates are much higher for the aged, and so are the amounts spent on health care. Estimates broadcast in 2000 suggest that genetic predispositions account for about 30 percent of all human cancers. If genetic treatments achieve their promise, allowing people to redress some of the anomalies that now abbreviate life, the share of the population who are aged will rise still faster. The early decades of the twenty-first century will be a good time to concentrate energies and resources on the full democratization of survival. Then, in the longer run, it may be easier to meet the next challenge.

[10] For the estimates, see Yvonne J. Gist and Victoria A. Velkoff, "International Brief: Gender and Aging: Demographic Dimensions," issued in December 1997 by the U.S. Bureau of the Census.

[11] John R. Wilmoth, "Are Mortality Rates Falling at Extremely High Ages? An Investigation Based on a Model Proposed by Coale and Kisker," *Population Studies* 49 (1995): 281–95.

Index

accidents, 45
acute respiratory infection, 21, 101, 134
adenovirus, 99
advice manuals, 171, 208
affluence, and disease, 192
Africa, 24, 30, 38, 48, 51, 71, 75, 109, 115, 144, 150–2, 159, 163, 187, 205, 210–12, 227, 230; AIDS in, 46–7; *see also* sub-Saharan Africa; *individual countries*
aged, as cause of death, 17
aging of populations, 2, 231–2
AIDS, 30, 41, 46–7, 48, 79, 97; mortality from, 41; in Africa, 46–7
air, as mode of disease transmission, 61, 63
Alameda County Study, 85–6
Albania, 130–2, 135, 214, 225
alcohol poisoning, 45
alcoholism, 171, 191
anthrax, 95, 97
antibiotics, 28, 52, 102–5, 114–15, 154, 222, 229
antimicrobials, 101–6
antisepsis, 96
apothecaries, 86–7
Argentina, 118, 130, 132

Arnold, David, 72
asepsis, 96
Ashkenazi Jews, 180
Asia, 24, 30, 38, 40, 51, 71, 75, 115, 152, 163, 187, 210, 230; *see also* South Asia; *individual countries*
aspirin, 103
Australia, 36
Austria, 125
ayurvedic medicine, 90, 169

bacteria and disease, 28, 60, 64, 91–2, 95–6, 99, 102–4, 164; *see also* germ theory
bacterial meningitis, 99
Baldwin, Peter, 55
Bangladesh, 142, 151, 190, 218
Banting, Frederick, 107
barefoot doctors, 94
Barker, David, 14
Bassi, Agostino, 95
bathing, 53, 180–1
BCG (bacillus Calmette-Guérin), 13, 74, 97
behavior, and health, xiv, 56, 169–72, 191–3

233

Behr-Pinnow, Carl von, 183
Belgium, 6, 118, 125–6; *see also* Low
    Countries
Belize, 122
beriberi, 53
bills of mortality, 16–18
biomedicine, 8, 27, 51–5, 81–3, 89–94,
    104–6, 110, 117, 119–20; conflict with
    traditional medicine, 89–94; and
    disease course, 106–7; and germ theory,
    95–6; shortcomings of, 230; *see also*
    technomedicine
Black, William, 16–18, 19, 21
Black Report, 140
bloodletting, 86, 88, 169
body mass index, 55, 165; *see also* stature
Bolivia, 138
Bombay, 175
books of the dead, 68
Booth, Charles, 72
Botswana, 90–92
bourgeoisie, *see* middle class
Brazil, 118, 166
breastfeeding, 112, 113, 154, 183, 185
Britain, 6, 9–10, 51, 55, 65, 72–3, 76, 83,
    124, 128, 140, 142, 173, 183–4, 208,
    210; causes of death in, 16–18; income
    distribution and life expectancy,
    135–36; *see also* England; United
    Kingdom
Broad Street pump, 64
bronchitis, 21, 23; *see also* chronic
    bronchitis
bubonic plague, 19–20, 21, 41, 59, 61, 68,
    74, 99
Buchan, William, 85
Burkina Faso, 130, 131

Calcutta, 65
Caldwell, John C., 111, 132, 134–5, 200,
    203–4, 213
Canada, 36, 116, 119, 130–1, 183
cancer, 17, 18, 23, 27, 55, 91, 98, 190–1,
    221, 232; lung, 194, 195; *see also*
    neoplasms

cardiovascular disease, 23, 25, 45, 166; *see
    also* heart disease
case fatality rates, 20
Castro, Fidel, 109
cause of sickness information, 11, 224
centenarians, 29
Chadwick, Edwin, 65, 72
chemotherapy, 103; *see also* antibiotics;
    individual drugs
Chen, L. C., 12–13
Cheney, George, 84
child health, and material education,
    203–5, 215, 218–19
child mortality, 155–6, 159, 182–5; *see also*
    child survival; infant mortality
child survival, 223; factors behind, 156–8;
    and maternal education, 204–5
childbed fever, 101
childbirth, 113–15; *see also* maternal
    mortality
Chile, 118
China, 40–1, 75–6, 93–4, 105, 118, 131,
    150, 165, 209, 214, 225, 227, 231;
    famine in, 41, 44; and Western
    medicine, 54
cholera, 20, 29, 54–5, 60, 64, 66, 72, 78,
    80, 82–3, 95, 99
cholesterol, 192–3, 195
chronic bronchitis, 23, 195
chronic undernutrition, 147–48; *see also*
    malnutrition
cities: and disease, 34, 40, 58, 61, 115;
    growth and sanitation, 66; housing in,
    175–6
clothing, and health, 179
Colombia, 131
colonies, and literacy, 210–14
communicable diseases, 13, 17, 20, 22–4,
    30, 45–6, 49, 52, 58, 68, 78, 93, 95, 148,
    192–3, 224, 226, 229–31; fast decline of
    in developing countries, 106; and
    population density, 82; and
    malnutrition, 146; *see also*
    noncommunicable diseases; *specific
    diseases*

community medicine, 59
congestive heart failure, 23
consumer revolution, and health, 178
consumption, 17; *see also* tuberculosis
convalescence, 73, 88
convulsions, 17
cordon sanitaire, 58–9
Cornaro, Luigi, 84
Costa Rica, xii, 36, 76, 117, 135, 214, 225–7
cowpox, 70
crowding, 173–5; in housing, 73; *see also* tuberculosis
Cuba, 109, 117, 212, 214, 225
Cyprus, 117
Czech Republic, 118

DDT, 75
deaths, world total of, 220–1; *see also* mortality
decomposing matter, 60–1, 67; *see also* environmental theory
degenerative diseases, 16, 19, 23–4, 26, 30, 134, 145–6, 164, 167, 193–5; *see also* noncommunicable diseases
Demographic and Health Survey, 156
demographic transition, 7
Denmark, 125; *see also* Nordic lands
diabetes, 27, 103, 107, 134, 165, 192
diarrheal disease, 13, 67, 77, 134, 156–7, 174, 223, 225, 228–9; *see also* dysentery; enteric disease; *individual diseases*
diet, 191; early in life and later effects, 166; and health, 55, 166, 190–3; and health transition, 9; *see also* body mass index; nutrition; stature
digitalis, 103
diphtheria, 21, 22, 45, 97–9, 175
discrimination in provision of health services, 65, 173–4
disease: causes, 184–5, 224; early discovery of, 108; modes of communication, 20, 95; and nutrition, 155–6; signs and symptoms of, 21, 59; *see also* air; communicable diseases;

famine; noncommunicable diseases; vectors; water; *specific diseases*
disease avoidance, 11, 26–8, 46, 82, 146, 171, 201
disease management, 11, 26–8, 46, 82, 146, 171, 201
disease prevention, 11, 26–8, 82, 146, 171, 201
disease profile, *see* cause of sickness information
disease treatment, 11, 26–8, 82, 146, 171, 201
diseases of affluence, 143, 166, 192
diseases of the circulatory system, 17; *see also specific diseases*
diseases of the respiratory system, 17; *see also specific diseases*
disinfection, 188; *see also* antimicrobials
Domagk, Gerhard, 102
domesticity and health, 177–80
Dominica, 117
drugs, pathogen resistance to, 103–4; *see also* antibiotics
Dutch hunger winter, 149
dysentery, 60; *see also* diarrheal disease

East Asia, 163
Eastern Europe, 36, 44; *see also individual countries*
economic development, 8, 122–3
economic modernization, *see* modernization
edema, 162
education, xii; and child health, 219; of females, 159; and health 200–3, 205, 218–19, 230–1; hypotheses about relating to health, 201–2, 204; maternal, 157; prestige associated with, 202; and socialization , 201–3; as a tactic, 56
Ehrlich, Paul, 89, 102
emotional diseases, 81–2, 90–3
emphysema, 194
endemic disease, 20, 21, 162
England, 8–10, 12, 22, 34–9, 113, 124, 139–40, 146, 160, 162, 172, 179, 212,

Index

England (*cont.*)
225; life expectancy in, 32; literacy in, 205–9; *see also* Britain; United Kingdom
English model of sanitary reform, 225; *see also* public health; sanitary improvements
enteric disease, 21, 60, 72, 76, 78; *see also* diarrheal disease
entitlement theory, 149–50, 152
entitlements and famine, 149
environmental theory, 61–4, 68
environmental toxins, 45
EPI (Expanded Program on Immunization), 98, 100–1
epidemic disease, 63; *see also* mortality crises
epidemiologic transition, 10–11, 15–25, 26–8; *see also* Omran, Abdel
Ernakulam district, 213–14
Ethiopia, 150
eugenics, 183
Europe, 7, 10, 18–20, 33–4, 52–3, 59–66, 72–5, 77–9, 83–4, 86–7, 123–4, 127–8, 159–67, 173–4, 177–8, 205–10; *see also* Northwest Europe; *individual countries*
European and tropical diseases, 110
excess female mortality, 189–91
excess male mortality, 189–91
expert advice, 53, 170–2; *see also* advice manuals

famine, 41, 145, 146–53, 166–7; interpretation of causes, 147–50; and natural disaster, 150–1; relief of 151–2
females: autonomy of, 132, deprivation of, 157–8; domestic responsibilities of, 170, 177–80; education of, 53, 216–18; excess mortality, 189–91; and knowledge of health factors, 178–9; status of, 157–9; survival of, 189–90, 209; *see also* gender; maternal education; mothercraft
feminism, 158

fertility: decline of and maternal mortality, 114–15; and infant/child mortality, 186
fever, 17, 21, 103, 154
fevers, 17, 67, 85; *see also specific diseases*
Fiji, 130, 132, 135
filth theory, 67, 89, 96, 173, 187–88; *see also* environmental theory
Finland, 21, 36, 125, 146; *see also* Nordic lands
flush toilets, 67
Fogel, Robert, 160–1
food: distribution of in population, 53; shortage and market mechanisms, 148–9; *see also* famine
fowl cholera, 97
Framingham Heart Study, 191–92
France, 3–4, 33–4, 36–7, 55, 72, 119, 124–6, 142, 146, 173, 180, 183, 185, 207
Furet, François, 207

Gabon, 130–1
GDP, *see* gross domestic product
gender: and education, 207, 209; and survival, 209; *see also* females; males
genetic factors, and life span, 2, 30
germ theory, 12, 51–2, 64, 67–8, 78, 89, 95–6, 101, 104–5, 106, 108, 111, 169, 179–82, 194, 209, 216, 224, 229; and behavior, 187–9; and relationship of life expectancy and income, 127
Germanin, 102
Germany, 55, 118, 125–6, 149, 173, 183
germicides, 68; *see also* antibiotics
Global Burden of Disease project, 13–14
goiter, 163
Greece, 117, 118, 131, 164
green revolution, 152–3
gross domestic product (GDP): and health spending, 108, 116, 118–20; and life expectancy, 117–19, 124, 128–31, 135, 137–9; *see also* income
growth, *see* stature

236

Haines, Michael, 208–9
Haiti, 48
Hamburg, 83
harvest failure, 21, 147–8; *see also* famine; mortality crises
healers, unconventional, 86–7; *see also* physicians; traditional medicine
health advice, 84–6, 106–7; *see also* advice manuals
health care: democratization of, 110; spending on, 115–17; *see also* barefoot doctors; physicians; primary health care
health clinics, 203, 230; and mothercraft, 183–4
"health for all by the year 2000," 111–12, 220
health infrastructure, 46, 56, 159, 223
health spending, and GDP, 118–19
health strategies, efficiency of, 225–6
health transition, 1, 3, 6, 26, 56, 105, 200, 208, 221–4; chronology and geography of, 33–40; determinants of, 11–2; and economic growth, 124; end of, 29–31; and epidemiologic transition, 16; history of, 7–15, 40–7; human agency in, 24–5; incomplete, 224–5; investigation of, 17–18; and morbidity, 48–50; and nutrition, 145–6; particularism of, xii; and redundancy, 28; strategies of, xii–xiii, 222–4; *see also* behavior; income; literacy; medicine; nutrition; public health
health visitors, 184
healthy life expectancy, 48–9, 50
heart disease, 17, 23, 27, 134, 143, 165, 190–5; *see also* cardiovascular disease
height, *see* stature
Helvétius, Claude Adrien, 206
hepatitis B, 98, 99, 101
Hinduism, 72, 90; *see also* ayurvedic medicine
Hippocratic ideas, 61; *see also* environmental theory
HIV, 46–8; *see also* AIDS

Hollingsworth, T. H., 139
Holocaust, 44
Honduras, 152
Hong Kong, 176
hospitals, 46, 56, 68–9, 74, 91–2, 109, 114, 120, 123, 136, 173
households and health, 169–72, 178–9, 197–8
housing, 53, 174, 176, 178; and disease, 105; as factor in health transition, 8; and filth, 174–5, 182; and health, 172–7; and isolation of sick, 175; *see also* crowding
human capital theory, 202; *see also* education
Human Development Index, 36, 155
human waste, 58, 60, 64–8; *see also* sanitary improvements
humoral medicine, 84, 85, 88, 119, 169, 194, 196
hygiene, *see* bathing; personal hygiene; public health

Iceland, 118
illiteracy, *see* education; literacy
immune response, 102
immune system, 88
immunization, 14, 45, 52, 97, 98–101
immunotherapy, 103, 222
income: and life expectancy, xii, 56, 122–31, 138, 143–4; conclusions about, 127–8; individuals' use of to control survival hazards, 139–43; over time, 125–6; in the twentieth century, 128–39
income distribution, and health, 54, 135–6
India, 72, 83, 90, 118, 131, 133–4, 149, 153, 169, 190, 212–14, 226, 227; survival in, 3–5; and malaria, 75–6
individual behavior, and health, 194–6; responsibility for health, 197–8
Indonesia, 118
industrial revolution, and literacy, 206
infant feeding, *see* infant nutrition

infant mortality, 3, 22, 30, 34–5, 45, 155–6, 159, 182–7; *see also* infant survival
infant nutrition, 145–6, 184–5
infant survival, 223; factors behind, 156–7; and maternal education, 204–5
infectious disease, 18; *see also* communicable disease; *individual diseases*
influenza, 21, 23, 73, 99, 141; epidemic of 1918–19, 24, 41
injuries, 26, 50, 80–1, 89, 107–8, 133, 180, 208, 221, 223–4, 226
insulin, 27, 103, 107
insult accumulation, *see* sickness
International Classification of Disease, 18
iodine deficiency, 145, 163
Iran, 131
Ireland, 146
Islam, 90, 218
isolation of the sick, 68, 175; *see also* hospitals; quarantine
isoniazid, 74
Italy, 12, 59, 118, 125–6, 163, 180

Jamaica, 117, 122
Jamison, Dean, 13
Japan, 12, 29, 35, 36, 38–9, 52, 53–5, 76, 116, 119, 130–1, 164, 226–7; income distribution and life expectancy, 135–6; life expectancy in, 32–3; public cooperation with authorities, 54; survival in, 3–5
Jenner, Edward, 26, 51, 70, 71, 97
Jhuggies, 175
Johansson, Sheila, 12

Kant, Immanuel, 177
Kenya, 118, 180, 211
Kerala, 38–9, 53, 112, 132–5, 164, 213–14, 225, 231
Kinshasa, 175
Klee, Philipp, 102
Koch, Robert, 51, 67, 89, 95, 96, 97

Korea, 75, 118
Kumar, Gopalakrishna, 134
Kunitz, Stephen, 25
Kuznets, Simon, 141

Lagos, 175
larvicides, 75
Latin America, 36, 75, 135, 205, 230; and epidemiologic change, 24; life expectancy in, 38–39; *see also individual countries*
Leblanc process, 179
Leeds, 172
Leeuwenhoek, Antony van, 95
Leicester, 71, 79
LeVine, Robert, 207
life expectancy, 19, 29–31; in Africa, 39; in China, 93; convergence among countries, 138; democratization of, 221; and economic development, 122–3; future of, 7; gender and, 55; and health spending, 116–19; high in some poor countries; 223, 225; history of 1, 32, 33, 35, 221–4; and income, 122, 128–31, 138–9; and income, routes of mediation, 122–3; and infant mortality, 185–6; in Latin America, 38–9; and literacy, 206–7; in medium income countries, 128–9; overachievers and underachievers, 131–9; projected, 36–8; social differentiation in, 128–9; and stature, 161–5; stratification in, 139–43; world, 40, 42–3; *see also* mortality; survivorship
life span, 2, 29
life table, 3n3
lifestyle, 30; *see also* risk factors
Lister, Joseph, 96
literacy, 202, 206, 216; adult, 211–17; beneficiaries of, 214–16; campaigns, 211–13; and economic development, 202, 226–30; functional, 234–5; and health, 200–2, 205, 213, 215, 217–19, 223, 226; history of, 205–9, 211–12;

information as a tactic in, 201; male and female, 133; meaning of, 201–2; measurement of, 207; and politics, 211–12, 215; and socialization, 207, 211; and survival, 208–9
London, 16–18, 63–5
Lopez, Alan, 13, 228
low birth weight, 101, 159
Low Countries, 36, 124, 173; *see also individual countries*
lung cancer, 194, 195; *see also* cancer; tobacco

McKeown, Thomas, 8–11, 159–60
malaria, 21, 74–6, 97, 102, 152, 187, 229, 230
Malaysia, 118
males, 209; excess mortality of, 189–91
malnutrition, 145–8, 153–9
Malthus, Thomas, 11, 22, 70, 146–8, 153
Malthusian model, 148
Manchester, 162
Mao Zedong, 93–4
marasmus, 153
Marx, Karl, 141, 177
Marxism, 202–3
mass immunization, *see* immunization
mass vaccination, *see* vaccination
maternal education, 203–7, 210–19; *see also* females
maternal mortality, 113–15, 226; and traditional medicine, 120
measles, 21, 25, 59, 98–100, 151, 175, 228, 229
medicalization, 87–8, 171
medicine, xii, 103; cost, 108–9, 111; democratization of, 117; and health transition, 81–3, 222–3; popular access to formal practitioners, 87–8; profession of, 89–90; as a tactic, 56; use in developing countries, 109–10; *see also* apothecaries; physicians; surgeons
menopause, 192
Mexico, 36

microbial unification, 82–3
middle class: as agent of health, 171–2; and health, 177–80; and mothercraft, 183
midwives, 87, 114
milk depot, 182–3
Minor, Charles, 88
Mitch, David, 206
modernization, as factor in the health transition, 9; *see also* education; literacy
modernization theory, 202, 211
Molenaer, Jan, 62
Monod, Henri, 72
Montesquieu, Charles Louis, baron de, 79
morbidity, 14, 107; forms, 48; as a gauge of population health, 48–50; in Kerala, 134; *see also* sickness; *specific diseases*
Morocco, 209
mortality, xi–xiii; adult, 22, 226; age structure of, 3–5, 22, 25, 34–5, 45, 49, 128, 221; in children under five, 154–5; and health spending, 116–17; *see also* life expectancy; survivorship
mortality crises, 20–1, 41, 146–8; *see also* epidemic disease
mortality decline, 7–8; *see also* health transition
mortality transition, *see* health transition
Moscow, 83
Mosk, Carl, 12
Mosley, W. H., 12–13
mosquitoes and disease, 74–5; *see also* vectors
mothercraft, 170, 182–5, 204
Mozambique, 211–12
mumps, 99
Murray, Christopher, 13, 228

Nasrin, Taslima, 218
National Health Conference of 1949, 93
National Health Service, 116, 140
neoplasms, 17, 134; *see also* cancer
Netherlands, 37, 118, 125, 174; *see also* Low Countries

New York City, 142
New Zealand, 36
Nicaragua, 118, 152, 212, 215
Nigeria, 39–40, 106, 111, 118, 151, 175, 203–4, 227
noncommunicable diseases, 13, 24, 46, 49, 192, 224; *see also* degenerative diseases; *specific diseases*
non-naturals, 194–5
Nordic lands, 32, 35, 36, 124, 142; *see also individual countries*
Northwest Europe, 27, 32–4, 40; and mortality decline, 21–25
Norway, 118, 124, 125; *see also* Nordic lands
numeracy, 215
nutrition, 10–11; and disease, 53, 155–6, 162; and European mortality decline, 159–65; and health, xii, 145–6; and mineral needs, 163–4; prenatal, 145; programs, 154; as a tactic, 56
nutrition transition, 165–6

obesity, *see* overnutrition
odor, and disease, 60–1
Omran, Abdel, 10–12, 15–16, 18–19; *see also* epidemiologic transition
opium, 103
oral rehydration therapy, 13, 112, 157, 216, 229
Orubuloye, I. O., 111
overachievers, and life expectancy-income association, 131–9
overnutrition, 145–6, 165–7
Oxfam, 151
Ozouf, Jacques, 207

Pakistan, 118, 190, 227
Papua New Guinea, 110, 196
Paraguay, 36
parents: educational status of and health, 200–1, 203–4; and the health transition, 223; views on education, 206, 210
Paris, 65, 173, 181

Paris green, 75
Pasteur, Louis, 51, 67, 95–7
pasteurization, 74, 169, 182–3, 186
patients, and expectations of doctors, 88
peers, of England, 139–40
pellagra, 163
penicillin, 102, 104
personal freedom, 79, 201, 231; and literacy, 207, 210–14; and public health, 79–80
personal hygiene, 180–2
pertussis, 98
Peru, 131
PHC, *see* primary health care
physicians, 87, 108, 171–2; and hand washing, 181–2; and health, 83–8; modern, 89–94; ratio to population, 93–4, 133; traditional, 89–94; and training to communicate with patients, 109; *see also* medicine, surgeons
pit latrines, 66, 77–8, 196
placebo effect, 86
plague, *see* bubonic plague
Plasmoquine, 102
pneumonia, 99
Poland, 118
polio, 98, 99
poor countries, and life expectancy gains, 138–9
population density, and disease, 63–4
Portugal, 130–1
poverty, 61, 159, 182; and disease, 64, 72, 105; housing and, 172–3; and life expectancy, 127, 133, 136, 144; and malnutrition, 145
pregnancy, and tuberculosis, 73
Preston, Samuel, 127, 208–9
primary health care (PHC), 109–13, 159
prontosil, 102
prospective health studies, 191–2
protein-energy malnutrition, 153–4; *see also* nutrition
proteins, 2, 161, 164
proximate determinants, of health transition, 12

public health, xii, 58–59, 66, 77–8; and disease surveillance, 68–72; and germ theory, 67–8; and the health transition, 8, 202–3; and public consensus, 69; and sociology of disease, 72–4; as a tactic, 56; and waterborne disease, 76–80; *see also* sanitary improvements
puerperal fever, 101, 114

quarantine, 58, 68
quinine, 75, 84–5, 102–3

rabies, 97
rational expectations model of health, 91
recovery, 86
Red Cross, 151
redundancy, in health system, 46
Reed, Walter, 75
relapsing fever, 102
Renoir, Louis, 170
respiratory disease, 17, 19, 21–4, 72, 101, 134, 156, 175, 187, 191, 193; *see also individual diseases*
rheumatic fever, 50
rich countries, and life expectancy gains, 138–9
rickets, 163
risk factors, 14, 23, 55, 169, 191–3; education about, 196–7; theory of, 194–6, 199
Rockefeller Foundation, 112
rodenticides, 74
Roehl, Wilhelm, 102
Romanovskii, D. L., 102
Ross, Ronald, 74–5
Rountree, Seebohm, 72
Rousseau, Jean-Jacques, 88
rubella, 99
Russia, 44–6; *see also* Soviet Union
Rwanda, 211

Salvarsan, 89, 102–3
sand filtration, 63
sanitary improvements, 8, 54, 63, 64–8,

77–8, 128, 142; alternatives to, 76–7; cost, 76, 115; *see also* public health
Saudi Arabia, 118, 132, 134
scarlet fever, 22, 25, 97, 99, 175
schistosomiasis, 75, 93
Schmoller, Gustav, 141
Schöfer, Fritz, 102
Schofield, R. S., 32, 139, 208
Schröder, Peter, 90–2
Scola, Roger, 162
scurvy, 163
selective primary health care (SPHC), 112
self-treatment, 27, 81, 83–4
Semmelweis, Ignaz, 101–2
Sen, Amartya, 149, 152
Senegal, 118
sheep anthrax, 95
sickness, 7, 13–4, 20, 48–50, 56, 73, 88–91, 107, 134, 140, 224–5, 232; responses to, 83–4; sickness rates and death rates, 49; *see also* morbidity, recovery; *individual diseases*
Sierra Leone, 29
silkworm disease, 95
Simon, John, 67
Singapore, 130–1
sleeping sickness, 102
smallpox, 17, 19, 21–2, 24–6, 54–5, 59, 67, 70–1, 79, 84, 89, 97, 99, 101, 105, 148, 182, 222; eradication, 71–2; inoculation, 89; vaccination, 51, 54, 70–1, 89, 185, 222
smoking, *see* tobacco
Snow, John, 64
social development, 143–4
social justice, 132
social medicine, 104–5
socialism, 177; and high life expectancy, 136
socialization theory, 203
Somalia, 211
South Asia, 48, 144, 151, 159, 186, 205; *see also* Asia; *individual countries*
Soviet Union, 39; *see also* Russia
Spain, 118, 125–6, 130–1

Sri Lanka, 76, 112, 118, 130–2, 135, 225, 231
standard of living, 8–9, 72, 141, 160, 213; see also income
stature, 53, 161–3, 165, 167; and life expectancy, 141; and nutrition, 145–6, 161–2
Stolnitz, George, 8, 12, 14
streptomycin, 74, 103–4
stroke, 55
Stromquist, Nelly, 216
sub-Saharan Africa, 27, 47–8, 186
sulfa drugs, 102–3; see also sulfonamides
sulfonamides, 102, 114; see also sulfa drugs
surgeons, 86–7, 120, 182
surplus mortality, 226–7
survivorship: in Africa, 38; in Asia, 38; in Europe, 32–36; in Latin America, 36; in world, 36–38; see also life expectancy; mortality
Sweden, 34–5, 37, 55, 70, 114, 118, 125–8, 131, 185, 227; see also Nordic lands
swine erysipelas, 97
Switzerland, 118, 130–1
syphilis, 55, 89, 102

Tanzania, 131, 211, 213
technomedicine, 107–8; see also biomedicine
tetanus, 97–9
Thailand, 118
Tianjin, 175
tobacco, 49, 190–1, 193–9, 226
Total Literacy Campaign, 213
toxins, and immunization, 97
traditional medicine, 51–5, 81–3, 117, 119–20; conflict with biomedicine, 89–94; and efficacy of treatment, 83–8
transgenic modifications, 153
tuberculin, 89, 99
tuberculosis, 13, 89, 95–6; drug resistance, 92; generality of infection, 72–3; modes of transmission, 72–3; mortality, 73–4; treatments, 90–2; see also consumption
Turkey, 131, 152, 190
typhoid fever, 22, 54, 60, 66–7, 78, 97, 181; vaccine, 97
Typhoid Mary, 69
typhus, 21, 61, 67, 181

Uganda, 48, 130–1, 180
unani medicine, 90
underachievers: in life expectancy-income association, 131–9; and overachievers, 143–4
undernutrition, see malnutrition
UNESCO, 217
United Kingdom, 53, 116, 127–6; see also Britain; Wales
United Nations, 8, 36, 151
United States, xiii, 36, 75, 108, 122, 130–1, 142, 166, 177, 183, 193, 209, 227; spending on health, 116–18, 168–9
urbanization, see cities

vaccination, 26, 71, 77, 79, 97–9, 101; history of, 98–9
vaccine matter: effectiveness of, 99; preservation of, 97
vectors, of disease, 74–6, 174–5; see also individual examples
Vienna, 101
Vietnam, 40, 118, 150
Villermé, Louis, 12, 72
vital revolution, see health transition
vitamins, 53, 162–4, 198

Waksman, Selman, 102
Wales, 8–9, 12, 22, 34, 160
Wang, Jia, 137
waste disposal, 76–7; see also sanitary improvements
water: contamination of, 63; as disease carrier, 63–5; treatment, 53, 64–8, 77, 128